THE All Beef Cookbook

On the cover: Ranch Ribs, Flank Steak Supreme, Tacos

THE All Beef Cookbook

Recipes compiled and tested
by the
AMERICAN NATIONAL COWBELLES, INC.

A BENJAMIN COMPANY BOOK
Distributed by CHARLES SCRIBNER'S SONS
NEW YORK

Special cowboy material written by	LUCILLE ANDERSON
Cowboy illustrations by	KEITH SOWARD

Senior Editor	BARBARA BLOCH
Editorial Production	DIANE MATHESON
Associate Editor	PHYLLIS BENJAMIN
Art Director	WILLIAM BROOKS

Photos courtesy of California Beef Council (pages 86, 155, 157, 158); National Live Stock and Meat Board (pages 49, 50, 51, 85, 120, 121, 122, 156, 191, 192); Wine Institute (pages 52, 119).

Cover Photo: RICHARD JEFFREY

"CowBelles" has a dual meaning
for the cowboy:
His way of handling cattle
in the brush was "to bell 'em,"
and to the rest of the world his gal was
his BELLE.

The AMERICAN NATIONAL COWBELLES, INC. has a membership of over sixteen thousand women who come from thirty affiliated states. Each member is dedicated to the goals of encouraging a spirit of cooperation among members of the cattle industry and the promotion of beef by acquainting others with the many ways it can be used.

Acknowledgments

Grateful acknowledgment to the following
for their time, help, and materials.
State CowBelle Organizations
American Dairy Association
American National Cattlemen's Association
California Beef Council
National Beef Industry Council
National Live Stock and Meat Board
Adolph's
American Spice Trade Association
Wine Institute

And a special thanks to
Bud Gunterman and Al Johnson
who not only gave us great moral support
but also ate most of the dishes tested and
answered our urgent questions:
"Did you like it?," "Would you add or
subtract anything?," and perhaps most
important, "Will you eat it again?"

Preface

This book about beef and how to cook it has been compiled by the CowBelles for everyone who delights in eating America's favorite food and everyone who is charged with the responsibility of preparing it.

The early Western cowboy started beef production as we know it today. In tribute to his pioneer spirit, this book features the cowboy, who tells part of the story of beef and shares his outdoor recipes with us.

When you buy beef, among the questions you should ask are, "What new ways can beef be cooked and served?" and, "What can be done with the leftovers?"

As long as you are familiar with the proper cooking method, beef can be prepared in any form, from whole to finely ground. You can wrap it around other food (as in "beef birds") or the beef itself can be wrapped (as with leaves or dough). It can be stuffed with dressings inserted in pockets cut in the beef, shaved in thin slices or left in large pieces. It can be pounded, chopped, or ground—coarse or fine.

Hundreds of members of the American National CowBelles contributed their favorite recipes and the Committee cooked, tested, and retested over five hundred of them. Unfortunately space limitations do not permit inclusion of all the recipes contributed. Like the cowboy, we had to "cull."

The recipes included are divided according to the size and shape of the beef—roast, steak, cube and strip, and ground. Veal, variety cuts, and processed and prepared beef are in separate sections. Ribs and oxtails are included with bony chunks in the variety section. The final chapter on beef complements provides recipes for foods that go well with beef along with a few special beef "extras."

The traditional "three square meals" habit has given way to more casual eating and as we have changed our pattern of living, beef with its enormous versatility, increasingly becomes the ideal food for breakfast, brunch, lunch, snacks, or dinner. Beef, a natural source of protein, is used almost universally and is as good as it is nutritious.

We hope you enjoy our recipes and that you will find the special tips and "Bell Ringers" helpful in answering any questions you may have concerning beef.

CowBelle Cookbook Committee

Mrs. F. J. Gunterman, Chairman
Mrs. Raymond Adams, Sr.
Mrs. John R. Anderson
Mrs. Walter Condon
Mrs. N. K. Dekle

Mrs. Alfred G. Johnson
Mrs. Preston Larson
Mrs. Claire D. Owen
Mrs. George B. Pond
Mrs. Floyd Stone, Jr.

Dedicated to Pat Stevenson
Past President, American National CowBelles,
whose interest in spreading information about beef
and the beef industry was the impetus for this cookbook.

Contents

Stories of the Western Cowboy tell that he'd "hang his line" on anything—including the devil himself. But a century ago when this cowboy "punched a hole in his sea grass" to throw at a steer, how could he possibly know that his rope would encircle the world?

All About Beef

Beef: An Important Food

Beef belongs to the meat group, one of the basic four food groups that comprise a balanced, nutritious diet. Two or more daily servings from the meat group are recommended in order to provide essential nutrients needed by the body. Beef is high in protein, and contains all the amino acids necessary to build, maintain, and repair body tissues, and to strengthen the body's mechanism against disease and infection. It is an excellent source of the B vitamins, iron, and phosphorus. Beef is one of the most completely digestible and easily utilized foods. Most beef cuts contain fewer than 250 calories per 3½-ounce serving of cooked lean meat so even weight watchers can enjoy it. Those on low-carbohydrate diets will be pleased to learn that beef contains no carbohydrates at all.

What Determines the Cost of Beef?

Just as the old Western cowboy has become a modern businessman, so has the cattle business undergone change and growth. No longer able to operate with the simple equipment of "horse and gear," the cattle industry now supports many other industries. Beef production is the largest single segment of total agriculture in the United States today.

Between birth and consumption, a steer is handled by a multitude of people, each of whom contributes to the retail cost of beef. In raising cattle, the rancher must cover the costs of land and livestock, taxes and/or leases, feed, veterinarian and medicine, feedlot fattening, and marketing.

It would be nice if every 1000-pound steer yielded 1000 pounds of steaks and rib roasts, or even edible meat, but unfortunately cattle just aren't built that way. A steer must be bought at live weight—on the hoof. After slaughtering it is resold to the retail distributor at "hanging weight," the weight of the carcass after removing head, feet, hide, and offal (all of which are sold separately). The retail distributor sells meat to the consumer in the familiar meal-sized cuts, after trimming away fat, bone, and waste.

A 1000-pound live steer produces a 615-pound carcass. The carcass loses another 183 pounds of bone, fat, waste, and shrinkage, leaving 432 pounds of retail cuts that reach the consumer. These are average figures—actual percentages vary among individual animals. Since at every level more weight must be bought than can be resold, the price per pound must rise in compensation. The 432 pounds of retail beef you buy is all the salable beef that remains from the original 1000-pound live steer.

Retail prices for beef also cover costs of transportation, processing. refrigeration, and packaging, which involves additional equipment and labor all along the production line. The vigorous expansion of the cattle industry has made beef production more efficient at every stage, and improvement in quality is evidenced by the amount of beef consumed annually by each and every American—115 pounds, more than double that of twenty years ago.

1000 lb. Steer

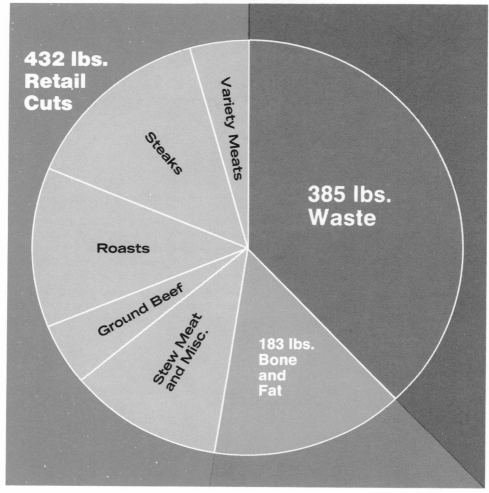

432 lbs. Retail Cuts

Variety Meats

Steaks

Roasts

Ground Beef

Stew Meat and Misc.

385 lbs. Waste

183 lbs. Bone and Fat

Buying Beef without Beefing

The wide variety of fresh, cured, cured-and-smoked, frozen, canned, and ready-to-serve beef cuts offers the consumer almost unlimited selection.

When buying fresh or frozen beef, it is imperative for the consumer to deal with a retailer who stakes his reputation on consistently high-quality products and service.

Watch newspapers for special sales on certain cuts of beef. They can save you money, especially if you have a freezer and can stock up on large quantities bought at a good price. Beware, however, of deceptively low prices, especially with an unfamiliar dealer. Sometimes these low prices represent "bait-and-switch" selling—an attempt to "bait" you with low prices and, once in the store, "switch" you to a better-quality product at a much higher price.

Fresh beef is available in a wide range of cuts from the individual steak or patty to the steamboat round, which will serve one hundred or more people. Beef may also be bought in large quantities—an entire quarter or side of a steer. A flat price per pound hanging weight is charged, which means you pay for the weight of the entire carcass "as it hangs," before trimming. You can get excellent steaks and roasts at a lower price, and buying beef this way can be economical if you have the space to store it. Be certain, however, that the price per pound is low enough to justify buying a large amount of ground beef in proportion to filet mignon.

Beef cuts vary in natural tenderness, but any cut can be made tender through proper preparation. Therefore, it is important to select beef with the cooking method in mind. Another important factor to consider in buying meat is the number of servings a cut will yield per pound. Some cuts are very inexpensive but yield only two servings per pound. Beef yielding two servings at $1.00 per pound costs 50¢ per serving. Beef bought at $1.20 per pound, but yielding three servings, costs 40¢ per serving and is more economical in the long run. In general, boneless beef will yield three to four servings per pound; "bone-in" cuts will give two or three servings per pound; very bony cuts will average one to two portions per pound. Be sure to allow for seconds and for hearty appetites.

When buying beef, consider not only the size and kind of cut you need, but also the quality of meat. Young beef is usually tenderer than beef from a more mature animal, even though it may not contain as much fat. Bones from young animals are reddish and porous; from older animals, they are white and flinty. The term "aging" has nothing to do with the age of the animal, but refers instead to a process applied to high-quality beef in order to increase tenderness and flavor. Meat is held in a vacuum or at a controlled temperature for two days to six weeks, depending on the method used. Aged beef gives the ultimate in tenderness and succulence, which makes it relatively expensive. Keep in mind, then, that high-quality beef does not necessarily have to be bright cherry red. The deep, rich wine-red color that appears with aging promises a meal *par excellence*.

Your assurance that the beef you buy is wholesome and was processed under sanitary conditions is provided by this stamp.

All meat sold in interstate commerce must have been federally inspected and stamped. Meat processed and sold within the state must pass an equivalent local inspection.

While the mandatory Federal inspection guarantees wholesomeness, it says nothing about the quality of beef. The U.S. Department of Agriculture provides a voluntary meat grading service for those who request it and who pay a fee. A large percentage of meat packers take advantage of this service, and most beef sold bears the familiar shield-shaped grademark that indicates the quality of the meat.

There are eight grades given to beef, but the lowest three—USDA Utility, Cutter, and Canner—are almost never sold as retail cuts. They are used instead in ground beef or processed items such as hot dogs.

The top grade, USDA Prime, is usually sold to hotels and restaurants, but is sometimes available in supermarkets and butcher shops. It has generous marbling—flecks of fat distributed throughout the meat—which help make it the most tender, juicy, and flavorful of any cut of beef. The next grade, Choice, is the most popular grade purchased. Though it has slightly less marbling than Prime meat, Choice grade beef is still of very high quality. USDA Good beef usually comes from grass-fed or short term pen-fed cattle, and is a wise choice for economy-minded shoppers. Rather than carrying a U.S. grade stamp, it is sometimes sold under a "house" brand name. Relatively tender, this grade of beef may lack some of the juiciness and flavor of Prime and Choice beef because it has less marbling.

15

Round

Round Steak ③

Top Round Steak ③

Ground Beef

Heel of Round ④

Eye of Round ③

Cubed Steak ③

③ Bottom Round Roast or Steak

Rolled Rump ①

Sirloin

Pin Bone Sirloin Steak ①

Flat Bone Sirloin Steak ②

Wedge Bone Sirloin Steak ③

Boneless Sirloin Steak ① ② ③

Short Loin

Top Loin Steak ① ② ③

T-Bone Steak ②

Porterhouse Steak ③

Boneless Top Loin Steak ① ② ③

Tenderloin (Filet Mignon) Steak or Roast (also from Sirloin 1a) ② ③

Rib

Rib Eye (Delmonico) Roast or Steak ← ②

Rib Steak, Boneless ②

Rib Steak ②

Rib Roast ②

Chuck

② Boneless Chuck Eye Roast

① Beef for Stew

Boneless Shoulder Pot-Roast or Steak ③

Blade ② Roast or Steak

① Ground Beef

Arm ③ Pot-Roast or Steak

Cross Rib Pot-Roast ④

Chuck Short Ribs ③ ④

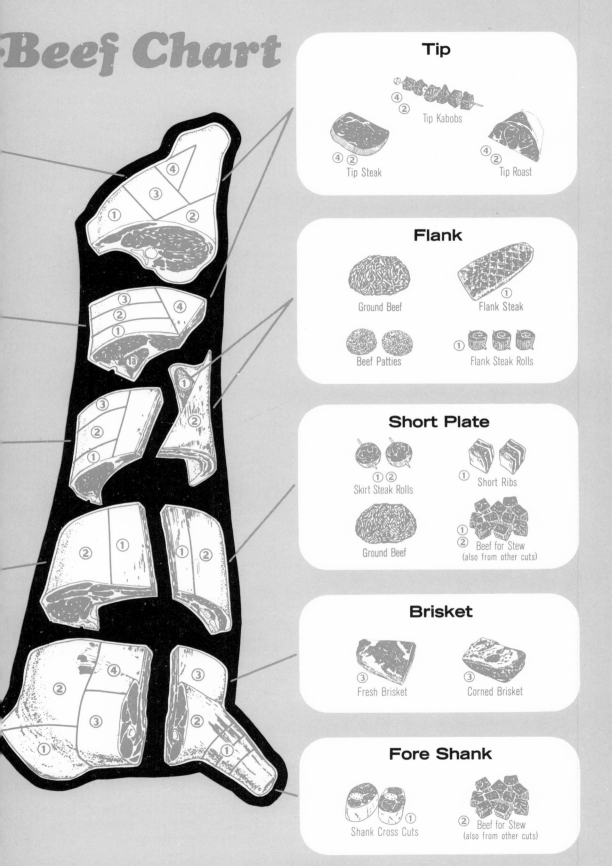

Beef Chart

Tip

Tip Kabobs

④ ②

Tip Steak
④ ②

Tip Roast
④ ②

Flank

Ground Beef

Flank Steak ①

Beef Patties

Flank Steak Rolls ①

Short Plate

Skirt Steak Rolls ① ②

Short Ribs ①

Ground Beef

Beef for Stew ① ②
(also from other cuts)

Brisket

Fresh Brisket ③

Corned Brisket ③

Fore Shank

Shank Cross Cuts ①

Beef for Stew ②
(also from other cuts)

Information courtesy of National Live Stock and Meat Board.

Only tender cuts from the higher grades of beef—Prime, Choice, and Good—are suitable for cooking by dry heat. Meat of this type can be successfully roasted, broiled, pan broiled, and pan fried. Standard and Commercial grades are not widely available and are not tender. All cuts from the lower grades, and all grades of the less tender cuts, such as chuck roast, need long, slow cooking by moist heat for maximum flavor and tenderness.

Standardization of Cuts

One of the biggest problems the consumer faces at the meat counter is the mind-boggling array of meat cuts labeled with confusing or obscure names. There are an estimated one thousand names for some 250 to 300 retail cuts on the market, with inconsistencies often occurring at two different supermarkets in the same neighborhood. Besides confusing the consumer, this practice has caused countless headaches for meat packers involved in interstate commerce, who receive requests for shipments of meat cuts whose nomenclature is totally unfamiliar to the shipper.

The Industrywide Cooperative Meat Identification Standards Committee (ICMISC), with the cooperation of the National Live Stock and Meat Board and under the guidance of several governmental agencies, has developed a system of Uniform Retail Meat Identity Standards (URMIS). This program is designed to standardize retail meat cuts of beef, pork, lamb, and veal; to eliminate consumer confusion; and to facilitate interstate commerce by insuring that each retail cut is given the same name everywhere in the United States. It is expected that the URMIS system, already enforced by law in some states, will eventually replace local statutes and enable consumers to purchase meat with ease and confidence all over America.

Under the uniform meat identity labeling program, each retail cut of meat is labeled according to species, primal cut, and accepted anatomical term. "Species" refers to the animal from which the cut comes—beef, pork, lamb, or veal. "Primal cut" refers to the seven basic wholesale cuts of meat, and tells you what part of the carcass the meat comes from. These seven categories are breast (brisket and short plate), shoulder (chuck) arm, shoulder (chuck) blade, rib, loin, sirloin (hip), and leg (round).

The anatomical designation pinpoints the cut according to location (e.g. Under Blade Roast), identifying bones (Wedge Bone Steak), or shape (Beef for Stew). Familiar fanciful names may be used as long as the standard name also appears on the price-weight label. For instance, a retailer may identify his familiar "California Roast" with a pressure-sensitive label, but the meat must also bear the new standard nomenclature: Beef Chuck/Under Blade Roast.

In addition to the uniform meat identity labels, which will identify the same meat cut everywhere the system is used, retailers are advised to indicate the recommended cooking method on the label, or to post a conspicuous chart with recommended cooking methods for every cut sold.

Ground beef is labeled somewhat differently from other beef cuts. It has been traditionally identified according to primal cut—"ground round," "ground chuck," "ground sirloin," or simply "hamburger." Many experts feel, however, that the true difference between types of ground beef lies in the ratio of lean beef to fat. Fat adds flavor and juiciness, but an excessive amount is uneconomical and adds calories.

Under the new standard identity system, ground beef will be labeled according to lean/fat ratio, and will bear the legend "Not less than X% lean." "Ground beef," for example, may contain 70 to 77% lean and 23 to 30% fat; 77 to 84% lean and 16 to 23% fat; 84 to 90% lean and 10 to 16% fat. Even the leanest ground beef, from which all visible fat has been trimmed, contains 7–10% fat as a result of marbling. At least this much fat is necessary to give the meat flavor and juiciness.

ICMISC has determined that meat labeled "ground beef" must not contain any pork, lamb, veal, or variety meats. Pork, lamb, and veal may be sold ground separately; beef, pork, and veal may be ground together and sold as "ground meat loaf."

The Uniform Retail Meat Identity Standards program has been developed for the benefit of consumers—to help them buy familiar meat cuts no matter where they happen to be shopping, and save them money indirectly by standardizing and streamlining the entire wholesale distribution process. The more states that enforce these standards the more effective the system will be.

The following table will explain what to look for when buying meat. Look up the old familiar name of meat cut; the new name is in the column to the left.

Top quality beef is always well-marbled!

Find out how your butcher cuts his beef and make a special effort to familiarize your-self with the new names of the particular cuts he carries. No retailer carries every cut listed in the table, but everyone carries some of them.

Primal Cut	Meat Board Recommended Name for Retail Beef Cut	Commonly Used Names for Retail Cut	Recommended Cooking Methods
Chuck	Chuck Arm Pot-Roast	Arm Chuck Roast; Chuck Arm Roast; Chuck Round Bone Cut; Round Bone Pot-Roast; Round Bone Roast	Braise
	Chuck Arm Pot-Roast Boneless	Chuck Arm Pot-Roast	Braise
	Chuck Cross Rib Pot-Roast	Boston Cut; Bread and Butter Cut; Cross Rib Roast; English Cut Roast; Thick Rib Roast	Braise
	Chuck Cross Rib Pot-Roast Boneless	Boneless Boston Cut; Boneless English Cut; Cross Rib Roast, Boneless; English Roll	Braise
	Chuck Shoulder Pot-Roast Boneless	Boneless English Roast; Cross Rib Roast, Boneless; Honey Cut; Shoulder Roast; Shoulder Roast, Boneless	Braise
	Soup Bone	Knuckle Bone; Knuckle Soup Bone; Soup Bone	Cook in Liquid
	Chuck Arm Steak	Arm Chuck Steak; Arm Steak Beef Chuck; Arm Swiss Steak; Chuck Steak for Swissing; Round Bone Steak; Round Bone Swiss Steak	Braise
	Chuck Arm Steak Boneless	Boneless Arm Steak; Boneless Round Bone Steak; Boneless Swiss Steak	Braise
	Chuck Short Ribs	Barbecue Ribs; Braising Ribs; English Short Ribs, Extra Lean; Fancy Ribs; Short Ribs	Braise, Cook in Liquid
	Chuck Shoulder Steak Boneless	English Steak; Shoulder Steak; Shoulder Steak, Boneless; Shoulder Steak, Half Cut	Braise
	Chuck Shoulder Pot-Roast Boneless	Center Shoulder Roast; Chuck Roast, Boneless; Chuck Shoulder Roast; Clod Roast	Braise
	Chuck Shoulder Steak Boneless	Chuck for Swissing; Clod Steak, Boneless; London Broil; Shoulder Clod Steak, Boneless; Shoulder Cutlet, Boneless; Shoulder Steak	Braise, Panfry

Primal Cut	Meat Board Recommended Name for Retail Beef Cut	Commonly Used Names for Retail Cut	Recom- mended Cooking Methods
	Beef for Stew	Beef Cubed for Stew; Boneless Beef for Stew; Boneless Stew Beef	Braise, Cook in Liquid
	Chuck Flat Ribs	Barbecue Ribs; Bottom Chuck Ribs; Chuck Spareribs	Braise, Cook in Liquid
	Chuck Short Ribs	Barbecue Ribs; Braising Ribs; Brust Flanken; Flanken Short Ribs	Braise, Cook in Liquid
	Chuck Flanken Style Rib	Barbecue Ribs; Braising Ribs; Brust Flanken; Flanken Short Ribs; Kosher Ribs	Braise
	Chuck Marrow Bones	Clear Bones; Marrow Bones; Soup Bones	Cook in Liquid
	Chuck Neck Pot-Roast	Neck Boiling Beef; Neck Pot-Roast; Neck Soup Meat; Yankee Pot-Roast	Braise, Cook in Liquid
	Chuck Neck Pot-Roast Boneless	Beef Neck, Boneless; Neck Pot-Roast, Boneless; Yankee Pot-Roast, Boneless	Braise, Cook in Liquid
	Chuck Neck Bones	Braising Bones; Meaty Neck Bones; Neck Bone; Neck Soup Bone	Cook in Liquid
	Beef for Stew	Beef for Stew	Braise, Cook in Liquid
	Chuck Pot-Roast Boneless	Boneless Chuck Roast; Chuck Pot-Roast, Boneless; Chuck Roast, Boneless	Braise
	Chuck 7-Bone Pot-Roast	Center Cut Pot-Roast; Chuck Roast Center Cut; 7-Bone Roast	Braise
	Chuck 7-Bone Steak	Center Chuck Steak; Chuck Steak Center Cut; 7-Bone Steak	Braise
	Chuck Blade Roast	Blade Chuck Roast; Chuck Blade Roast; Chuck Roast, Blade Cut; Chuck Roast, 1st Cut	Braise, Roast—high quality
	Chuck Blade Steak	Blade Steak; Chuck Blade Steak; Chuck Steak, Blade Cut; Chuck Steak, 1st Cut	Braise, Broil or Panbroil—high quality

Primal Cut	Meat Board Recommended Name for Retail Beef Cut	Commonly Used Names for Retail Cut	Recommended Cooking Methods
	Chuck Blade Steak	Blade Steak; Chuck Blade Steak; Chuck Steak, Blade Cut; Chuck Steak, 1st Cut	Braise, Broil or Panbroil— high quality
	Chuck Blade Steak Cap Off	Char Broil Steak; Chuck Barbecue Steak; Chuck Steak, 1st Cut; Chuck Steak for Bar B Q	Braise, Broil or Panbroil— high quality
	Chuck Top Blade Pot-Roast	Blade Roast, Bone-In; 7-Bone Roast; Top Chuck Roast	Braise
	Chuck Top Blade Steak	Blade Steak, Bone-In; Top Blade Steak; Top Chuck Steak, Bone-In	Braise
	Chuck Under Blade Pot-Roast	Bottom Chuck Roast; California Roast; Semiboneless Roast; Under Cut Roast	Braise, Roast
	Chuck Under Blade Steak	Bottom Chuck Steak; California Steak; Semiboneless Chuck Steak; Under Cut Steak	Braise, Broil, Panbroil, Panfry
	Chuck Under Blade Pot-Roast Boneless	Boneless Roast Bottom Chuck; Bottom Chuck Roast, Boneless; California Roast, Boneless; Inside Chuck Roast	Braise, Roast
	Chuck Under Blade Steak Boneless	Boneless Chuck Steak; Bottom Chuck Steak, Boneless; Chuck Fillet Steak; Under Cut Steak, Boneless	Braise, Broil, Panbroil, Panfry
	Chuck Mock Tender	Chuck Eye; Chuck Fillet; Chuck Tender; Fish Muscle; Medallion Pot-Roast; Scotch Tender	Braise
	Chuck Top Blade Roast Boneless	Flat Iron Roast; Lifter Roast; Puff Roast; Shoulder Roast, Thin End; Triangle Roast	Braise
	Chuck Top Blade Steak Boneless	Book Steak; Butler Steak; Lifter Steak; Petite Steak; Top Chuck Steak, Boneless	Braise, Panfry
	Chuck Eye Roast Boneless	Boneless Chuck Roll; Boneless Chuck Fillet; Chuck Eye Roast; Inside Chuck Roll	Braise, Roast
	Chuck Eye Steak Boneless	Boneless Chuck Fillet Steak; Boneless Steak Bottom Chuck;	Braise, Broil, Panbroil,

Primal Cut	Meat Board Recommended Name for Retail Beef Cut	Commonly Used Names for Retail Cut	Recommended Cooking Methods
	Chuck Eye Steak Boneless (con't)	Chuck Boneless Slices; Chuck Eye Steak; Chuck Fillet Steak	Panfry
	Chuck Eye Edge Pot-Roast	Boneless Chuck Pot-Roast; Chuck Boneless Roast; Inside Chuck Roast; Chuck Rib Pot-Roast	Braise
Shank	Shank Cross Cuts	Center Beef Shanks; Cross Cut Shanks; Fore Shank for Soup Meat, Bone-In	Braise, Cook in Liquid
	Shank Cross Cuts Boneless	Boneless Beef Shanks; Cross Cut Shank, Boneless; Fore Shank for Soup Meat, Boneless	Braise, Cook in Liquid
	Shank Center Cut	Center Shank Soup Bone; Shank Soup Bone	Braise, Cook in Liquid
	Shank Soup Bones	Beef Bones; Clear Bones; Soup Bones	Cook in Liquid
Brisket	Brisket Whole Boneless	Boneless Brisket; Brisket Boneless; Fresh Beef Brisket; Whole Brisket	Braise, Cook in Liquid
	Brisket Point Half Boneless	Brisket Front Cut; Brisket Point Cut; Brisket Thick Cut	Braise, Cook in Liquid
	Brisket Flat Half Boneless	Brisket First Cut; Brisket Flat Cut; Brisket Thin Cut	Braise, Cook in Liquid
	Brisket Point Cut Boneless	Brisket Front Cut; Brisket Point Cut; Brisket Thick Cut	Braise, Cook in Liquid
	Brisket Middle Cut	Brisket Center Cut; Brisket Flat Cut	Braise, Cook in Liquid
	Brisket Flat Cut Boneless	Brisket Flat Cut	Braise, Cook in Liquid
	Brisket Edge Cut Boneless	Brisket Edge Cut; Brisket Side Cut	Braise, Cook in Liquid
	Brisket Half Point Boneless	Brisket Front Cut; Brisket Point Cut; Brisket Thick Cut	Braise, Cook in Liquid
	Brisket Corned Boneless	Corned Beef; Corned Brisket; Corned Beef Brisket	Cook in Liquid

Primal Cut	Meat Board Recommended Name for Retail Beef Cut	Commonly Used Names for Retail Cut	Recommended Cooking Methods
Plate	Plate Short Ribs	Plate Short Ribs	Braise, Cook in Liquid
	Plate Spareribs	Plate Spare Ribs	Braise, Cook in Liquid
	Plate Ribs	Boiling Beef; Plate Beef, Plate Boiling Beef	Braise, Cook in Liquid
	Plate Skirt Steak Boneless	Skirt Steak, Diaphragm	Braise, Broil, Panbroil, Panfry
	Plate Skirt Steak Cubed Boneless	Cubed Skirt Steak; Skirt Steak, Cubed, Diaphragm	Broil, Panbroil, Panfry
	Plate Skirt Steak Rolls Boneless	London Broil; London Broil; Skirt Fillets; Skirt London Broil; London Grill Steak	Braise, Broil, Panbroil, Panfry
	Plate Rolled Boneless	Plate Roll; Rolled Plate; Yankee Pot-Roast	Braise
Flank	Flank Steak	Flank Steak Fillet; Plank Steak; London Broil; Jiffy Steak	Braise, Broil
	Flank Steak Cubed	Flank Steak Cubed	Braise, Broil, Panbroil, Panfry
	Flank Steak Cubed, Rolled	Flank Steak Cubed, Rolled	Braise, Roast
	Flank Steak Rolls	London Broil; Cubed Flank Steak; Flank Steak Fillets; Flank Steak London Broil	Braise, Broil, Panbroil, Panfry
Rib	Rib Roast, Large End (Ribs 6 to 7)	Rib Pot-Roast, Short Cut; Standing Rib Roast; Rib Roast, Short Cut; Rib Roast Oven Ready	Roast
	Rib Roast, Large End (Ribs 6 to 8)	Standing Rib Roast; Rib Roast Oven Ready	Roast
	Rib Roast, Large End (Ribs 8 to 9)	Standing Rib Roast; Rib Roast Oven Ready	Roast
	Rib Extra Trim Roast, Large End (Ribs 6 to 8)	NewPort Roast; Rib Roast Deluxe; Club Rib Roast	Roast

Primal Cut	Meat Board Recommended Name for Retail Beef Cut	Commonly Used Names for Retail Cut	Recommended Cooking Methods
	Rib Steak, Large End (7th Rib)	Rib Steak; Rib Steak, Bone-In	Broil, Pan-broil, Panfry
	Rib Roast, Small End (Ribs 9 to 10)	Rib Roast Oven Ready; Standing Rib Roast	Roast
	Rib Roast, Small End (Ribs 10 to 12)	Rib Roast Oven Ready; Standing Rib Roast	Roast
	Rib Roast, Small End (Ribs 11 to 12)	Rib Roast Oven Ready; Standing Rib Roast; Sirloin Tip Roast	Roast
	Rib Steak, Small End (Ribs 11 to 12)	Rib Steak; Rib Steak, Bone-In	Broil, Pan-broil, Panfry
	Rib Steak, Small End Boneless (Ribs 11 to 12)	Rib Steak Boneless; Spencer Steak, Boneless	Broil, Pan-broil, Panfry
	Rib Eye Steak	Delmonico Steak; Boneless Rib Eye Steak; Fillet Steak; Spencer Steak; Beauty Steak	Broil, Pan-broil, Panfry
	Rib Eye Roast (Ribs 6 to 12)	Delmonico Pot-Roast; Delmonico Roast; Rib Eye Pot-Roast; Regular Roll Roast	Roast
	Short Ribs	Short Ribs	Braise, Cook in Liquid
	Back Ribs	Riblets; Rib Bones; Finger Ribs	Braise, Cook in Liquid
	Rolled Cap Pot-Roast	Cap Meat Rolled; Top Rib Roll Boneless	Braise
Loin	Loin Top Loin Steak or Loin Strip Steak	Shell Steak; Strip Steak; Club Steak; Chip Club Steak; Bone-In Club Sirloin Steak; Country Club Steak; Sirloin Strip Steak, Bone-In; Delmonico Steak	Broil, Pan-broil, Panfry
	Loin Top Loin Steak Boneless or Loin Strip Steak	Strip Steak; Kansas City Steak, N.Y. Strip Steak; Sirloin Steak, Hotel Style; Loin Ambassador Steak; Loin Strip Steak, Hotel Cut; Boneless Club Sirloin Steak	Broil, Pan-broil, Panfry
	Loin T-Bone Steak	T-Bone Steak	Broil, Pan-broil, Panfry

Primal Cut	Meat Board Recommended Name for Retail Beef Cut	Commonly Used Names for Retail Cut	Recommended Cooking Methods
	Loin Porterhouse Steak	Porterhouse Steak	Broil, Pan-broil, Panfry
	Loin Sirloin Steak, Pin Bone or Loin Sirloin Steak	Sirloin Steak, Pin Bone; Sirloin Steak	Broil, Pan-broil, Panfry
	Loin Sirloin Steak, Flat Bone or Loin Sirloin Steak	Sirloin Steak, Flat Bone; Sirloin Steak; Flat Bone Sirloin Steak	Broil, Pan-broil, Panfry
	Loin Sirloin Steak, Round Bone or Loin Sirloin Steak	Sirloin Steak	Broil, Pan-broil, Panfry
	Loin Sirloin Steak, Wedge Bone or Loin Sirloin Steak	Sirloin Steak, Wedge Bone; Sirloin Steak, Short Cut; Sirloin Steak	Broil, Pan-broil, Panfry
	Loin Shell Sirloin Steak	Sirloin N.Y. Steak, Bone-In; N.Y. Sirloin Steak	Broil, Pan-broil, Panfry
	Loin Sirloin Steak, Boneless	Sirloin Steak, Boneless; Rump Steak	Broil, Pan-broil, Panfry
	Loin Top Sirloin Steak, Boneless	Top Sirloin Steak	Broil, Pan-broil, Panfry
	Loin Tenderloin Roast	Tenderloin Tip Roast; Tenderloin, Fillet Mignon Roast; Tenderloin, Chateaubriand	Roast, Broil
	Loin Tenderloin Steak or Loin Fillet Mignon	Fillet Mignon; Fillet Steak; Tenderloin, Fillet De Boeuf; Tender Steak	Broil, Pan-broil, Panfry
	Loin Tenderloin Tips	Tenderloin Tips	Broil, Pan-broil, Panfry
Round	Round Steak	Round Steak; Round Steak, Center Cut; Round Steak, Full Cut	Braise, Panfry
	Round Steak, Boneless	Round Steak; Round Steak, Center Cut Boneless; Round Full Cut, Boneless	Braise, Panfry
	Round Rump Roast	Round Rump Roast, Bone-In; Round Standing Rump	Braise, Roast—high quality
	Round Rump Roast, Boneless	Round Boneless Rump; Round Rump Roast, Rolled	Braise, Roast—high quality

Primal Cut	Meat Board Recommended Name for Retail Beef Cut	Commonly Used Names for Retail Cut	Recommended Cooking Methods
Round	Heel of Round	Round Heel Pot-Roast; Pikes Peak Roast; Diamond Roast; Denver Pot-Roast; Horseshoe Roast	Braise, Cook in Liquid
	Beef for Stew	Stew Beef	Braise, Cook in Liquid
	Top Round Steak 1st Cut	First Cuts of Top Steak; Short Cuts; Top Round London Broil	Broil, Pan-broil, Panfry
	Top Round Steak	Top Round Steak; Top Round Steak, Center Cut	Broil, Pan-broil, Panfry
Round	Top Round Steak, Butterfly	Braciole Round Steak; Braciole Steak; Top Round Braciole Steak	Braise, Panfry
Round	Top Round Roast	Top Round Roast; Top Round Roast, Center	Roast
	Cubed Steak	Cube Steak	Braise, Panfry
Round	Bottom Round Rump Roast	Round Tip Roast; Round Back of Rump Roast	Braise, Roast–high quality
Round	Bottom Round Roast	Bottom Round Pot-Roast; Bottom Round Oven Roast; Bottom Round Steak Pot-Roast	Braise, Roast—high quality
Round	Bottom Round Steak	Beef Bottom Round Steak; Bottom Round Steak	Braise, Panfry
Round	Eye Round Roast	Eye Round Roast; Round Eye Pot-Roast; Eye Round Pot-Roast; Round Eye Roast	Braise, Roast—high quality
Round	Eye Round Steak	Eye Round Steak; Round Eye Steak	Braise, Pan-broil, Panfry
Round	Tip Roast	Sirloin Tip Roast; Face Round Roast; Tip Sirloin Roast; Round Tip Roast; Crescent Roast	Braise, Roast—high quality
Round	Tip Steak	Sirloin Tip Steak; Top Sirloin Steak	Broil, Pan-broil, Panfry
Round	Tip Steak, Cap Off	Ball Tip Steak; Trimmed Tip Steak	Broil, Pan-broil, Panfry
Round	Tip Roast, Cap Off	Ball Tip Roast; Full Trimmed Tip Roast	Braise, Roast—high quality
Round	Tip for Kabobs	Sirloin Tip, Kabob Cubes	Braise, Broil

27

Refrigerator Storage

Fresh meat which is not to be frozen should be stored in the coldest part of the refrigerator or, when available, in the compartment designed for meat storage. The temperature should be as low as possible without freezing the meat (see chart below).

Prepackaged meat should be stored in the refrigerator in the original wrapping for not more than two days.

Fresh meat, not prepackaged, should be removed from the market wrapping paper, wrapped loosely in waxed paper or aluminum foil (often, the inner-wrapping paper used by the meat dealer makes an excellent wrap for storage) and refrigerated for not more than two days.

Variety meats and ground or chopped meats are more perishable than other meats and should be cooked in one or two days if not frozen.

Cured, cured and smoked meats, sausage and ready-to-serve meats also should be stored in the refrigerator. They should be left in their original wrapping.

Cooked meats which are left over should be cooled within one to two hours after cooking, then covered or wrapped promptly to prevent drying, and stored in the refrigerator. Bones may be removed to conserve storage space, but meat should be left in as large a piece as possible.

Meats cooked in liquid for future serving should be cooled uncovered, within one to two hours, then covered and stored in the refrigerator. To speed cooling, when meat is cooled in liquid, the pan containing the cooked meat may be set where there is good circulation of cool air, or it may be cooled by setting the pan in cold or running water.

REFRIGERATOR STORAGE TIMETABLE
Refrigerator Temperature 35° to 40°

	Type of Meat	Maximum Recommended Storage Time
Uncooked Beef	Roasts	3 to 5 days
	Steaks	2 to 3 days
	Ground beef	1 to 2 days
	Stew meat	2 days
	Variety meats (heart, liver, etc.)	1 to 2 days
	Frankfurters	4 to 5 days
Uncooked Veal	Roasts	2 to 4 days
	Chops	2 to 4 days
	Ground veal	1 to 2 days
	Stew meat	2 days
	Variety meats (liver, sweetbreads, etc.)	1 to 2 days
Cooked Meat	Roasts	4 days
	Steaks, Ground beef	2 to 3 days
Cured Beef	Corned beef	7 days

FREEZER STORAGE TIMETABLE

0° or colder

	Type of Meat	Maximum Recommended Storage Time
Beef	Roasts	6 to 12 months
	Steaks	6 to 12 months
	Ground beef	3 to 4 months
	Stew meat	3 to 4 months
	Variety meats	3 to 4 months
	Frankfurters	1 month
Veal	Roasts	6 to 9 months
	Chops	6 to 9 months
	Ground veal	3 to 4 months
	Stew meat	3 to 4 months
	Variety meats	3 to 4 months
Cooked meat	All types	2 to 3 months
Cured meat	Corned beef	2 weeks

Note: *Times given are for separate-door freezers only. For smaller freezers that average about 5°, cut storage time by ⅓ to ½.*

Freezer Storage

Most meat may be frozen satisfactorily if properly wrapped, frozen quickly and kept at 0° or below.

Freeze meat while it is fresh and in top condition. Meat will be no better in quality when it is removed from the freezer than when it was put in.

Select proper wrapping materials. Choose a moisture-vapor-proof wrap so that air will be sealed out and moisture locked in. When air penetrates the package, moisture is drawn from the surface of the meat and the condition known as "freezer burn" develops. There are several good freezer wraps on the market. Pliable wraps such as aluminum freezer foils and transparent moisture-vapor-proof wraps and certain types of plastic bags are good for wrapping bulky, irregular-shaped meats, since these wraps may be molded to the meat. Freezer papers and cartons coated with cellophane, polyethylene or wax; laminated freezer paper; plastic bags and certain types of waxed cartons are suitable for some cuts of meat.

Prepare meat for freezing before wrapping. Trim off excess fat and remove bones when practical to conserve freezer space. Meat should not be salted as salt shortens freezer life. Wrap in "family-size" packages. When several chops, patties or individual pieces of meat are packaged together, place double thickness of freezer wrap between them for easier separation during thawing.

Wrap tightly, pressing out as much air as possible.

Label properly. Indicate name of cut and date on package. If content is not obvious, it is helpful to indicate the weight or approximate number of servings.

Freeze at once at −10° or lower, if possible. Allow space for air between packages during initial freezing time. Try to avoid freezing such a large quantity of meat at one time that the freezer is overloaded and temperature thereby raised undesirably.

Maintain freezer temperature at 0° or lower during freezer storage. Higher temperatures and fluctuations above that temperature impair quality.

Refer to freezer storage chart for suggested maximum storage times. Frozen meat will be of best quality if used before the maximum time indicated.

Refreezing of defrosted meat is not recommended except in emergencies. There is some loss of juices during defrosting and the possibility of deterioration of the meat between the time of defrosting and refreezing.

Meat purchased frozen should be placed in the freezer immediately after purchase unless it is to be defrosted for cooking. The ice cube compartment of a refrigerator is not intended as a substitute (for more than a week) for a regular freezer or freezer storage section.

Freezing and Reheating Precooked Foods

Many cooks find it convenient to prepare two batches of a recipe and freeze one for later use, or to prepare a meal well ahead of time and freeze it. Most beef dishes, especially casseroles, freeze beautifully if properly done. Food should be prepared for immediate serving, but very slightly underdone, to allow it to cook to perfection when reheated. It should be cooled quickly in the refrigerator or on ice. Package when cool in moisture- and vapor-proof containers or materials such as freezer paper or heavy-duty aluminum foil. Pack tightly, eliminating as much air as possible, but leaving ½ inch to 1 inch head space for expansion of liquids. Seal tightly with airtight lid or freezer tape and freeze immediately. Mark date frozen on each package.

When reheating precooked dishes, only those in ovenproof containers may go directly from freezer to oven. Otherwise, transfer to an ovenproof container after partially thawing in a pan of warm water. Food should be completely thawed only in the refrigerator.

A double boiler is preferable when reheating frozen food on the stove. If direct heat must be used, keep it low, stir often, and distribute blocks of food evenly in the pan.

Thawing Uncooked Beef

Raw meat is best thawed either in the refrigerator or during cooking. Beef may spoil rapidly if thawed at room temperature and allowed to stand after completely defrosted. Cook beef promptly after thawing, or refrigerate. Do not remove wrapping while thawing, and do not immerse in water unless meat is to be cooked in water. It is not a good idea to refreeze thawed, uncooked meat, as it both loses juices during thawing, and is susceptible to spoilage between time of thawing and refreezing.

Note: It is possible, in an emergency, to refreeze uncooked beef that has thawed but not become warm. However, to do so increases the danger of undetected spoilage and does nothing to enhance the quality of the meat.

Cooking Methods

DRY HEAT

Roasting (large, tender cuts)

1. Preheat oven to 325° (425° for loin tenderloin roast, 350° for rib eye roast).
2. Season meat with salt and pepper.
3. Place meat, fat side up, on rack in open roasting pan.
4. Insert meat thermometer in meatiest part of roast, so that tip does not rest on bone or in fat.
5. Do not cover, add water, or baste.
6. Cook to desired degree of doneness.

BEEF ROASTING CHART

Cut of beef	Weight	Cooking Time Minutes per Pound[1]
Rib Roast, Large End	4 to 8 pounds	23–32 rare 27–38 medium 32–42 well-done
Rib Roast, Large End, Boneless	4 to 6 pounds	28–30 rare 32–35 medium 37–40 well-done
Round Rump Roast, Boneless	4 to 6 pounds	28–30 rare 32–35 medium 37–40 well-done
Rib Eye Roast	4 to 6 pounds	18–20 rare 20–22 medium 22–24 well-done
Rib Roast, Small End	3 to 5 pounds	30 rare 35 medium 40 well-done
Loin Tenderloin Roast	4 to 5 pounds	10 rare

(If you don't like rare beef, please don't buy fillet!) Rare beef should register 140° on the meat thermometer; medium beef, 160°; well-done, 170°. Fillet should register 140°.
[1] *Meat at refrigerator temperature at start of roasting.*

Broiling (tender steaks, usually thicker than ¾ inch)

1. Preheat broiler.
2. Place meat on rack set in broiling pan, or on outdoor grill.
3. Place thinner cuts 2 to 3 inches from heat, thicker cuts 3 to 5 inches from heat.
4. Broil until one side is brown.
5. Turn meat over and season cooked side.
6. Broil second side until brown.
7. Season and serve promptly.

STEAK BROILING CHART
Approximate time each side in minutes:

Thickness	Rare	Medium	Well-done
¾"–1"	5	7	9
¾"–1½"	8	10	12
2"	15	18	20

Pan Broiling (for steaks ¾ inch to 1 inch thick)

1. Place meat in preheated heavy skillet.
2. Do not add cooking oil or water. Do not cover.
3. Cook over moderate heat, turning occasionally.
4. Pour off fat as it accumulates.
5. When cooked to desired doneness, season and serve at once.

Pan Frying (for thin, tender or tenderized cuts of steak)

1. Heat a small amount of cooking oil in heavy skillet.
2. Brown meat on both sides.
3. Season as desired.
4. Do not cover.
5. Cook at moderate temperature, turning occasionally, until done.
6. Serve at once.

MOIST HEAT

Braising (for less tender cuts)

1. If desired, dredge meat with flour.
2. Brown on all sides in small amount of cooking oil.
3. Season as desired.
4. Add small amount of liquid.
5. Cover tightly.
6. Simmer at low temperature on top of range (or between 325° and 350° in oven) until tender.

Cooking in Liquid (for less tender cuts; stews; soups)

1. Brown meat on all sides, in cooking oil or in its own drippings.
2. Season as desired.
3. Cover meat with liquid.
4. Cover pot tightly.
5. Simmer until tender; do not boil.
6. If adding vegetables, add to pot just long enough before serving so vegetables finish cooking at the same time as the meat.

Microwave Cooking

The microwave oven has proved a boon to modern time-conscious cooks. It can cut cooking time up to two-thirds, provide speedy defrosting, and warm leftovers without adding additional moisture or fat. Instead of surrounding food with heat as in a conventional oven, microwave cooking causes the moisture molecules in food to vibrate very quickly. This friction, created by vibration, produces heat energy which allows the food to cook itself. Since paper, plastic, some glass and china contain no moisture molecules, microwaves pass right through them, so food can be defrosted, cooked, reheated, and served on a plastic, paper, or a suitable glass or china plate.

The microwave oven is an invaluable aid in quick and imaginative meal preparation, and a helpful addition to the conventional oven. Texture and appearance may be somewhat different in microwave cooking; for example, foods do not brown unless the oven is equipped with a special electric browning unit. You can roast a standing rib roast quickly, or cook a ground beef casserole in a flash. Cooking losses for the roast will be greater and the degree of doneness may not be uniform. Most less tender cuts of meat cook better with conventional slow, moist heat cooking.

It is not possible to give specific directions for using a microwave oven since each brand is different. Consult the manufacturer's instructions and specially written microwave cookbooks for exact directions, cautions, cooking timetables, and other tips. They will make it possible to prepare meals with amazing speed, requiring minimum effort and yielding maximum compliments.

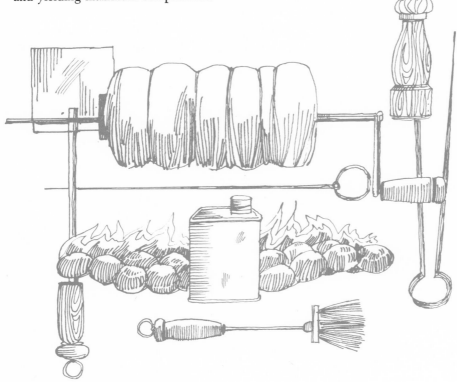

BARBECUING

Nothing beats a barbecue! For informal entertaining, good eating, and just plain fun, there isn't anything that compares to the tantalizing aroma of barbecuing meat. There are numerous ways to barbecue, from using the tiny Japanese hibachi to the all-out mammoth pit barbecue with several hundred pounds of meat. Folding grills, braziers, cooking wagons, cooking kettles, gas or electric grills, and stationary barbecue fireplaces all provide acceptable methods available for barbecuing.

Follow manufacturer's instructions for the equipment you choose. In case the instructions happen to be lost, stolen, or strayed, here is a general outline of how to build a fire with charcoal briquets and what to do with it once it's built.

1. Line the grill base with heavy-duty aluminum foil and cover it with a shallow layer of gravel or vermiculite.
2. About 30 to 45 minutes before cooking begins, pile briquets in a pyramid in center of grill base (the number of briquets will depend on grill size and amount of food to be cooked).
3. Start fire with an electric starter; or by pouring liquid starter over briquets and then igniting; or by igniting kindling under briquets.
4. When coals are covered with ash and glowing in the center, spread in a uniform layer and place grid over coals. Keep a few ignited briquets along edge of fire bowl.
5. Cook meat, controlling heat by rearranging, adding, or removing coals, or by using adjustment feature peculiar to your equipment (6 to 8 inches from coals is average).

Grill Barbecuing

1. When briquets are coated with gray ash, rearrange them and knock off the ash with a rake or fire tongs.
2. Rub grill grid with cooking oil to prevent food from sticking.
3. Place meat on grill.
4. When meat is browned on one side, turn with long-handled tongs and season as desired. Turn beefburgers with a spatula. Wear gloves when turning kabob skewers.
5. If dripping fat flares up, squirt or sprinkle with water.
6. Baste throughout cooking as desired unless glazes or sauces that burn easily are used. In this case, wait until cooking time is almost complete before basting.
7. Cooking time will vary from 5 to 10 minutes per side for beefburgers. A 1½ inch steak cooked 6 to 8 inches from the coals will be rare if cooked 4 to 7 minutes per side; medium if cooked 7 to 9 minutes per side; well done if cooked 9 to 12 minutes per side. Adjust time for variation in width of steak or distance of grid from coals. Kabobs require from 15 to 30 minutes total time, depending on the size of cubes.

 To make your own drip pan from heavy-duty aluminum foil: Tear off a sheet twice the length of the roast plus 4 or 5 inches. Fold in half, and then again lengthwise to make quadruple thickness. Turn up all four sides to make a 1 inch rim, folding corners tightly to reinforce. Arrange coals around drip pan or at rear of fire bowl.

Spit Barbecuing

1. When briquets are coated with gray ash, arrange in rear of fire bowl, or according to manufacturer's directions. Knock off gray ash with a rake or fire tongs. Food should cook at moderate temperature.
2. Tie or truss beef to make as compact as possible.
3. Insert spit rod through center of gravity of the beef.
4. Secure beef with spit forks, and make sure meat rotates evenly with the spit and does not wobble.
5. Insert meat thermometer in center of roast, at a slight angle so it won't fall out. Tip must not rest in fat, on bone, or on spit rod. Place thermometer so that it will clear coals, drip pan, and grill.
6. Attach spit rod to motor.
7. Place a drip pan under meat in front of coals to catch fat and juices for basting, and to prevent flareups. Use any shallow metal pan, or make one from heavy-duty aluminum foil.
8. Turn on motor. As meat revolves on the spit, the natural juices on the surface will baste the food. Additional basting with drippings or with special sauce is optional.
9. Sauces that burn easily should be applied only during the last 10 minutes of cooking.
10. Remove roast when thermometer is about 5° below desired degree of doneness. Allow to set 20 minutes before serving. It will continue to cook while standing and will carve more easily.

 When inserting spit rod into meat, check balance by rotating spit on palms of hands. It should rotate evenly.

**TIMETABLE FOR ROASTING BEEF
ON A SPIT**

Rare	12 to 20 minutes per pound
Medium	15 to 25 minutes per pound
Well-done	35 to 40 minutes per pound

Carving

A perfectly cooked roast or steak, properly carved, is a triumph. Poor carving can turn it into a disaster. Good carving is not difficult, but it is impossible without a very sharp knife. A few strokes of the knife against a sharpening steel each time the knife is used make the difference between a carved roast and a mangled one.

When carving a slice, use a light sawing motion, as smooth as possible, to obtain even slices. Don't hack at the meat, and don't change the angle of the knife blade once a slice is started.

Rib Roast:

1. Place roast flat on the platter, rib bones on side opposite from carving hand.
2. Slice across the top, against the grain, to the rib bone.
3. Free slice from bone with knife tip.
4. Lift slice on knife, steadying with fork, and remove to serving platter.

Note: Some people prefer to stand a roast on its ribs to carve it. If you do, turn the diagram sideways.

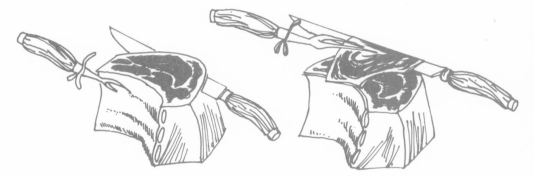

Rolled Roast:

1. Place roast on the platter, cut end upright.
2. Slice evenly across the top. As each cord-tie is reached, cut with knife and remove.
3. Lift slice on knife, steadying with fork, and remove to serving platter.

Flank Steak (London Broil):

1. Place on platter with long side towards carver.
2. Cut very thin slices at an angle.

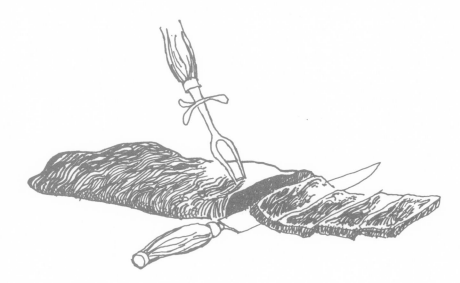

Loin Porterhouse or Loin T-bone Steak:

1. Cut around the bone and remove it.
2. Slice across the width of the steak. Be sure to include tenderloin and top loin in each portion.

Loin Shell Sirloin Steak:

1. Cut around the bone and remove it.
2. Slice across the width of the steak.

Cooking Terms

Bake: To cook by dry heat in an oven.

Barbecue: To roast or broil on a rack or revolving spit over hot coals or in an oven, usually basting with a highly seasoned sauce.

Barbecue, Pit: To cook large cuts of meat, wrapped in paper and burlap and dipped in water, by placing over beds of hot coals, covering with damp soil, and allowing to steam 12 to 24 hours.

Baste: To moisten foods during cooking with a liquid, usually pan drippings or a sauce, to prevent drying and to add flavor.

Blanch: Either to pour boiling water over food in order to facilitate removal of outer skin; or to place meat in cold water to cover, bring to a boil, simmer for a specified length of time, and then plunge into cold water.

Blend: To combine ingredients by stirring, rather than beating.

Boil: To cook in liquid at a temperature of 212°; bubbles rise to the surface and break.

Braise: To cook at low temperature with small amount of liquid in tightly covered pan.

Bread: To coat food with dry bread or cracker crumbs; usually the food is dipped in milk or beaten egg between breadings to make crumbs adhere.

Broil: To cook by direct heat, usually in a broiler or over coals.

Brown: To darken the surface of food by cooking quickly in hot fat on top of stove or at high heat in the oven or broiler.

Chill: To make food cold without freezing it.

Chop: To cut into small pieces about the size of peas.

Coat: To cover food lightly but thoroughly with a dry or liquid substance.

Cool: To allow to stand until food or utensil is no longer warm to the touch.

Correct seasoning: To taste food during cooking and add seasoning if necessary.

Cube: To cut into small, even pieces, generally ¼ to ½ inch.

Deep fry: See fry.

Dice: To cut food into very small uniform cubes.

Dilute: To thin or weaken a substance by adding liquid to it.

Dissolve: To make a solution by adding liquid to a solid substance, or by melting over low heat.

Dot: To place small pieces of butter or other substance over the surface of food.

Drain: To remove liquid, usually by allowing it to drip off as food stands in a colander or strainer.

Dredge: To coat food heavily with flour or other fine, dry substance.

Dust: To lightly sprinkle the surface of food with sugar, flour, or crumbs.

Flour: To cover evenly with a thin layer of flour.

Fry: To cook in hot fat.

  Deep fry: To cook completely immersed in hot fat.

  Pan fry: To cook in fat about ⅛ inch deep.

  Stir fry: To fry small pieces of food in a very small amount of oil as quickly as possible at a very high temperature. Food must be stirred constantly, or turned over and over, to bring all surfaces into brief contact with the hot, oiled cooking utensil. A metal, bowl-like utensil called a wok is usually used. It is balanced on a metal ring to hold it stable above the source of heat. However, if no wok is available, it is still possible to stir fry in a large skillet, 12 to 14 inches, with high flaring sides.

Garnish: To decorate food before serving by adding small attractive foodstuffs, such as parsley sprigs or lemon wedges.

Grate: To separate food into very fine particles by rubbing on a grater.

Grease: To rub fat onto the surface of cooking utensils.

Grill: To cook on a gridiron, over hot coals or under a broiler.

Grind: To cut into very small pieces with a meat grinder or food mill.

Lard: To insert thin strips of fat salt pork into meats lacking natural marbling, such as veal, and which are to be cooked by dry heat. A thin tool, a larding needle, is used.

Marinate: To allow food to stand in a seasoned liquid (marinade) to tenderize and/or to add flavor.

Mince: To cut or chop into very fine pieces.

Pan broil: To cook uncovered in a skillet, removing fat as it accumulates.

Pan fry: See fry.

Parboil: To boil in a liquid until partially cooked, prior to completion by another cooking method.

Poach: To cook by simmering, completely submerged, in a liquid.

Precook: To partially cook by simmering, before final cooking.

Preheat: To heat an oven or broiler to desired temperature before cooking.

Reduce: To decrease the volume of a liquid by boiling rapidly.

Render: To liquefy fat from solid form by heating slowly.

Roast: To cook by dry heat without added liquid, usually in an oven.

Sauté: To brown or cook in a small amount of hot fat.

Scallop: To bake in layers, usually with cream or other sauce.

Sear: To brown the surface of meat very quickly with intense heat.

Season: To add salt, herbs, spices, or other ingredients to enhance the flavor of food.

Shred: To break or cut into long, very narrow pieces.

Simmer: To cook over low heat at a temperature of 185° to 210°; bubbles form slowly and burst beneath the surface.

Skim: To remove a substance, usually fat, from the surface of a liquid. Skimming is facilitated if liquid is chilled so that fat rises to the surface, or by using a cold spoon drawn across the surface of the hot liquid.

Steam: To cook by means of vapor from boiling liquid rising through the food.

Steep: To extract color or flavor from a solid substance by letting it stand in liquid just below the boiling point.

Stew: To simmer slowly, covered with a seasoned liquid.

Stir: To move a utensil through a substance with a circular motion, in order to cool, mix, dissolve, or agitate the substance.

Stir fry: See fry.

Tenderize: To make meat tender by marinating, pounding, or applying a commercial tenderizer, such as M.S.G.

Thicken: To make a liquid substance more dense by adding an agent such as flour, egg yolks, cornstarch, arrowroot, potatoes, or rice.

Food Terms

Acidulated water: Water to which one tablespoon vinegar or lemon juice has been added to each quart of water.

Aspic: Flavored gelatin substance used to "trap" food.

Au jus: Applies to meat served with unthickened natural pan juices.

Bouillon: Stock or broth made by simmering meat, fish, or vegetables in liquid; may be in concentrated form.

Bouquet garni: Small bundle of herbs wrapped in cheesecloth or tied together, added to cooking for flavoring, and removed before serving.

Broth: Liquid in which meat, fish, poultry, or vegetable has been cooked.

Casserole: Baked dish combining several elements, usually including meat, fowl, or fish; pasta, potatoes, or rice; and a variety of vegetables.

Châteaubriand: Thick slice of beef from the center of the fillet, usually grilled and garnished with Château potatoes and a special sauce.

Condiment: Any seasoning added to food in order to enhance flavor; usually refers to prepared sauces and relishes.

Consommé: Clear, strongly seasoned soup made from stock.

Drippings: Fat and juices of meats that drip into the roasting pan while cooking.

Empanada: Small pastry filled with meat.

En brochette: Cooked on a skewer.

Fillet or filet: Boneless cut of lean meat, taken from the loin of beef.

Fondue Bourguignonne: Hot dish consisting of cubes of lean, tender beef cooked by dipping briefly into very hot fat.

Garbanzos: Chick peas.

Gnocchi: Dumplings made with wheat or potato flour.

Goulash: Thick, Hungarian meat and vegetable stew, usually flavored with paprika.

Guacamole: Mixture of mashed avocado, onion, spices, and lemon.

Hors d'oeuvre: A variety of light and delicate snacks served, hot or cold, before a meal to stimulate the appetite.

Julienne: Cut into very thin strips.

Kneaded butter: A blend made by kneading flour into an equal amount of softened butter; used for thickening.

Monosodium glutamate (MSG): White, crystalline substance used to enhance flavor.

Offal: Variety meats, or innards, such as heart, kidney, liver, or sweetbreads.

Pasta: Generic name for any product made with a dough of semolina and water, such as macaroni, noodles, or spaghetti.

Polenta: Thick cornmeal mush often served with a sauce, or a gravy. It can also be served as a side dish for stew.

Ragoût: Highly seasoned stew of meat and vegetables.

Roux: Smooth blend of butter and flour, which is cooked together briefly and then used for thickening.

Scallopini: Thin slices of meat, usually veal.

Skewer: Wooden or metal pin, used to hold meat in place during cooking or to thread small pieces of meat and vegetables onto for grilling.

Spit: Long metal rod onto which meat or poultry is threaded and then roasted or grilled.

Stew: Thick combination of foods, usually including meat, fish, or poultry, cooked for a long time in liquid at a low temperature.

Stock: Liquid in which meat, poultry, fish, bones, or vegetables and seasonings have been cooked.

Suet: Crumbly white fat deposited around the kidneys and loin of beef.

Tortilla: Flat unleavened bread made of corn flour. If made with wheat, it is called a flour tortilla.

Weights and Measures

Liquid volume

Dash or pinch	less than ⅛ teaspoon
1 tablespoon	3 teaspoons
2 tablespoons	1 fluid ounce
4 tablespoons	¼ cup
5⅓ tablespoons	⅓ cup
8 tablespoons	½ cup
16 tablespoons	1 cup
1 cup	8 fluid ounces
2 cups	1 pint
4 cups	1 quart
1 liter	1.05 quarts
1 deciliter	3.3 fluid ounces

Dry weight

16 dry ounces	1 pound
1 ounce	28.35 grams
1 pound	454 grams
1 gram	0.035 ounces
1 kilogram	2.2 pounds

Can Size	Weight	Approximate Cups
8 oz.	8 oz.	1
Picnic	10½ to 12 oz.	1¼
12 oz. vacuum	12 oz.	1½
No. 300	14 to 16 oz.	1¾
No. 303	16 to 17 oz.	2
No. 2	20 oz. (1 lb. 4 oz.) or 1 pt. 2 fl. oz.	2½
No. 2½	29 oz. (1 lb. 13 oz.)	3½

Equivalents

Avocado	1 medium	2 cups chopped
Beans		
dried	1 cup uncooked	2½–3 cups cooked
Beef	1 lb. raw	2 cups ground, raw
		3 cups diced, cooked
Bread crumbs		
dry	1 slice bread	⅓ cup
soft	1 slice bread	¾ cup
Butter or margarine	¼ lb.	½ cup (8 tablespoons)
Cabbage	1 lb.	4 cups shredded
		2 cups cooked
Carrots	1 lb. (8–10)	2½ cups cooked or shredded
Celery	1 stalk	½ cup finely chopped
Cheese, American		
or Cheddar	1 lb.	4 cups shredded
Cornmeal	1 cup uncooked	4 cups cooked
Flour, all-purpose	1 lb.	4 cups
Gelatin, unflavored	¼ oz. envelope	1 tablespoon
Green bell pepper	1 large (6 oz.)	1 cup diced
Lemon	1 medium	2½ tablespoons juice
Macaroni	8 oz. (2 cups) uncooked	4 cups cooked
Mushrooms	1 lb. fresh	4 cups sliced, raw
		6 oz. canned
Noodles	8 oz. (5½ cups) uncooked	4–6 cups cooked
Onion	1 medium	½ cup chopped, fresh or frozen
Potatoes	1 lb. (3 medium)	2½ cups diced, cooked
Rice	1 lb. (2 cups) uncooked	6 cups cooked
Rice, precooked	1 cup	2 cups cooked
Spaghetti	8 oz. uncooked	3½ cups cooked
Tomatoes	1 lb. (3–4 medium)	1½ cups chopped, cooked

Substitutions

Beef stock base
  1 teaspoon powdered
  4 teaspoons powdered + 1¼ cups
    water

1 beef bouillon cube
1 10½ oz. can undiluted beef bouillon or
  consommé

Catsup or chili sauce
  1 cup

1 cup tomato sauce + ½ cup sugar + 2
  tablespoons vinegar

Flour (for thickening)
  1 tablespoon

1½ teaspoons cornstarch
1½ teaspoons arrowroot
2 teaspoons quick-cooking tapioca

Garlic
  1 clove

⅛ teaspoon garlic powder

Ginger
  1 teaspoon fresh, chopped

2 teaspoons crystallized, chopped
¼ teaspoon ground

Herbs
  3 teaspoons fresh

1 teaspoon dried

Horseradish
  2 tablespoons bottled, prepared

1 tablespoon dry, + 1 tablespoon water
  + 1 tablespoon vinegar + sugar
  and salt to taste

Milk
  1 cup whole

½ cup evaporated + ½ cup water
1 cup nonfat dry, reconstituted + 2 teaspoons butter or margarine

Onion
  1 medium

1 tablespoon instant minced

Pepper, green bell
  1 tablespoon fresh, chopped

1 teaspoon dried

Pepper, red bell
  1 tablespoon fresh, chopped

1 teaspoon dried
2 teaspoons pimiento, chopped

Ricotta cheese

Cottage cheese

Tomato juice
  1 cup

½ cup tomato sauce + ½ cup water

Roasts

Cowboy way of
cooking a big
chunk of beef:
over th' spit
or in th' pit

THEN as NOW
His spit cooking—
dry-heat method
His pit cooking—
moist-heat method

Fact is, a roast is a big hunk of beef, and if yore inter'sted in my horseback opinion, beef is about th' best eatin' there is!

In th' old days we'd string beef roasts on a spit rigged up out of metal or a length of green wood laid accrost two stout, forked posts pounded deep into th' ground. We'd cook over th' coals an' holler, "Hey, somebody keep that spit aturnin'!" Or we'd bury beef (wrapped in sacks or covered over in tubs) with hot coals in a hole in th' ground an' let th' beef steam in its own juices. It wuz th' only way we knowed how to cook big hunks of beef.

Now today some of th' cooks an' equipment has changed but not th' Barbecue! It's still bein' cooked, served, an' bragged about from coast to coast.

PIT BARBECUE

First set a couple of th' hands to work diggin' a pit four-foot wide, three an' a half-foot deep, an' long enuf to hold all th' roasts. Th' pit should have straight sides an' be dug in well-drained clay or loamy soil.

For yore beef, boneless roasts weighin' twelve to fifteen pounds each is th' best. (Five roasts 'll serve a hunnerd to a hunnerd an' twenty people.) Season each roast with salt, pepper, and garlic or yore fav'rite seasonin's. Wrap each roast in heavy-duty aluminum foil and then in burlap, pokin' a hole here an' there to let steam out. Tie up each bundle with twine or wire.

Sixteen to eighteen hours before you figger on eatin', build a good fire in th' pit with th' hardest wood you can rustle up. Git a lot of wood, 'cuz th' woodpile should be at least three times bigger'n th' pit. Keep addin' wood 'til th' bed of coals is about two-and-a-half-foot deep. This'll take about six hours.

Then rake th' coals level an' cover 'em with an inch of gravel or coarse sand an' put th' bundles of roasts in th' pit, leavin' some air space around each bundle. Be shore ya c'n see red glow thru gravel. Cover th' pit fast with a metal lid. Ya can use metal pipes covered with sheet iron or corrugated roofing. Cover th' lid with dirt an' seal it good by hosin' with water and trompin' with feet, so's no heat or steam can git out.

Leave th' meat alone to cook in th' pit for ten to twelve hours. Then jist open th' pit real careful. Take th' roasts out with a pitchfork, unwrap, slice, slosh on some barbecue sauce, holler, "Come 'n git it!" and stand back!

HEAVENLY ROAST BEEF

Ribs	Boneless Weight	Total Roasting Time at 500°
2	4½ to 5 pounds	25 to 30 minutes
3	8 to 9 pounds	40 to 45 minutes
4	11 to 12 pounds	55 to 60 minutes

Roast must be brought to room temperature before it is put in oven. Preheat oven to 500°. Rub roast lightly with flour. Season with salt and a generous amount of freshly ground pepper. Place roast on rack in uncovered shallow roasting pan and place in preheated oven. When cooking time is finished (see chart above), turn off oven. **Do not open oven door.** Leave roast in closed oven at least 2 hours and no more than 4 hours, depending on size of roast. Outside of roast will be crunchy. If a meat thermometer is used, insert it so that dial is visible through window in oven door.
Serve with Yorkshire Pudding (see page 205).

VARIATION FOR SLOW ROASTING: *Preheat oven to 200°. (It is not safe to cook meat at a lower temperature.) Roast 6 hours for a 4- to 6-pound roast, with or without ribs. During last 30 minutes of cooking, turn up oven to 325° to brown surface of meat.*

FLAMING ROAST BEEF
WITH MUSHROOM SAUCE 10 TO 12 SERVINGS

6½-pound boned, rolled rib roast
Salt and pepper to taste

Mushroom Sauce (see recipe below)

Preheat oven to 325°. Rub surface of meat with salt and pepper. Place, fat side up, on a rack in roasting pan. Roast to desired doneness. Turn off oven, remove roast to another pan and return it to the warm oven. Reserve pan with drippings. Leave oven door open and allow meat to stand while preparing sauce.

MUSHROOM SAUCE ABOUT 2½ CUPS

Roast drippings, divided
1 can (4 ounces) sliced mushrooms
1 teaspoon salt
2 tablespoons cornstarch

1 can (10½ ounces) condensed beef
*   broth or consommé*
½ cup rosé wine
½ cup brandy

Place 2 tablespoons roast drippings in a medium size saucepan and sauté mushrooms 3 minutes. Reserve remaining pan juices. Stir in salt and cornstarch, dissolved in water. Add beef broth and enough hot water to meat juices in roasting pan to make 1 pint liquid. Stir this liquid into mushroom-cornstarch mixture slowly, and simmer, stirring constantly, until slightly thickened. Add wine and simmer about 5 minutes. When ready to serve, place meat on warm platter or serving dish with a rim to hold juices. Place gravy in separate dish. Warm brandy. Spoon over the hot roast and flame at table. Serve immediately.

 You cooked a two-ton roast for dinner and the boss didn't come after all? See Leftovers, page 184.

opposite: RIB ROAST
page 50: BRAISED STEAK
page 51: GRILLED STEAK

BEEF WELLINGTON 10 TO 12 SERVINGS

5-pound loin tenderloin roast, trimmed	*1 bay leaf, crumbled*
2 tablespoons butter or margarine,	*2 stalks celery*
melted	*½ onion, sliced*
½ teaspoon salt	*4 sprigs parsley*
¼ teaspoon pepper	*Easy Pâté (see recipe below)*
Pinch of rosemary	*Pastry (see recipe below)*

Preheat oven to 450°. Brush melted butter over meat. Season with salt and pepper. Place on rack uncovered in shallow roasting pan. Sprinkle with rosemary and bay leaf. Place celery, onion, and parsley on top of meat. Roast 15 minutes for rare, slightly longer if medium is preferred. Remove roast from oven and brush off vegetables and as much seasoning as possible. Cool while making pâté.

EASY PATE

¾ pound liverwurst	*¼ cup heavy cream*
1 medium onion, finely chopped	*¼ cup Cognac*
¼ cup butter or margarine	

Remove casing from liverwurst and place in bowl. Sauté onion in butter until soft but not browned. Add to liverwurst. Slowly add cream and Cognac and mix well. Spread pâté evenly on top and sides of roast.

PASTRY

3 cups flour	*1 cup shortening*
1 teaspoon salt	*1 egg yolk*

Sift together flour and salt. Cut in shortening with pastry blender or fork. Slowly add 7 to 8 tablespoons cold water, a few tablespoons at a time to make smooth dough. Roll pastry into ⅛ inch thick rectangle, large enough to surround roast.
Place pâté-covered meat on pastry. Surround meat with pastry and seal with water. If oven has been turned off, preheat again to 450°. Place meat on lightly-oiled baking sheet. Make egg wash by beating egg yolk with 1 or 2 tablespoons water or milk. Brush on pastry. Bake 15 minutes or until golden.
Garnish with fluted mushrooms.
NOTE: *This recipe is not recommended for those who prefer well-done meat.*

 Cook frozen beef roasts at 300° to 325°, allowing ⅓ to ½ additional time for cooking. Braise frozen pot roasts in the same way nonfrozen roasts are braised.

Don't crowd carving area with garnishes, extra dishes, wine glasses, or other obstructions. You'll give the carver—not to mention the roast—claustrophobia.

opposite: SAUERBRATEN

HAM STUFFED FILLET 10 TO 12 SERVINGS

6- to 7-pound loin tenderloin roast
4 tablespoons butter or margarine
4 tablespoons olive oil
2 large onions, chopped
2 cloves garlic, minced
2 cans (2¾ ounces each) chopped ripe
    olives

½ cup finely chopped cooked ham
Salt and pepper to taste
1 teaspoon thyme
2 tablespoons chopped parsley
2 egg yolks, lightly beaten
1 tablespoon butter or margarine,
    melted

Preheat oven to 300°. Combine butter and olive oil in medium skillet. Sauté onion until soft but not browned. Add garlic, olives, ham, salt, pepper, thyme, and parsley. Cook until just warm and well mixed. Carefully stir in egg yolks and cook about 3 minutes longer. Cut long pocket in center of fillet. Fill pocket with ham mixture. Tie in at least two places and set on rack in uncovered roasting pan. Brush with melted butter. Roast about 50 minutes or to desired doneness (rare is recommended). Allow to stand several minutes before serving.
Serve with mushroom gravy (see page 203).

ROAST FILLET OF BEEF WITH WINE SAUCE 8 TO 10 SERVINGS

4-pound loin tenderloin roast, wrapped
    in thin layer of suet
Salt and pepper to taste
2 cups Burgundy or other dry red wine,
    divided

¼ cup flour
1 cup beef broth

Preheat oven to 450°. Rub meat with salt and pepper and place on rack uncovered in shallow pan. Roast to desired doneness, basting twice with ½ cup wine after meat has cooked 20 minutes. Remove roast to heated serving platter. Skim fat from drippings, reserving ¼ cup. Pour ½ cup wine into roasting pan; stir and scrape up all brown bits; strain. Heat reserved drippings in skillet, gradually add flour. Slowly stir in strained liquid, beef broth and 1 cup wine. Cook, stirring, until sauce thickens. Add a few drops of gravy coloring, if desired, and correct seasoning.
Garnish roast with mushroom caps, parsley, and crab apples. Serve Wine Sauce on the side.

MARINATED PATIO ROAST 12 TO 16 SERVINGS

6- to 8-pound boneless round rump,
    eye, or tip roast
½ cup finely chopped onion
⅓ cup butter or margarine

1 cup dry white wine
2 teaspoons salt
2 tablespoons chopped parsley
1 tablespoon crushed mint leaves

Sauté onion in butter until soft but not browned. Slowly stir in wine and salt. Bring to a boil, reduce heat, and simmer 5 minutes. Remove from heat, add parsley and mint, mix well. Cool. Marinate roast in cooled wine mixture 2 hours in refrigerator, turning occasionally. Cook on rotisserie, basting every 30 minutes with marinade. (See page 35 for timing.)

VARIATION: Roast in 325° oven 2½ to 3 hours, basting at 30 minute intervals.

MARINATED BARBECUED BEEF 6 TO 8 SERVINGS

*3½-pound chuck blade or 7-bone
    pot roast
Instant meat tenderizer
½ cup soy sauce
2½ tablespoons brown sugar*

*1½ tablespoons granulated sugar
1 tablespoon tarragon vinegar
1 tablespoon ginger
1 clove garlic, crushed*

Pierce meat with a fork, sprinkle tenderizer on both sides. Combine remaining ingredients and pour over meat. Marinate 3 or 4 hours, turning several times. Barbecue meat over slow fire about 1 hour, or to desired doneness. Baste with marinade during last 10 minutes of cooking.

ROLLED ROAST
WITH BARBECUE SAUCE 6 TO 8 SERVINGS

*3½-pound boneless rolled round rump,
    eye, or tip roast
4 teaspoons catsup
4 teaspoons vinegar
4 teaspoons butter or margarine
4 teaspoons Worcestershire sauce
½ teaspoon cayenne*

*4 teaspoons lemon juice
2 teaspoons prepared mustard
2 teaspoons salt
2 teaspoons paprika
1 teaspoon chili powder
4 teaspoons brown sugar
3 drops liquid smoke*

Preheat oven to 350°. Place meat on rack uncovered in roasting pan and cook to desired doneness. Set aside. Combine all ingredients, except meat, with 8 teaspoons of water in saucepan. Simmer 10 to 15 minutes. Slice roast and arrange slices in shallow pan. Cover with sauce and return to 350° oven until sauce and meat are hot.

Watch beef when basting. It burns more quickly than unbasted beef.

BEEF BRISKET 6 TO 8 SERVINGS

*3½-pound brisket
Garlic powder
Salt and pepper to taste
Instant meat tenderizer*

*2 teaspoons liquid smoke
2 teaspoons lemon juice
Pinch of cayenne*

Preheat oven to 300°. Sprinkle garlic powder, salt, pepper, and tenderizer on meat. Mix liquid smoke, lemon juice, and cayenne and brush surface of meat with mixture. Wrap meat completely in foil or baking bag, place in roasting pan, and bake 2½ to 3 hours, or until tender.

Remove roasts from oven about 5° underdone and allow to "set" 15 to 30 minutes, depending on size. This makes it easier to carve—also easier for the pets to get at, so watch out!

PINEAPPLE FLAVORED ROAST 6 TO 8 SERVINGS

*3-pound boneless round rump, eye, or
   tip roast
2 tablespoons lemon juice
Flour
1 teaspoon sugar*

*1 teaspoon salt
¼ teaspoon rosemary
¼ teaspoon thyme
¼ cup chopped onion
2½ cups pineapple juice*

Cut slits in roast and fill with lemon juice. Allow to stand overnight in refrigerator, well covered. Preheat oven to 325°. Dredge roast with flour; mix dry ingredients and sprinkle over meat. Place in roasting pan, add onion and pineapple juice. Roast 2½ hours, or until tender, basting several times during cooking.

EASY OVEN POT ROAST 6 TO 8 SERVINGS

*3- to 4-pound boneless chuck top or
   under blade roast
1 package (1⅜ ounces) dry onion soup
   mix*

Flour

Preheat oven to 350°. Place meat on large piece of heavy-duty foil in roasting pan. Sprinkle soup mix around it. Close foil with double fold to make airtight package. Roast 2½ to 3 hours. When finished remove meat to warm platter. Pour juice into saucepan. Skim off excess fat and thicken liquid with flour (1 tablespoon flour to 1 cup liquid). For added zest, flavor gravy with red wine (see Wine Chart page 198).

 Hate cleaning the oven? Special cooking bags save spills and splatters—and they're self-basting, too. Consult manufacturer's instructions for details—but for Heaven's sake, don't use any old plastic bag unless you want melted plastic all over everything.

HAWAIIAN POT ROAST 6 TO 8 SERVINGS

*3½-pound boneless chuck shoulder or
   round rump roast
2 tablespoons cooking oil
Salt and pepper to taste
¼ cup soy sauce
1 can (9 ounces) pineapple chunks,
   (reserve juice)*

*¼ teaspoon ginger
1 medium onion, sliced
1 can (4 ounces) mushroom stems and
   pieces
⅓ cup sliced celery
Flour*

Sear meat on all sides in cooking oil in large skillet or dutch oven. Drain off oil, season meat with salt and pepper. Mix soy sauce, pineapple juice, ginger, and onion. Pour over meat. Cover and simmer 2¾ hours. Add more liquid if necessary. Add mushrooms, celery, and pineapple chunks and simmer 15 minutes or until meat is tender. Correct seasoning. Thicken gravy with flour, if desired (1 tablespoon flour to 1 cup liquid).

POLYNESIAN POT ROAST 6 TO 8 SERVINGS

3½-pound boneless round rump roast,
   tied
1½ teaspoons instant meat tenderizer
1 large onion, sliced
1 cup pineapple juice
3 tablespoons soy sauce
1½ teaspoons ginger

½ teaspoon salt
4 stalks celery, sliced diagonally
4 carrots, cut in julienne
½ pound spinach, washed,
   stems removed
1 tablespoon cornstarch

Sprinkle meat with tenderizer. Place onion slices in bottom of 3-quart casserole or bowl. Set meat on top. Combine pineapple juice, soy sauce, ginger, and salt and pour over meat. Cover and refrigerate several hours or overnight. Place onion and meat in dutch oven, add marinade, cover and simmer 1½ to 2 hours, or until meat is tender. Add celery and carrots and continue cooking about 8 minutes. Add spinach and cook until it wilts and other vegetables are tender. Remove roast and vegetables to heated platter. Blend cornstarch with 2 tablespoons of water and stir into gravy. Cook, stirring, until it thickens (about 3 minutes). Serve separately.

 Slice off excess fat from roasts while meat is still half-frozen.

FRUITED POT ROAST 8 SERVINGS

4-pound boneless chuck shoulder or
   round rump roast
2 tablespoons cooking oil
Salt and pepper to taste
½ teaspoon rosemary
1 teaspoon cinnamon

¼ teaspoon nutmeg
1 can (11 ounces) mandarin oranges
1 package (12 ounces) mixed dried fruit,
   cut in small pieces
1½ cups dry vermouth
3 tablespoons cornstarch

Sear meat on all sides in cooking oil in heavy skillet or dutch oven. Drain off oil. Season meat with salt, pepper, rosemary, cinnamon, and nutmeg. Add oranges, dried fruit, and vermouth. Cover and simmer 3½ hours, or until tender. Remove meat. Combine cornstarch with ½ cup water. Add cornstarch to gravy and simmer until clear and thickened.

 If you need to skim fat off the top of the liquid in which a pot roast is simmering, use a fat-catcher—a cloth filled with a few ice cubes which is skimmed over the surface of the liquid.

BOEUF NICOISE 6 TO 8 SERVINGS

*4½-pound chuck top or under blade
    roast, trimmed
1 teaspoon rosemary
4 tablespoons flour
2 teaspoons seasoned salt
Salt and pepper to taste
3 tablespoons olive oil
1 cup dry red wine
1 large whole onion studded with
    10 whole cloves*

*2 cloves garlic, mashed
1 can (28 ounces) peeled whole toma-
    toes, drained, or 7 peeled fresh
    tomatoes
⅓ cup brandy or dry vermouth
1 can (2¾ ounces) sliced ripe olives,
    drained
Flour*

Mix rosemary with 4 tablespoons flour and seasonings and pound into meat. Brown meat on both sides in olive oil in heavy kettle. Remove meat, drain fat, and pour wine into sizzling hot pan. Return meat to pan. Add onion and garlic. Cover and simmer 2 hours. Turn meat, add tomatoes and simmer another 1½ hours or until tender. Just before serving, add brandy and olives. Remove meat and thicken sauce with a little flour mixed with water, if desired.

 Running out of time with a simmering pot roast? Remove from pot, slice thin, and return to pot. It will cook faster.

SAUERBRATEN 12 SERVINGS

*6-pound boneless chuck top blade or
    round rump roast
1½ cups dry red wine
½ cup wine vinegar
1 bay leaf
6 whole cloves
5 peppercorns*

*Salt to taste
2 large onions, diced
¼ cup cooking oil
4 tablespoons butter or margarine
5 tablespoons flour
1 tablespoon sugar
¾ cup crushed gingersnaps*

Place meat in earthen or glass dish (not metal). Combine wine, vinegar, seasonings, onion, and 2 cups water. Pour over meat, cover, and let stand in marinade 2 days in refrigerator, turning each day. Remove meat from liquid, pat dry, and brown in heavy skillet in cooking oil. Drain off fat. Strain marinade, pour over meat, cover, and simmer about 3 hours, or until tender. Remove meat to platter and keep warm. Pour off liquid and set aside. In same skillet melt butter, add flour and sugar, stir until smooth. Add liquid from meat slowly and cook until thickened. Add gingersnaps and cook until dissolved. Return meat to skillet and cook covered 30 minutes.
Serve with hot noodles.

CIDER POT ROAST 8 TO 10 SERVINGS

4- to 5-pound boneless chuck top
    or under blade roast
2 tablespoons flour
1 tablespoon salt
¼ teaspoon pepper
¼ teaspoon ginger
2 tablespoons cooking oil
1½ cups apple cider or apple juice,
    divided

1 can (1 pound 7 ounces) sweet pota-
    toes, drained and mashed
1 tablespoon brown sugar
2 tablespoons butter or margarine
½ teaspoon salt
6 baking apples, cored, top half peeled
¾ cup currant jelly
Flour

Preheat oven to 325°. Combine 2 tablespoons flour, 1 tablespoon salt, pepper, and ginger. Dredge meat in seasoned flour and brown in cooking oil in heavy skillet. Transfer meat to baking dish, add 1 cup cider. Cover tightly and cook 3 to 4 hours, or until meat is tender. When meat has been cooking about 2½ hours, mix sweet potatoes with brown sugar, butter, and ½ teaspoon salt. Spoon mixture into cored apples and place in ovenproof baking dish. Heat remaining cider and currant jelly in saucepan until jelly is dissolved, and pour over apples. Bake in oven with meat 50 minutes, or until apples are cooked. Remove meat to heated platter; arrange apples around it. Combine cooking liquids and thicken with flour (1 tablespoon flour to 1 cup liquid). Serve as gravy.

 Pot roast can be seared under the broiler as well as on top of the stove. This is a great method for diet watchers.

GREEK POT ROAST 6 TO 8 SERVINGS

3½-pound boneless chuck shoulder or
    round rump roast
2 tablespoons cooking oil
Salt and pepper to taste
1 large onion, chopped
1 can (8 ounces) tomato sauce
½ cup dry red wine
1 tablespoon wine vinegar
1 tablespoon brown sugar

1 bay leaf
1 clove garlic, mashed
½ teaspoon ground cumin
1 large eggplant, peeled and cut
    in chunks
2 green bell peppers, seeded and cut
    in squares
1 can (16 ounces) whole onions,
    undrained

Sear meat on all sides in cooking oil in large skillet or dutch oven. Remove meat, season with salt and pepper, and set aside. Sauté onion until transparent. Drain off oil and add next 7 ingredients plus 1 cup water. Bring to slow boil. Return meat to skillet. Cover and simmer 2½ hours, or until tender. Add more liquid if needed. Add vegetables. Cover and simmer 30 minutes, or until eggplant is tender. Correct seasoning and serve.

CRANBERRY POT ROAST 6 TO 8 SERVINGS

3½-pound boneless chuck shoulder or
    round rump roast
Instant meat tenderizer
2 tablespoons cooking oil
Salt and pepper to taste
1 medium onion, sliced

1 teaspoon celery salt
1 teaspoon Worcestershire sauce
1 pound cranberries (fresh, cooked,
    sweetened to taste) or 1 can
    (16 ounces) whole cranberry sauce

Preheat oven to 325°. Sprinkle meat tenderizer over beef and let stand at room temperature 20 minutes. Sear beef on all sides in oil in heavy skillet. Remove meat to ovenproof dish and season with salt and pepper. Sauté onion until soft but not browned. Mix onion, celery salt, Worcestershire, and ½ cup boiling water. Add to meat. Place 1 cup cranberries (or ½ can) on top of meat. Cover and bake in oven 2½ hours, or until tender. After 1 hour place remainder of cranberries on meat. Add more water during cooking if necessary. Correct seasoning and serve.

 Snap up loads of fresh cranberries when they're available and freeze for use out of season. Place unopened box directly in the freezer and they'll always be on hand.

OVEN-BRAISED BEEF 8 TO 10 SERVINGS

4- to 5-pound boneless chuck top or
    under blade roast
2 teaspoons salt
¼ teaspoon pepper
1 medium onion, thinly sliced
1 carrot, thinly sliced
1 rib celery, cut in thin crescents
1 cup dry red wine

¼ cup brandy
1 tablespoon tomato paste
3 sprigs parsley
1 clove garlic, minced
1 teaspoon crushed thyme
2 bay leaves
2 whole cloves
Cornstarch

Line bottom and sides of a shallow roasting pan with heavy-duty foil with overlap large enough to cover meat later. Arrange meat in the center. Place meat under broiler and brown lightly, turning several times. Remove pan from broiler and reset oven to 325°. Sprinkle meat with salt and pepper, and surround with onion, carrot, and celery. Combine wine, brandy, and tomato paste. Add parsley, garlic, thyme, bay leaves, and cloves. Pour over meat. Seal foil with double fold, return meat to oven, and roast until tender, 3½ to 4 hours. Remove beef to a warm platter. Strain juices into a quart measure. Skim off fat. Mix 1 tablespoon cornstarch with 1 tablespoon cold water for each 1¼ cups liquid. Add cornstarch mixture to pan. Stir in strained liquid and cook over moderate heat, stirring constantly, until slightly thickened. Correct seasoning.
To prepare this dish ahead, refrigerate cooked meat and strained liquid separately. When ready to use, remove fat from top of liquid and make sauce as directed. Slice meat fairly thin and reheat in sauce.

 To recycle used cooking oil, fry slices of raw potato in the oil until the potatoes are brown. They will absorb even the strongest flavors and be either delicious or inedible, depending on what was cooked in the oil previously.

ONION POT ROAST 6 TO 8 SERVINGS

*3½-pound boneless chuck shoulder or
    round rump roast*
2 tablespoons cooking oil
Salt and pepper to taste
*1 package (1⅜ ounces) dry onion soup
    mix, diluted in 1 cup water*

8 medium carrots, cut in 3 pieces each
3 stalks celery, cut in 2-inch pieces
Flour

Sear meat on all sides in cooking oil in large skillet or dutch oven. Drain off oil. Season meat with salt and pepper. Add onion soup, cover, and simmer 2½ hours. Add more liquid if necessary. Add carrots and celery and continue cooking 30 minutes, or until meat and vegetables are tender. Thicken cooking liquid with flour, if desired (1 tablespoon flour to 1 cup liquid).

POT ROAST WITH HERB GRAVY 6 TO 8 SERVINGS

*3½-pound boneless chuck shoulder or
    round rump roast.*
2 tablespoons cooking oil
Salt and pepper to taste
*1 beef bouillon cube, dissolved in 1 cup
    water*

2 bay leaves
½ teaspoon marjoram
¼ teaspoon basil
½ teaspoon garlic powder
1 teaspoon chopped parsley
Flour

Sear meat on all sides in cooking oil in large skillet or dutch oven. Drain off oil. Season meat with salt and pepper. Combine all other ingredients and pour over meat. Cover and simmer 3 hours, or until tender. Add more liquid if necessary. Discard bay leaves. Thicken gravy with flour, if desired (1 tablespoon flour to 1 cup liquid).

 Keep your carving knives razor-sharp. Don't use them to pry off jar tops or to open packages. Always use them on a cutting board. It doesn't have to be a fancy butcher block; even a plain piece of plywood will do.

SOUTHERN POT ROAST 6 TO 8 SERVINGS

3½-pound boneless chuck shoulder or
*   bottom round roast*
2 tablespoons cooking oil
Salt and pepper to taste
¼ cup dry vermouth
1 can (15 ounces) stewed tomatoes
1 can (8 ounces) tomato sauce
1 can (6 ounces) tomato paste

1 teaspoon sugar
1 large onion, chopped
1 green bell pepper, diced
6 potatoes, halved
6 carrots, cut in 2-inch sections
1 can (16 ounces) whole white onions,
*   drained*

Sear meat on all sides in cooking oil in large skillet or dutch oven. Remove meat, season with salt and pepper, and set aside. Drain off oil. Reduce heat. Add vermouth to skillet and scrape to loosen meat particles. Add stewed tomatoes, tomato sauce, tomato paste, sugar, chopped onion, and bell pepper. Return meat to skillet, cover, and simmer 2½ hours. Add potatoes and carrots, and simmer 15 minutes. Add whole onions and simmer 15 minutes more or until meat and vegetables are tender. Correct seasoning and serve.

CURRY POT ROAST 6 TO 8 SERVINGS

3½-pound boneless chuck shoulder roast
2 tablespoons cooking oil
Salt and pepper to taste

3½ teaspoons curry powder
½ teaspoon sugar
1 medium onion, sliced

Sear meat on all sides in cooking oil in large skillet or dutch oven. Drain off oil. Season meat with salt, pepper, curry powder, and sugar. Add ½ to ¾ cup water and onion. Cover and simmer 3 hours, or until tender. Add more liquid if necessary.

BURGUNDY BRISKET POT ROAST 6 TO 8 SERVINGS

3½-pound brisket
2 tablespoons bacon fat or cooking oil
Salt and pepper to taste
2 onions, sliced
3 tablespoons flour
1 beef bouillon cube, dissolved
*   in 1 cup boiling water*

½ cup catsup
1 tablespoon bottled browning sauce
2 teaspoons salt
½ teaspoon thyme
½ teaspoon garlic powder
1 cup red Burgundy wine
2 tablespoons dry sherry

Sear meat on all sides in bacon fat in large skillet or dutch oven. Remove meat, season with salt and pepper, and set aside. Add onion and sauté until soft but not browned. Drain off fat. Return meat to skillet. Mix flour, dissolved bouillon cube, catsup, and browning sauce and pour over meat. Add seasonings, Burgundy and sherry. Simmer, covered, 3 hours or until meat is tender. Add more liquid if needed. Carrots and potatoes may be added 30 minutes before meat is done. Correct seasoning and serve.

POTTED BEEF IN BEER 6 TO 8 SERVINGS

3½-pound boneless chuck shoulder
    pot roast
1 large onion, sliced
1½ cups chopped celery
Peel of ½ lemon
1 teaspoon salt
¼ teaspoon pepper

1 bay leaf
1 can (4 ounces) mushroom stems and
    pieces
1 can (12 ounces) beer
1½ cups sliced carrots
3 medium potatoes, halved
⅓ cup flour

Place all but last 3 ingredients in a large kettle. Cover and simmer over low heat (or bake at 300°) 3 hours, or until meat is fork-tender. Add carrots and potatoes during last 30 minutes of cooking. Place meat and vegetables on warm platter. Discard lemon peel and bay leaf. Blend flour to a smooth paste with ½ cup water. Stir into pan liquid slowly and cook, stirring, until thickened. Serve as gravy.

 When searing pot roast on all sides prior to braising or cooking in liquid, turn it over with two large spoons. Don't use a long-handled fork, which will pierce the meat and allow juices to escape.

Always use level measures. Measure liquids at eye level. Make sure dry ingredients are leveled off with a knife or other flat utensil.

A quick, easy, and calorie-conscious way to brown meatballs is to place them in a shallow pan in a 400° oven and roast until browned.

PRESSURE COOKER BOILED BEEF 6 SERVINGS

2-pound boneless chuck under blade
    roast or brisket
1 onion studded with 2 whole cloves
    and 4 peppercorns
2 stalks celery

2 cans (10½ ounces) condensed
    consommé
1 envelope unflavored gelatin,
    softened in 2 tablespoons water

Place meat in pressure cooker. Add onion, celery, and consommé. Mix softened gelatin with 2 soup cans of water. Add to meat. Cook 20 minutes, or according to pressure cooker directions. Bring pressure down immediately by running cold water over sides of cooker. Remove cover. Simmer slowly, uncovered, on top of stove 10 minutes or until done (last cooking to remove steamy taste). Serve the broth garnished with parsley. Slice beef about 1 inch thick and serve with pickled gherkins and horseradish.

 Don't be afraid to buy prefrozen beef—its quality is as good or better than unfrozen meat. Prefrozen beef has been frozen scientifically at high speed and low temperature, so it retains maximum moisture and flavor. Added bonus: meat is already professionally freezer-wrapped!

MEAT FILLINGS FOR MEXICAN TREATS

SHREDDED BRISKET

4- to 5-pound brisket
2 teaspoons salt

1 teaspoon garlic powder
6 to 8 peppercorns

Place meat in dutch oven, cover with water, add salt, garlic, and peppercorns. Cover and cook 2 to 3 hours, or until tender. Cool and shred meat. Use for fillings below.

CHIMICHONGAS 2 DOZEN

Shredded brisket (see recipe above)
2 medium onions, chopped
2 tablespoons cooking oil
2 tablespoons olive oil
Salt, pepper, oregano, and garlic
 powder to taste

2 cans (4 ounces each) diced green
 chilies
Flour Tortillas (see page 206)

Brown onion in combined oils. Add shredded meat and brown. Add seasonings and chilies. Preheat oven to 425°. Place 2 or 3 tablespoons of filling near end of flour tortilla. Roll once, fold sides toward center, and continue rolling. Place, seamed side down, in baking dish and brush with small amount of cooking oil. Bake in hot oven until brown and crisp, about 15 minutes. Turn and allow other side to brown.

If desired, just before removing from oven, top with grated cheese or dairy sour cream. Or, after removing from oven, top with mashed avocado. Serve on shredded lettuce. These may be frozen before baking.

MACHACA BURROS 2 DOZEN

Same filling as above with 1 can (30 ounces) tomatoes added. Simmer until nearly dry. Follow filling and cooking instructions for Chimichongas.

NOTE: Fillings may also be added to scrambled eggs, or shredded brisket and green onions may be browned in cooking oil and served on buns.

TAMALES 3 DOZEN MEDIUM SIZE

SHREDDED BRISKET

4- to 5-pound brisket
3 teaspoons salt

36 (approximately) corn shucks,
 if available

The day before: simmer meat in salted water to cover, about 3 hours or until easy to shred. Allow to stand in broth overnight. Soak dry corn shucks separately overnight in water. Dry shucks may be purchased in bulk in some grocery stores or you can use fresh corn shucks which can be dried by placing in a warm, sunny spot 3 to 8 days until yellow. If corn shucks are not available use 6-x 8-inch pieces of aluminum foil or heavy plastic wrap.

Filling

Shredded brisket (see recipe above)
2 tablespoons cooking oil
2 tablespoons flour

1 jar (16 ounces) chili sauce
Few drops Tabasco sauce (optional)

Shred cooked beef. Reserve liquid. Place oil in a saucepan, blend in flour, add chili sauce. Thin with broth in which meat cooked if necessary for gravylike consistency. Add shredded beef and bring to a boil. Turn off heat and let stand while preparing masa. For hotter tamales, add a few drops of Tabasco to gravy.

Masa

2 cups bacon fat or lard (bacon fat is best)	2½ tablespoons salt
	8 cups liquid (beef broth plus water)
12 cups (5 pounds) masa flour (corn tamale or corn tortilla flour)	1 jar (16 ounces) chili sauce

Beat fat in electric mixer until fluffy. Blend in remaining ingredients. If necessary, add additional liquid to make masa spread easily.

TO ASSEMBLE TAMALES:

Hold a dampened corn shuck in one hand and spoon 1½ to 2 tablespoons masa onto it. Spread masa thin leaving a ½-inch margin at the sides and a 2-inch margin at the ends. Spoon filling along the center of masa. Bring side edges of shuck together, overlapping slightly, and fold ends under. Tie tamale with ¼-inch strip of shuck to hold ends flat. If aluminum foil or plastic wrap is used, twist ends to close. Once tamales are assembled, place them on edge on a steaming rack in a large kettle with 2 inches of water in the bottom. Place far enough apart so steam can circulate freely. Make sure boiling water can't touch tamales, especially if using plastic wrap. Cover and cook over medium heat. Water should boil gently. Steam about 2 hours. To test for doneness, remove a tamale from rack and open shuck. If masa does not stick to shuck, tamale is ready to eat, or ready to cool and wrap airtight for freezing. Reheat frozen tamales by steaming as above for 20 minutes.

HOMEMADE CORNED BEEF 12 SERVINGS

5-pound brisket	2 tablespoons pickling spices
1½ cups coarse salt	8 cloves garlic, divided
½ ounce saltpeter	1 onion, sliced
1 tablespoon brown sugar	½ cup vinegar
9 bay leaves, crumbled, divided	

Combine 4 quarts of water, salt, saltpeter, brown sugar, 6 bay leaves, and pickling spices. Boil 5 minutes, then cool. Place beef in large glass or stoneware crock. Add boiled mixture and 6 cloves garlic, slivered. Add extra water if needed to cover meat completely. Place heavy plate over meat and add weight to keep meat submerged. Tie a piece of muslin over top of crock. Muslin should be taut and tightly tied. Cover crock, leaving a gap to allow some air circulation. Let crock stand in cool place 2 weeks.
At end of 2 weeks, rinse meat well and place in dutch oven. Add fresh water to 1 inch above meat. Add 3 bay leaves, 2 cloves chopped garlic, onion, and vinegar. Bring to a boil, reduce heat, and simmer until meat is tender, 2½ to 3 hours.
Allow meat to stand, covered, 30 minutes. Drain well. Trim off fat and thinly slice meat.

Making corned beef from scratch is very rewarding. It also gives you something to do with that old crock that's been sitting around since "who knows when." But it takes two weeks. If you don't have two weeks, see recipe for New England Boiled Dinner, page 174.

Steaks

Cowboy way of
cooking a steak:
over th' coals
or in a dutch oven

THEN as NOW
His grilling—
dry-heat method
His dutch oven frying—
moist-heat method

We didn't always have beef on th' range, but when we did we ate it all—shoulders to shin bone, tail to tongue and most ever-thin' in between. Natch'raly there weren't no cut we liked better'n steak cut outa th' loin and served up for any meal.

Beef steaks are a dang sight tenderer now than they wuz in my day. These new cowmen know what they're about with pen-fed beef and select've breedin'—makes for real high qual'ty, tender beefsteak you c'n jist slap on a grill an' cook.

When we had tender steaks like that we'd plop 'em on a mesh wire to cook over th' coals, but if we had a tougher steak we'd fry it in th' dutch oven. We didn't know we'd roped ahold of dry an' moist methods of cookin' we jist did what come natural and wuz th' best eatin'.

I'm learnin' now that steaks can be grilled, char-broiled, baked, rolled, pan fried, broiled, basted, barbecued, mar'nated, or sauced up. You can cook a London Broil, Steak "My Tie," or even our ol' dutch oven fry steak, but you're still cookin' dry or moist. Cook dry an' there's nuthin' but air between th' beef and th' fire. (A pan is considered dry if collected fat or moisture is poured off as beef is cookin'.) Cook moist and there's water or steam or grease surroundin' th' beef and between it and th' fire. Most gen'rally we cook th' tender cuts with th' dry methods and th' less tender cuts with moist methods. Don't mix dry and moist cookin' on th' same steak or yore askin' for more trouble than tryin' to put a three-foot catch rope on a wild filly.

DUTCH OVEN FRY STEAK

First build a fire in a hole dug about nine inches deep and jist bigger than yore dutch oven. Give yoreself at least a half hour lead before you start to cook so's you'll have time to build up a good bed of coals to set th' dutch oven on.

Take any kind of steak and plunk it on a board. Mix up a handful of flour, a teaspoon salt, and half teaspoon pepper. Pound th' flour mixture into both sides of th' steak with a cleaver or whatever's handy.

When th' coals is ready, put th' dutch oven (half to three quarters full of some kind of cookin' oil) in th' hole. When th' fat is sizzlin' hot, drop in th' steak to deep fry 'til it's cooked jist th' way you like it.

STEAK DIANE INDIVIDUAL SERVING

½-pound tenderloin steak,
*   ½ inch thick, trimmed*
2½ tablespoons butter, divided
Salt and pepper to taste
1 teaspoon minced parsley

1 tablespoon minced chives
1 tablespoon minced shallots
1 tablespoon Cognac
2 tablespoons dry sherry
1½ teaspoons Worcestershire sauce

Use a chafing dish and cook meat at table, searing no more than one or two steaks at a time. Cream together 1½ tablespoons butter, salt, pepper, parsley, and chives. Set aside. Melt 1 tablespoon butter in chafing dish over medium heat and sauté shallots until just soft but not browned. Increase heat and sear steak quickly on each side. Remove meat to warm platter. Add Cognac to pan and flame. Reduce heat. Add seasoned butter, sherry, and Worcestershire and blend. Return meat to chafing dish just long enough to warm. Serve immediately with sauce.

NOTE: *All ingredients given are per portion.*

PEPPER STEAK FLAMBE 6 SERVINGS

2-pound porterhouse steak,
*   2½ inches thick*
2 tablespoons freshly ground pepper
1 tablespoon minced shallots

1 tablespoon minced parsley
3 tablespoons butter or margarine
1 teaspoon salt
⅓ cup bourbon

Press pepper into meat and allow to stand at room temperature 30 minutes. Broil steak on both sides to desired doneness. Salt meat on both sides. Remove to warm platter. In a small skillet sauté shallots and parsley in butter until shallots are soft but not browned. Pour heated bourbon over steak and ignite. Slice and serve with butter seasoned with salt, pepper, parsley, and chives.

For good cooking, preheat broiler. For best results, do this 5 minutes before you broil a steak.

Serving steak at an informal outdoor buffet? Slice thin and serve on hamburger rolls or French bread. Add corn on the cob and finger salad, and you can forget about silverware.

ROQUEFORT CHEESE STEAK 4 TO 6 SERVINGS

2-pound sirloin or porterhouse steak
1 clove garlic, mashed
¼ cup softened butter or margarine

¾ cup crumbled Roquefort cheese
Salt and pepper to taste

Combine garlic, butter, and Roquefort cheese. Blend well and set aside. Grill meat to desired doneness over hot coals, seasoning both sides with salt and pepper. Three minutes before steak is finished, spread top with cheese mixture.

BEEF BORDELAISE 6 SERVINGS

2½-pound sirloin steak, 1 inch thick
Salt and pepper to taste

1½ tablespoons butter or margarine
Bordelaise Sauce (see page 203)

Make Bordelaise Sauce and keep warm in double boiler. Dry steak thoroughly with paper towel, score edges and season with salt and pepper. Melt 1½ tablespoons butter in heavy skillet over medium heat until it foams. Cook steak 3 to 4 minutes on each side, then remove to heated platter and serve with hot sauce.

 Firebellringer for barbecuing: NEVER start a fire with gasoline or kerosene, and never add liquid starter after the coals are burning. But never!

RANCH GRILL 8 SERVINGS

3-pound sirloin steak, 2 inches thick
¼ cup olive oil
2 tablespoons soy sauce
1 can (12 ounces) beer
½ cup chili sauce
1 tablespoon prepared mustard

½ teaspoon Tabasco sauce
1 medium onion, chopped
2 cloves garlic, minced
⅛ teaspoon liquid smoke
Salt and pepper to taste

In a medium saucepan mix together all ingredients except meat, salt, and pepper. Simmer about 30 minutes. Coat meat with sauce on both sides, reserving remainder of sauce. Grill steak over hot coals to desired doneness, basting frequently. Remove to warm platter and season with salt and pepper. Reheat remaining sauce and serve as gravy.

For that special charcoal flavor, sear steak when barbecuing. Place meat very close to heat until browned; then move to desired distance from coals and continue cooking according to directions. Repeat for second side.

GRILLED MARINATED STEAK 6 TO 8 SERVINGS

3½-pound round steak or chuck eye
    steak boneless
1 large onion, chopped
1 cup cooking oil
½ cup dry red wine

¼ cup lemon juice
1 teaspoon salt
2 cloves garlic, minced
1 bay leaf
6 peppercorns

To make marinade, combine all ingredients, except meat, in large screw-top jar and shake. Let stand at room temperature 2 hours, shaking occasionally. Place beef in shallow pan, pour marinade over and marinate meat a least 1 hour. Allow 45 minutes to get coals hot. Place steak 5 inches above coals, turning often and basting frequently with marinade. Grill to desired doneness. Slice meat and serve.

Use long-handled tongs to turn steaks on the grill. A fork will pierce meat and allow the juices to escape.

MAI TAI STEAK 6 SERVINGS

2-pound flank steak
1 package (⅝ ounce) instant meat
    marinade
1¼ cups pineapple juice, divided

3 tablespoons dark rum, divided
½ teaspoon ginger
1 teaspoon cornstarch

Combine marinade, ½ cup pineapple juice, 2 tablespoons rum, and ginger. Mix well. Pierce all surfaces of meat thoroughly and deeply with fork. Place steak in a shallow non- metal dish and pour marinade over. Marinate 15 minutes, turning several times. Remove steak to broiler rack and place 2 inches from heat. Reserve marinade for sauce. Broil steak to desired doneness, turning once. Place 1 teaspoon of drippings from broiler pan in small saucepan and stir in cornstarch to make smooth paste. Add reserved marinade, ¾ cup pineapple juice and 1 tablespoon rum. Blend well and bring sauce to a boil. Simmer 5 minutes. Meanwhile, transfer steak to carving board and carve in very thin, diagonal slices. Serve hot sauce over sliced steak.

BAKED CHEESE STEAK 6 SERVINGS

3-pound round steak or rib eye steak
Salt and pepper to taste
½ cup butter or margarine, divided

1 onion, sliced, divided
¾ cup grated American process cheese,
    divided

Preheat oven to 300°. Divide steak in half and season with salt and pepper. Place half the meat in a 2-quart casserole and dot with half the butter. Add half the onion and sprinkle with half the cheese. Repeat layering. Cover and bake 1½ hours, or until meat is tender.

For easier cleanup, line broiling pan with aluminum foil and broil meat on a rack placed in pan, allowing fat to drip off.

ROLLED STEAK BRAISE 4 SERVINGS

2-pound flank steak
Salt and pepper to taste
2 tablespoons flour
4 cups soft bread cubes
2 small onions, chopped
3 tablespoons butter or margarine

¾ cup chopped celery
½ teaspoon sage
2 tablespoons cooking oil
1 can (10¾ ounces) condensed tomato
    soup, diluted with ¼ cup water

Preheat oven to 350°. Pound steak lightly. Sprinkle with salt and pepper, dredge with flour, and pound again. In a small skillet sauté onion in butter until soft but not browned. Combine with bread cubes, celery, and sage. Moisten with about 1 cup of water and season with salt and pepper. Spread stuffing over steak, roll, and tie with string. Brown rolled steak in cooking oil. Remove to ovenproof dish, add soup, and bake in oven about 1½ hours, or until tender. Baste occasionally.

 Use a child's water pistol to control flareups while barbecuing.

RICE FILLED FLANK STEAK 6 SERVINGS

2-pound cubed flank steak,
    thin enough to roll
3 tablespoons chopped onion
2 tablespoons cooking oil, divided
4 tablespoons raisins (optional)
2 cups cooked rice
½ teaspoon sage

2 teaspoons poultry seasoning
½ teaspoon salt
¼ teaspoon pepper
1 bay leaf
8 medium carrots, halved
8 small white onions

In a large skillet or dutch oven, sauté chopped onion in 1 tablespoon oil until soft but not browned. Add raisins, rice, sage, poultry seasoning, salt and pepper. Spread on meat, roll, and tie with string. Add 1 tablespoon oil to skillet and brown meat on all sides. Add 2 cups of boiling water, bay leaf, and carrots. Cover and simmer about 1 hour, until almost tender. Add whole onions and cook 30 minutes more.

Security blanket: Keep a few individual steaks and a loaf of garlic bread in the freezer for unexpected guests. Add a crisp green salad, and voila! A gourmet meal tout de suite.

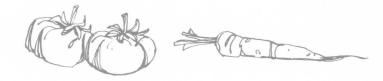

FLANK STEAK SUPREME 6 TO 8 SERVINGS

2½-pound flank steak
1-pound lean ground beef
2 cups soft bread cubes (for croutons)
6 tablespoons butter or margarine,
    divided
2 eggs, lightly beaten
1½ cups chopped onion, divided
1 cup diced carrots, divided

1 tablespoon chopped parsley
½ cup diced celery
Salt and pepper to taste
1¼ teaspoons thyme, divided
1 can (8¼ ounces) stewed tomatoes
½ cup dry red wine
½ cup beef broth
Flour

Cut large pocket in steak. In a large skillet, sauté bread cubes in 3 tablespoons butter. In a large bowl, combine ground beef, eggs, ¾ cup onion, ½ cup carrots, parsley, celery, salt, pepper, and ¼ teaspoon thyme. Drain croutons. Add to ground beef mixture and blend. Place mixture in pocket of steak. Tie steak in several places. Season with salt and pepper. Melt remaining 3 tablespoons of butter in skillet and brown meat on all sides. Drain off fat. Add ¾ cup onion, ½ cup carrots, 1 teaspoon thyme, and tomatoes. Simmer 5 minutes. Add wine and beef broth. Cover and simmer 1¼ hours. Remove meat to warm platter. Drain liquid. Thicken with flour, if desired (1 tablespoon flour to 1 cup liquid), and serve as gravy.

TAMALE STEAK ROLLS 6 SERVINGS

6 cubed flank steaks
1 can (6 ounces) tomato paste
1 tablespoon chopped pimiento
1 can (2¾ ounces) chopped ripe olives
⅓ cup tomato sauce

Salt, pepper, and cayenne to taste
⅛ teaspoon marjoram
1 teaspoon chili sauce
1 teaspoon Worcestershire sauce
⅓ cup grated Parmesan cheese

Preheat oven to 325°. Combine all ingredients, except steaks and cheese. Reserving at least half, spread each steak with mixture. Roll steaks and secure with wooden picks. Place steaks in an oiled baking dish. Cover with remaining sauce mixture. Sprinkle with cheese and bake uncovered 30 minutes.

NOTE: This may be prepared the day before and reheated, covered, in about 20 minutes.

 For a hickory flavor in barbecued steaks, sprinkle damp hickory chips on coals a few minutes before coals are ready. Cover meat with grill cover or sheet of aluminum foil during last few minutes of grilling for stronger flavor.

Help! The power went off! If you don't want to give up and go out for dinner, grill a steak over a hibachi.

SPINACH STEAK ROLLS 6 SERVINGS

2 1-pound top round or cubed flank
    steaks, thin enough to roll
1 can (4 ounces) button mushrooms
1 package (10 ounces) frozen chopped
    spinach, cooked and well drained
1 tablespoon chopped onion

½ teaspoon salt
1½ cups cooked rice, half long grain
    rice and half wild rice
3 tablespoons cooking oil
1 can (10¾ ounces) condensed cream of
    mushroom soup

Pound or lightly score flank steaks on both sides. Drain and chop mushrooms, reserving liquid. Combine mushrooms, spinach, onion, salt, and rice. Spread on steaks and roll as jelly roll. Tie steaks with string. In a large skillet or dutch oven brown steaks in oil. Drain off oil. Combine mushroom soup, mushroom liquid, and ½ cup water. Pour over steaks. Cover tightly and simmer 1½ hours, or until tender.

 To avoid the bother of turning meat to marinate evenly, place meat and marinade in extra-strength plastic bags. Close bag tightly and place in large bowl to avoid messy leaks in refrigerator.

MARINATED HERB STEAK 8 SERVINGS

2½-pound round or chuck eye steak,
    1 inch thick
2 tablespoons flour
1½ teaspoons paprika
½ teaspoon hickory smoke salt
½ teaspoon seasoned salt
½ teaspoon lemon-pepper seasoning
½ teaspoon chili con carne seasoning
2 tablespoons garlic-flavored wine
    vinegar, divided

1 tablespoon olive oil
2 tablespoons cooking oil
¼ cup finely chopped green bell pepper
¼ cup finely chopped onion
¾ cup dry red wine
1 can (15 ounces) tomato sauce
    with bits, divided
Cornstarch

Trim fat from steak and score lightly with a sharp knife on both sides. Combine flour with dry seasonings, 1 tablespoon vinegar, and olive oil. Rub into both sides of meat. Cover and refrigerate several hours. Heat cooking oil in heavy skillet and brown meat well on both sides. Drain off oil. Add green pepper, onion, wine, and all but ½ cup of tomato sauce. Cover tightly and simmer about 3 hours, or until meat is fork tender. Place meat on hot serving platter. Skim excess fat from pan liquid. Add remaining tomato sauce and remaining vinegar. If desired, thicken sauce slightly with a little cornstarch mixed with cold water. Spoon a little gravy on meat to keep it moist. Serve remainder of gravy separately.
Garnish with green pepper rings.

 You can prevent steaks from curling while broiling by making diagonal slashes at 2 inch intervals in fat along the outer edge of steak.

SWISS STEAK 4 SERVINGS

1-pound boneless chuck arm or
   shoulder steak
2 tablespoons flour
1 teaspoon seasoned salt
¼ teaspoon pepper

1 tablespoon cooking oil
¼ teaspoon dry mustard
¼ cup brown sugar
½ cup catsup
1 onion, sliced

Pound flour into steak, add salt and pepper and brown on both sides in oil in medium size skillet. Drain off oil. Mix mustard, brown sugar, catsup, and 1 cup of water. Pour over steak, add onion, and cook 1½ hours, or until tender.

Steaks thinner than ¾ inch are not recommended for broiling. Pan fry instead.

SAVORY ROUND STEAK SURPRISE 8 SERVINGS

2 2-pound round or top round steaks,
   thin enough to roll
1½ cups rice
6 green onions or 1 white onion,
   chopped
¼ green bell pepper, diced
3 tablespoons chopped celery
1 teaspoon salt
¼ teaspoon black pepper
⅛ teaspoon cayenne

⅛ teaspoon garlic powder
1 egg, beaten
Salt and pepper to taste
3 tablespoons cooking oil
1 can (10¾ ounces) condensed cream of
   mushroom soup
1 package (1⅜ ounces) dry onion soup
   mix
1 tablespoon Worcestershire sauce

Cook rice with vegetables and seasonings according to package directions. Slowly stir in beaten egg. Season steaks with salt and pepper. Put ½ rice dressing on each steak and fold over or roll as jelly roll and tie. In a medium skillet brown meat rolls in oil. Drain off oil. Mix soups with ½ soup can of water and Worcestershire. Add to meat. Simmer, covered, about 2 hours, or until tender. Remove to warm platter, slice, and serve with gravy.

NOTE: *This may be made a day ahead, placed on a large ovenproof platter with gravy poured around and between slices. Cover well, refrigerate, and reheat when needed.*

FLEMISH STEAK 4 SERVINGS

1-pound top round steak
1 tablespoon cooking oil
1 tablespoon flour

1 tablespoon brown sugar
6 ounces beer

Trim fat from steak. Heat oil in medium size skillet and brown meat quickly, turning once. Sprinkle flour and sugar on both sides of steak and swish in pan so flour and sugar are well moistened with pan juices. Add beer to skillet and cook over moderate heat, turning occasionally, until liquid is reduced to sauce consistency. Remove steak to hot platter and pour sauce over.

CHUCK STEAK SPECIAL 6 SERVINGS

2-pound chuck eye steak,
    1½ inches thick
1 tablespoon cooking oil
Salt and pepper to taste
1 medium onion, chopped
1 large clove garlic, chopped
1 tomato, chopped

1 large rib celery
Several celery leaves
1 carrot, sliced
2 green onions, chopped
1 tablespoon lemon juice
2 tablespoons orange juice
1 tablespoon flour

In heavy skillet or dutch oven, brown meat in oil. Remove meat and season with salt and pepper. In the same skillet, sauté onion and garlic until onion is soft but not browned. Pour off oil. Return the meat to skillet. Add ¾ cup of water and remaining ingredients except flour. Let come to a boil, lower heat, and simmer 1½ to 2 hours. Remove meat to warm platter and thicken gravy with 1 tablespoon flour mixed with ¼ cup water.

SHERRY STEAK 6 SERVINGS

2-pound boneless round or chuck eye
    steak, ¾ inch thick
1 teaspoon salt
¼ cup flour
2 tablespoons cooking oil
¾ cup dry sherry

1 can (10¾ ounces) condensed golden
    cream of mushroom soup or 1 can
    (10½ ounces) condensed beef broth
1 can (4 ounces) sliced mushrooms
    and liquid
1 tablespoon lemon-pepper seasoning

Cut meat into 6 serving pieces. Salt meat and coat with flour. Pound on both sides. Brown steak in oil in medium size skillet. Pour off oil. Add sherry, soup, mushrooms, and lemon-pepper seasoning. Cover and simmer until meat is tender, approximately 1½ to 2 hours.

VARIATION: *Preheat oven to 350°, place meat in covered baking dish, and bake 2 hours.*

LEMON STEAK BAKE 6 TO 8 SERVINGS

2-pound round or chuck eye steak,
    1 inch thick
1 tablespoon softened butter
    or margarine
1 teaspoon salt

½ teaspoon pepper
4 lemon slices
1 medium onion, sliced
½ cup catsup
½ tablespoon Worcestershire sauce

Preheat oven to 350°. Wipe steak with damp cloth. Score diagonally with sharp knife and place in large baking dish. Rub with softened butter. Season, cover with lemon and onion slices. Combine catsup, Worcestershire, and ½ cup water, and pour over steak. Cover tightly and bake 2 hours, or until tender.

Wrap slices of bacon around individual tenderloin or sirloin steaks for added flavor. Secure with wooden toothpicks before broiling.

Cubes & Strips

Cowboy way
of cooking
cubes n' strips:
on a stick
or in a dutch oven

THEN as NOW
His wrapping
and toasting—
dry-heat method
His dutch oven
stewing—
moist-heat method

I'd say when yore cookin' with cubes 'n strips, yore cookin' Chuck-Wagon Chow. And lots of times you git it chuck-wagon style! 'Course today's "boofays" is kinda fancy for anybody who's used to havin' his bedroll tied and is ready to fork an ol' pony and high-tail it.

An' I notice some foods git hitched up with some funny soundin' handles. After all, what's a "shish kabob"? Now run that thru yore belt loop! I understand it's beef 'n stuff strung up on a long metal pin, grilled an' then maybe laid out accrost a bed of rice. Wouldn't beef "fondoo" make you wonder whether or not you was workin' with a tied rope or takin' dallies? I've got to where I can spear that little chunk of beef an' swizzle it around in th' pot of oil with th' best of 'em. But even if I went back to stabbin' with my pocketknife, I don't suppose I'd ever feel I had that little piece of beef *en brochette*. I haven't got *carbonnade* or *estofado* figgered out yet.

I admit I'm most comfortable with my hat on, but I shore have to take it off to today's pen-fed beef an' these new ways to cook it.

In th' old days most of our grub was cooked on an open fire. If we was afoot for wood, we'd use some "prairie coal" (dry cow chips).

I still believe th' ol' dutch oven is th' best all-round pot. And from th' recipes I see nowadays I'd say th' dutch oven is th' meltin' pot. I guess everbody in th' world has got his own special stew and a name to go with it. Natur'ly I put my personal brand on th' old-fashioned cowboy kind, but I'm not goin' to pass up good food jist because a cook gits heavy-handed with th' spice or calls his specialty "ragoo."

CHUCK WAGON BEEF STEW

Take three and a half to four pounds of lean beef chunks and roll 'em around in a handful of flour. Heat four tablespoons bacon drippings or cookin' oil in a dutch oven an' brown th' beef chunks in th' fat. Add four cups water and simmer with th' lid on over glowin' coals for sever'l hours until meat is tender. Half-hour before chow time, drop two or three cut up potatoes an' a couple of "skunk eggs" (onions) in th' pot. We didn't have no carrots, but if you do, toss 'em in. Season with salt an' pepper.

BEEF FONDUE

Kind of Beef to use: Tenderloin, boneless sirloin, or top round. Remove from refrigerator 30 minutes before meat is to be served. Trim off all fat, and pat dry. Just before serving, cut into 1 inch cubes.

VARIATIONS: *For a teenage party, serve frankfurter chunks or meatballs instead of beef cubes. For added flavor, marinate meat 2 hours before serving.*

Amount of Meat: Approximately ½ pound per person is a generous portion.

Cooking Oil: Butter, margarine, vegetable oil, salad oil, peanut oil, corn oil, or a combination of oils. Oil should be at least 2 inches deep in fondue pot, but no more than three-quarters full, and very hot.

Equipment: Ideally no more than 4 to 6 people to each fondue pot. Fondue forks (or any fork with a nonmetal handle). Washable tablecloth and lots of napkins.

Cooking: Bring meat to table uncooked. Spear cubes with fondue fork and dip in hot oil: approximately 15 seconds for rare, 35 seconds for medium, 1 minute for well-done.

SAUCES

Provide 3 to 6 sauces in which to dip cooked meat.

BEARNAISE SAUCE (SEE PAGE 202)

CURRY SAUCE 1¼ CUPS

4½ teaspoons curry powder	3 tablespoons milk
1 cup mayonnaise	Salt and pepper to taste
½ teaspoon Tabasco sauce	

Blend all ingredients well, using a blender if available. Chill before serving.

CHILI SAUCE 1¼ CUPS

1 cup chili sauce	½ cup minced onion
1 teaspoon brown sugar	1 clove garlic, crushed
¼ teaspoon dry mustard	3 tablespoons lemon juice
Few drops Tabasco sauce	2 tablespoons butter or margarine

Combine all ingredients. Bring to a boil. Simmer about 7 minutes. Serve warm.

CHUTNEY SAUCE 1 CUP

4 tablespoons chutney, chopped	1 teaspoon Worcestershire sauce
1 can (8 ounces) tomato sauce	½ teaspoon salt
1 teaspoon onion powder	

Combine all ingredients. Heat thoroughly. Serve warm.

TIPSY SAUCE 1 CUP

2 tablespoons Cognac	½ teaspoon Worcestershire sauce
1 cup mayonnaise	½ teaspoon lemon juice
2 tablespoons catsup	

Mix carefully, blend well. Chill before serving.

COLD BUTTER SAUCE ¼ POUND

¼ *pound butter*
Seasoning to taste:
  5 drops Tabasco, or
  2 cloves garlic, crushed, or

2 tablespoons prepared mustard, or
2 tablespoons anchovy paste, or
whatever you can dream up.

Soften butter, mix with seasoning, reshape as desired, and chill. Cooked meat is rubbed against small portion of chilled seasoned butter.

Different oils, in all sorts of combinations, contribute interest to a beef fondue.

Hollandaise sauce made in the blender is easy and guaranteed curdleproof. This is also true of mayonnaise.

PAPRIKA GOULASH WITH DUMPLINGS 8 TO 10 SERVINGS

3-pound boneless round or chuck
4 tablespoons cooking oil
1 can (4 ounces) sliced mushrooms
    liquid reserved
2 cups sliced onion
½ teaspoon salt
¼ teaspoon coarse black pepper

2 teaspoons paprika
½ teaspoon monosodium glutamate
1 cup beef broth
2 tablespoons flour
1 cup dairy sour cream
Dumplings (see recipe below)

Cut meat in 1-inch cubes. In large electric skillet or dutch oven, heat cooking oil over medium heat. Add beef cubes, a few at a time, and brown on all sides. Remove as they brown and set aside. Sauté mushrooms and onion in hot oil until onion is soft but not browned. Return beef cubes to pan. Sprinkle salt, pepper, paprika, and monosodium glutamate over meat and toss well to blend all ingredients. Add beef broth at the side of pan, cover, and simmer 1 hour, or until meat is tender. Add flour to reserved mushroom liquid and blend. Add about 2 tablespoons meat liquid to flour mixture, blend, and slowly stir into simmering beef mixture. Cook 5 minutes, stirring carefully. Add 6 to 8 tablespoons thickened meat liquid to sour cream, blend, and add slowly to beef mixture. Heat but do not boil. Keep warm until dumplings are ready.

DUMPLINGS

2 cups flour
2 eggs
¼ teaspoon salt
3 cups beef broth

¼ teaspoon pepper
½ teaspoon paprika
1 tablespoon chopped parsley

In large bowl, beat flour, eggs, salt, and ½ cup cold water. Beat at medium speed until dough is smooth. In a large saucepan, heat beef broth to boiling. Season with pepper, paprika, and parsley. Drop dough into boiling broth by teaspoonfuls. Lower heat to simmer, cover, and cook 12 minutes. Place meat with sauce in center of large warm platter. Arrange dumplings around meat.

CORNISH BEEF PASTIES 4 SERVINGS

¼-pound boneless round or chuck
¾ cup potatoes, finely diced
⅓ cup minced onion
½ teaspoon salt

Dash of pepper
Pastry for 2-crust pie (plain or
    seasoned with marjoram)
Milk or beaten egg

Preheat oven to 425°. Cut meat into tiny cubes. Combine beef, potato, onion, salt, and pepper. Divide pastry in half and roll into 2 squares, 10 x 10 inches. Quarter each to make a total of 8 small squares. Place 3 tablespoons of mixture on each square. Moisten edges with milk and fold over to make a triangle. Press edges together with fork to seal. Cut slits in tops to allow steam to escape. Brush tops with milk or beaten egg. Place pastries on ungreased baking sheet and bake 35 to 40 minutes until golden brown.
Delicious served with a cream sauce or gravy.

 Be certain stew meat is of a fairly uniform size, to prevent small pieces from overcooking and larger pieces from not cooking enough.

BEEF KABOBS 6 TO 8 SERVINGS

1½-pound loin tenderloin tip, chuck eye
    steak, or round tip
3 cups your favorite marinade
Three or four of the following
    ingredients:
Mushroom caps, medium size
Large green bell pepper, seeded and
    cut in squares
Large red bell pepper, seeded and
    cut in squares
Cherry tomatoes
Tomato wedges
Onion wedges, parboiled
Small whole white onions, fresh
    (parboiled) or canned

Celery chunks, parboiled
Zucchini, sliced
Summer squash, sliced
Eggplant, cubed
Pineapple chunks, fresh or canned
Apple chunks, unpeeled
Water chestnuts
All-beef frankfurters, cut in thirds
Chicken livers
Bacon, wrapped around lean beef,
    frankfurters, water chestnuts, or
    chicken livers
Stuffed green olives

Cut meat in 1½-inch cubes. Less tender cuts should be marinated in refrigerator in covered glass dish about 2 hours. Remove meat from marinade, reserving marinade for basting. Alternate meat with three or four other ingredients on skewer, being careful not to crowd food. Place on grill 4 inches from hot coals. Turn frequently and baste with reserved marinade or melted butter at frequent intervals. Grill approximately 15 minutes, until meat is browned and vegetables or fruit are tender.
NOTE: *An alternative method is to grill foods that have different cooking times on separate skewers.*

The secret of successful shish kebab is to have everything finish cooking at the same time. Many raw vegetables take longer to cook than the meat. Parboil them before cooking with kabobs, or cook vegetables on separate skewers and combine with meat when serving.

opposite: BEEF KABOBS

BEEF AND FRUIT CURRY 4 TO 6 SERVINGS

1½-pound boneless round or chuck
2 tablespoons cooking oil
1 can (8¾ ounces) crushed pineapple,
*   with juice*
1 small apple, finely chopped
1 banana, chopped
1 cup chopped celery
½ cup chopped green bell pepper

⅓ cup white raisins
2 teaspoons curry powder or to taste
Salt and pepper to taste
2 tablespoons flour
2 tablespoons instant beef bouillon,
*   dissolved in ¾ cup boiling water*
½ cup dry white wine
Garlic powder to taste

Cut meat into 1-inch cubes. In a large skillet, brown meat on all sides in cooking oil. Add pineapple, apple, banana, celery, green pepper, raisins, curry powder, salt, pepper, and flour. Combine bouillon with wine and garlic powder and add to meat. Simmer about 1 hour, or until meat is tender.
Serve over rice.

SOUR CREAM BEEF CASSEROLE WITH DUMPLINGS 6 TO 8 SERVINGS

2½-pound boneless round or chuck
⅓ cup flour
1 teaspoon paprika
¼ cup cooking oil
1 can (16 ounces) small onions, with
*   liquid*

1 can (10¾ ounces) condensed cream of
*   chicken soup or condensed cream*
*   of mushroom soup*
1 cup dairy sour cream
Butter Crumb Dumplings (see recipe
*   below)*

Preheat oven to 350°. Mix flour and paprika. Cut meat into 1½-inch cubes and coat meat with flour mixture and brown on all sides in cooking oil in medium skillet. Remove meat to 2-quart casserole. Combine onion and onion liquid, soup, and sour cream in a saucepan. Heat just to boiling and pour over meat. Bake uncovered 45 minutes. Reduce oven heat to 325° and top casserole with Butter Crumb Dumplings. Bake 25 minutes or until golden brown.

BUTTER CRUMB DUMPLINGS

2 cups sifted flour
½ teaspoon salt
4 teaspoons baking powder
1 teaspoon poultry seasoning (optional)
1 teaspoon celery seed

1 teaspoon onion flakes
1 cup milk
2 tablespoons butter or margarine
½ cup fine bread crumbs
Sauce (see recipe below)

Sift together flour, salt, baking powder, and poultry seasoning. Add celery seed, onion flakes, and milk. Mix batter well. Melt butter, add to bread crumbs, and mix well. Drop round teaspoonfuls of batter into crumb mixture. Put coated dumplings on top of the meat.
Serve meat and dumplings with additional sauce made from another can of condensed cream of chicken soup mixed with 1 cup dairy sour cream and heated just before serving.

opposite (top): BEEF STEW
(bottom): BEEF STROGANOFF

VEGETABLE-BEEF CASSEROLE
WITH CHIVE BISCUITS 4 TO 6 SERVINGS

1½-pound boneless chuck or round
½ cup prepared biscuit mix
Salt, pepper, and paprika to taste
1 tablespoon cooking oil
½ cup cooked tomatoes
2 small onions, chopped

3 large carrots, sliced
1 small clove garlic, minced
⅔ cup dairy sour cream
¼ teaspoon Worcestershire sauce
Chive Biscuits (see recipe below)

Season biscuit mix with salt, pepper, and paprika. Cut meat into 1½-inch cubes. Roll in mix and brown thoroughly on all sides in a dutch oven in cooking oil. Add vegetables and garlic, and sauté until onion is soft but not browned. Add enough water to cover meat and vegetables, cover tightly, and cook over low heat 1½ to 2 hours, or until meat is tender. Add more water during cooking if necessary. Stir in sour cream and Worcestershire and correct seasoning. Pour stew into 2-quart baking dish and cover with Chive Biscuits. Bake 15 to 20 minutes in preheated 425° oven.

CHIVE BISCUITS 12 BISCUITS

2 cups biscuit mix
⅔ cup dairy sour cream

1 tablespoon chopped chives

Combine all ingredients in a bowl with ⅓ cup water. Beat 20 hard strokes and knead 8 or 10 times. Roll out on lightly floured board and cut into approximately 12 biscuits.

BEEF BURGUNDY FLAMBE 2 SERVINGS

¾ pound boneless round or chuck
2 slices bacon
1 bay leaf
½ teaspoon salt
½ teaspoon oregano
¼ teaspoon monosodium glutamate
¼ teaspoon pepper
¼ cup garlic wine vinegar

1 cup red Burgundy wine
1 tablespoon flour
5 to 6 small onions
1 small green bell pepper, seeded and
*   chopped*
½ pound mushrooms, sliced
¾ cup cherry tomatoes, halved
¼ cup Cognac

Cut meat into 1½-inch cubes. Fry bacon in large skillet. Remove bacon and drain. Pour all but 2 tablespoons bacon fat from pan. Add beef and brown slowly on all sides. Combine bay leaf, salt, oregano, monosodium glutamate, pepper, vinegar, and Burgundy and pour over beef. Cover and simmer 1 hour or until beef is almost tender. Thicken gravy with flour mixed with a little water. Add onion, cover, and simmer 10 minutes. Add green pepper and mushrooms and simmer 5 minutes. Add tomatoes and simmer about 5 minutes more.

Transfer to serving dish. Warm Cognac slightly, pour over beef and ignite. Carry flaming to the table.

SIX HOUR CASSEROLE 8 SERVINGS

2-pound boneless chuck or round
8 carrots, cut coin-shaped and rather
    thick
1 cup sliced celery, cut in ½-inch pieces
1 can (16 ounces) whole tomatoes
1 package (1⅜ ounces) dry onion
    soup mix
½ cup dry sherry
3 tablespoons tapioca

2 slices white bread, cubed
1 tablespoon sugar
1 tablespoon salt
Dash of pepper
Dash of thyme
Dash of marjoram
Dash of rosemary
1 package (10 ounces) frozen peas

Preheat oven to 250°. Cut meat into 1½-inch cubes. Combine all ingredients except peas in 3-quart casserole. Bake, covered, 6 hours. Add frozen peas 20 minutes before done.

BEEF CARBONNADE 10 TO 12 SERVINGS

4-pound boneless chuck or round
4 tablespoons flour
Salt and pepper to taste
2 tablespoons cooking oil
12 medium onions, sliced
2 cloves garlic, minced
2 tablespoons salt

1 teaspoon crushed peppercorn
1 teaspoon oregano
2 cans (10½ ounces each) condensed
    consommé
1 can (12 ounces) beer
1 tablespoon sugar

Preheat oven to 325°. Cut meat into 1½-inch cubes, shake in bag with flour seasoned with salt and pepper. Brown coated meat on all sides in cooking oil in large skillet. Remove meat from skillet and set aside. Sauté onion and garlic in skillet until onion is soft but not browned. Place half the meat in 3-quart casserole. Cover with half the onion. Repeat. Add remaining ingredients to skillet, heat well, and pour over meat in casserole. Cover and bake 2½ to 3 hours, or until meat is tender.

ESTOFADO 6 SERVINGS

1½-pound boneless chuck or round
1 large onion, minced
1 clove garlic, minced
2 tablespoons olive oil
3 tablespoons vinegar
½ cup tomato sauce

1 cup dry red wine
1 bay leaf
1 teaspoon oregano
Salt and pepper to taste
1 can (7 ounces) green chili salsa
Beer Rice (see recipe below)

Cut meat into 1½-inch cubes. Place meat in large saucepan. Add all remaining ingredients. Cover and bring to boil. Reduce heat and simmer 2 hours or until meat is tender. Serve over Beer Rice.

BEER RICE

2 tablespoons olive oil
1 cup rice

1 can (10½ ounces) onion soup
1 soup can beer

Heat oil in saucepan. Add rice and brown carefully, stirring. Add onion soup and beer. Cover pan and cook over medium heat 20 to 25 minutes.

CHUCK WAGON CHOW 4 SERVINGS

1-pound boneless round or chuck
½ teaspoon salt
2 tablespoons chili powder
¼ teaspoon pepper
⅛ teaspoon garlic powder
2 tablespoons cooking oil

2 small onions, chopped
1 green bell pepper, chopped
1 can (15½ ounces) kidney beans, with
    liquid
1 can (17 ounces) whole-kernel corn,
    with liquid

Cut meat into ¾-inch cubes. Season meat with salt, chili powder, pepper and garlic powder. Brown slowly in cooking oil in medium skillet. Drain off oil. Add onion, green pepper, and liquid from beans and corn. Simmer 45 minutes. Add beans and corn and simmer an additional 15 minutes.

Chuck or round beef for stew can make delicious kabobs if marinated for extra tenderness.

CURRIED BEEF STEW 4 TO 6 SERVINGS

1½-pound boneless round or chuck
2 long red peppers or 2 green chilies
¼ cup lime juice
1 cup diced onion
3 tablespoons cooking oil
1½ cloves garlic, minced
1 teaspoon dry mustard
1 teaspoon ginger
¼ teaspoon thyme
½ teaspoon cumin
¼ teaspoon coriander

2 to 3 teaspoons curry powder
1 teaspoon brown sugar
1 cup fresh coconut milk or substitute
    1 package shredded sweet coconut
    boiled in 1½ cups water 2 minutes—
    drain and use water for liquid
1 tablespoon browning sauce
½ cup tomato sauce
1 cup finely chopped raw apple
2 tablespoons flour

Remove seeds from peppers, dice, and soak in lime juice. Sauté onion in cooking oil in large heavy skillet until soft but not browned. Remove onion to bowl with slotted spoon. Set skillet and oil aside. Add all ingredients except meat and flour to bowl with onion. Mix well. Cut meat into 1-inch cubes. Roll meat in flour and brown in reserved oil. Remove meat, drain off oil, return meat to skillet. Add onion mixture, cover, and simmer 1½ hours, or until tender.
Garnish with pineapple or coconut. Serve on rice with baked bananas.

ROUND STEAK TOMATO STEW 6 TO 8 SERVINGS

2½-pound boneless round or chuck
2 large onions, thinly sliced
2 tablespoons butter or margarine
1 teaspoon paprika
1 can (10¾ ounces) condensed tomato
    soup or 1 can (16 ounces) stewed
    tomatoes

1 clove garlic, minced
1 teaspoon sugar
Pinch of caraway seed
½ teaspoon shredded lemon peel
1 tablespoon flour

In a large skillet, sauté onion in butter until soft but not browned. Cut meat into 1½-inch cubes, add to skillet with paprika and tomato soup. Bring to a boil, cover, and simmer 1½ hours. Add garlic, sugar, and caraway seed and simmer another 1½ hours. Add lemon peel and cook about 40 minutes more or until tender. Remove meat and thicken gravy with flour.

BELGIAN BEEF STEW 6 TO 8 SERVINGS

2-pound boneless round or chuck
¼ cup flour
2½ teaspoons salt
½ teaspoon pepper
½ cup cooking oil, divided
2 pounds onions, sliced
1 clove garlic, crushed
1 can (12 ounces) light beer

1 tablespoon soy sauce
1 tablespoon Worcestershire sauce
1 tablespoon bottled steak sauce
2 bay leaves
½ teaspoon thyme
2 pounds potatoes, quartered
1 package (10 ounces) frozen peas,
    partially thawed

Cut meat into 1-inch cubes. Combine flour, salt, and pepper. Coat meat well with the mixture. Set aside. Heat ¼ cup cooking oil in dutch oven or kettle. Sauté onion and garlic until onion is soft but not browned. Remove and set aside. Heat remaining oil in the same pot. Add coated meat and brown well on all sides. Drain off oil. Return onion and garlic to pot. Add beer, soy sauce, Worcestershire, steak sauce, bay leaves, and thyme. Mix well and bring mixture to boil. Reduce heat and simmer, covered, 1½ hours. Add potatoes and simmer, covered, about 30 minutes, or until potatoes are almost tender. Add peas and simmer, covered, 8 minutes, or until peas are tender. Turn stew into serving dish. Garnish with 2 tablespoons chopped parsley.

 Do a fruit kabob along with your beef. Thread kumquats, watermelon pickle, spiced crab apples, even prunes and dates, between meat chunks.

BEEF STEW IN WINE 6 SERVINGS

2-pound boneless chuck or round
Juice of ½ lemon (optional)
½ cup dry red wine
1 can (10¾ ounces) condensed
    cream of mushroom soup

1 package (1⅜ ounces) dry onion
    soup mix

Preheat oven to 250°. Cut meat into 1½-inch cubes and place in 3-quart casserole. Cover with lemon juice and wine. Spread mushroom soup evenly over meat. Sprinkle dry onion soup over all. (Do not add salt.) Cover casserole with foil and bake 3 hours, or until meat is tender. Do not remove foil until ready to serve.

NEW ORLEANS BEEF STEW 6 SERVINGS

1½-pound boneless round or chuck
2 tablespoons butter or margarine
1 teaspoon sugar
1 cup chopped onion
1 cup chopped green bell pepper
2 beef bouillon cubes, dissolved in
    2 cups boiling water

½ teaspoon salt
¼ teaspoon pepper
Few drops Tabasco sauce
1 cup rice
¼ cup minced parsley

Cut meat into ¾-inch cubes. In heavy saucepan with tight cover, heat butter and sugar until bubbly. Add meat and brown well. Add onion and green pepper and stir until wilted. Add bouillon cubes, salt, pepper, and Tabasco. Bring to full boil, stir, cover, and lower heat. Simmer 30 minutes. Add rice and simmer another 30 minutes or until meat is tender. Add parsley, stir lightly, and cook 5 minutes longer.

BEEF BURRITOS ABOUT 16 BURRITOS

3-pound boneless chuck or round
4 tablespoons cooking oil
2 cloves garlic, minced
1 large bay leaf, crumbled
Salt to taste
2 medium green bell peppers, chopped

1 can (4 ounces) diced green chilies
1 onion, sliced
4 medium tomatoes, cut into
   6 wedges each
Pepper to taste
16 Flour Tortillas (optional) (see page 206)

Cut meat into ½-inch cubes. Heat oil in large skillet. Add meat, garlic, bay leaf, and salt. Sauté until meat is browned. Add green peppers and chilies. Cover and simmer 10 minutes. Add onion and cook 5 minutes. Add tomatoes and pepper and cook 5 minutes. Add a little water if necessary. Spoon into flour tortillas and wrap as burritos by placing about 4 tablespoons meat mixture in tortilla and rolling up. Fasten ends with toothpicks. Tortillas may be homemade or ready-made from store.
VARIATION: *Instead of filling tortillas, serve with refried beans or rice.*

BEEF CHOP SUEY 4 TO 6 SERVINGS

1½-pound boneless chuck or round
1 can (16 ounces) bean sprouts, drained
2 tablespoons flour
1 teaspoon salt
⅛ teaspoon pepper
2 tablespoons peanut or corn oil

1 cup chopped onion
1 cup celery, diagonally sliced
1 can (5 ounces) water chestnuts, sliced
1 can (8½ ounces) bamboo shoots
¼ cup soy sauce

Rinse bean sprouts, place in ice water, and set aside 30 minutes to restore crispness. Drain and dry well before cooking begins. Cut meat into ½-inch cubes. Mix flour with salt and pepper and coat meat. Brown meat on all sides in oil. Drain off oil. Add bean sprouts and remaining ingredients, soy sauce last. Add 1½ cups boiling water. Cover and simmer about 1 hour. You may, if you wish, thicken the sauce with a little cornstarch mixed with water.
Serve with chow mein noodles or hot rice.

SUKIYAKI 8 SERVINGS

2½-pound loin tenderloin steak
1 can (16 ounces) bean sprouts, drained
2 cups beef broth
¾ cup soy sauce
⅔ cup mirin (sweet saké) or dry sherry
6 medium onions, thinly sliced

½ pound fresh mushrooms, sliced
1 cake tofu (soy bean curd),
   cut in small cubes
2 bunches fresh spinach leaves
1 small piece beef suet

Trim fat from meat and slice into strips as thin as possible. Rinse bean sprouts, place in ice water, and set aside 30 minutes to restore crispness. Drain well. Combine bouillon, soy sauce, and saké and place in pitcher. Arrange meat, onion, bean sprouts, mushrooms, tofu, and spinach on platter. If electric skillet is available, this dish is easily cooked at the table. Heat skillet to 300° and rub suet in pan. Set aside. Cook by placing one third of meat and vegetables in skillet, add one third of combined liquids and cook about 7 minutes, turning meat and vegetables at least once. Vegetables should remain crisp, but tender. Meat should be rare. Serve small portions immediately and eat while second third is cooking. Repeat once more.
NOTE: *Be sure to grease skillet with suet before each addition of meat and vegetables.*

CHINESE STIR FRIED BEEF 4 SERVINGS

*½-pound flank steak or loin tenderloin
   steak
1 can (16 ounces) bean sprouts, drained
1 tablespoon cornstarch
½ tablespoon soy sauce
1½ tablespoons sherry
4 tablespoons peanut or corn oil,
   divided*

*1 clove garlic, crushed
2 thin slices ginger root, minced
¼ teaspoon salt
1 green bell pepper, cut in strips
1 onion, cut lengthwise in strips
1 chicken bouillon cube, dissolved
   in 4 tablespoons boiling water*

Cut meat across the grain into strips ⅛ inch thick, 2 inches long, and 1 inch wide. Rinse bean sprouts, place in ice water, and set aside 30 minutes to restore crispness. Drain and dry well before cooking begins. In a bowl, combine cornstarch with soy sauce and sherry and blend. Add meat and toss until well coated. Allow to stand 10 minutes. Heat 2 tablespoons of oil in large skillet or wok over high heat. Stir fry meat (see below) 2 minutes, or until meat has just lost color. Remove meat from wok and set aside. Add remainder of oil and heat. Add garlic, ginger root, and salt and stir fry 1 minute. Add pepper and onion and stir fry 1 minute more. Add bean sprouts and stir fry 1 minute. Add chicken broth and heat to boiling. Return meat to wok, stir fry 30 seconds, or just long enough to reheat. Inside of meat should still be pink.
Serve immediately with rice and Chinese tea.

Stir-fry cooking, Chinese style, is a marvelous way to cook food very quickly, pre-serving color and flavor. Food is usually cooked in a wok, a metal cooking vessel with a round bottom and high sloping sides. Since heat is conducted evenly and rapidly throughout the utensil, a very large cooking surface can be used. Stir-fry cooking needs your undivided and uninterrupted attention because food cooks in seconds and must be kept constantly in motion. It is especially important to have everything organized, prepared for cooking, and within easy reach before you start.

ORIENTAL BEEF STRIPS 8 SERVINGS

*2½-pound loin sirloin steak or top round
   steak, boneless
2 tablespoons peanut or corn oil
3 large green bell peppers, thinly sliced
3 medium size onions, thinly sliced
1 pound fresh mushrooms, sliced
1 pound fresh firm tomatoes,
   cut in small pieces*

*1 can (16 ounces) whole tomatoes
1 slice ginger root
1½ teaspoons salt
½ teaspoon pepper
1½ tablespoons cornstarch
¼ cup soy sauce*

Cut meat into strips ¼ inch thick and 3 inches wide. Heat oil in a large skillet and brown meat until juice evaporates, about 15 minutes. Add peppers, onion, mushrooms, and tomatoes and stir about 1 minute. Add ginger root, salt, and pepper. Cover and cook about 30 minutes over low heat. Add cornstarch mixed with ½ cup warm water, stir till smooth. Add soy sauce and simmer about 3 minutes, or until sauce is thick and clear.
Serve over steamed rice or Chow Mein noodles.

BEEF TERIYAKI 6 SERVINGS

2-pound loin tenderloin steak
½ cup mirin (sweet saké) or dry sherry
1 cup soy sauce
2 teaspoons powdered ginger

2 cloves garlic, minced
1 medium onion, minced
2 tablespoons sugar

Cut meat into ½ inch thick strips. Combine all ingredients except meat. Blend well and pour over meat. Allow to stand two hours. Broil or grill close to heat in broiler, or on hibachi about 1 minute on each side.
Serve with very hot mustard and garnish with parsley.

BEEF MANDARIN 8 SERVINGS

2½-pound chuck eye steak or round tip
    steak, boneless
¼ cup peanut or corn oil
1 can (15¼ ounces) pineapple chunks
    (reserve liquid)
1 cup celery, cut in ½ inch chunks
3 tablespoons cornstarch
½ teaspoon pepper
1 can (12 ounces) apricot nectar
1 cup brown sugar
½ cup vinegar

Juice from pineapple chunks and
    mandarin oranges plus water to
    make 2 cups
1 teaspoon salt
1 tablespoon soy sauce
1 large green bell pepper, cut in thin
    strips
3 tomatoes, cut in wedges
1 can (11 ounces) mandarin oranges
    (reserve liquid)

Cut meat into strips 2 inches by ½ inch. Heat oil in large skillet or wok over high heat. Stir fry meat (see page 93) 2 minutes or until meat has just lost color. Lower heat and stir in pineapple chunks and celery. Cover and cook 3 minutes. In a bowl, combine cornstarch and pepper with a small amount of apricot nectar to make smooth paste. Slowly add remaining nectar, sugar, vinegar, reserved fruit juices, salt and soy sauce. Stir into meat slowly and simmer briefly until sauce is thickened and clear. Shortly before serving, add green pepper, tomatoes, and mandarin oranges and simmer until heated through, lifting gently with spatula in order not to break tomatoes. Remove to platter. Garnish with toasted almonds and serve with rice.

BEEF STROGANOFF 6 SERVINGS

2-pound flank steak
2 onions, sliced
½ cup cooking oil
2 teaspoons instant beef stock broth
    or 2 bouillon cubes, dissolved in
    ½ cup boiling water
1½ teaspoons salt

½ teaspoon pepper
½ cup apple juice
Dash of Angostura bitters
½ teaspoon nutmeg
1 tablespoon cornstarch
1 cup sliced ripe olives
2 cups dairy sour cream

Cut meat into strips 2 inches wide by ½ inch thick. In a medium skillet sauté onion lightly in cooking oil until soft but not browned. Remove onion and brown meat. Drain off oil. Add beef broth to meat with salt, pepper, apple juice, bitters, and nutmeg. Cover and simmer 10 minutes. Mix cornstarch with 2 tablespoons cold water and blend into hot sauce. Cook until thickened, stirring constantly. Add cooked onion, olives, and sour cream and simmer about 2 minutes, or until just heated through.

QUICK STROGANOFF 4 TO 6 SERVINGS

1½-pound top round steak, boneless
2 tablespoons cooking oil
1 can (4 ounces) sliced mushrooms,
*   undrained*

1 package (1⅜ ounces) dry onion
*   soup mix*
1 cup dairy sour cream
2 tablespoons flour

Cut meat diagonally across grain into strips ¼ inch thick. Heat cooking oil in skillet or chafing dish and brown meat quickly. Drain off oil. Add ⅔ cup water and mushrooms with liquid. Stir in dry soup mix and heat just to boiling. Blend sour cream and flour and add to skillet. Simmer (do not boil), stirring, until mixture thickens a little (sauce will be rather thin).
Serve immediately over hot noodles.

CALIFORNIA STROGANOFF 6 SERVINGS

2-pound chuck eye steak or round tip
*   steak, boneless*
Instant meat tenderizer
2 tablespoons flour
2 tablespoons cooking oil
1 cup chopped onion

1 clove garlic, crushed, or ⅛ teaspoon
*   garlic powder*
Salt and pepper to taste
1 cup dairy sour cream
1 cup white port (do not substitute)

Cut meat into strips ¼ inch thick. Sprinkle meat with tenderizer. Flour meat and brown in cooking oil. Drain off oil. Add remaining ingredients. Cover, simmer very gently 15 to 20 minutes, or until onion is done and meat is tender.

BEEF AND NOODLES 4 SERVINGS

1-pound top round steak, boneless
2 tablespoons butter or margarine
1 can (10¾ ounces) condensed golden
*   cream of mushroom soup*

½ cup dairy sour cream

Cut meat into strips ¼ inch thick and 2 inches wide. Heat butter in large skillet over moderately high heat. Add meat strips and sauté, stirring occasionally, until brown. Remove from heat, add soup. Stir to blend all ingredients thoroughly. Cover and place over moderate heat. Simmer 1 hour or until meat is fork tender. Add sour cream and heat but do not boil.
Serve over hot noodles.

NEVADA STEAK FINGERS 4 SERVINGS

1½-pound round tip steak
½ cup tomato juice
½ cup vinegar
1 teaspoon salt

1 teaspoon pepper
2 cups flour or cornmeal
3 tablespoons cooking oil
1 small clove garlic, crushed (optional)

Trim meat to finger lengths, about ¼ inch thick and ½ inch wide. Mix tomato juice, vinegar, salt, pepper, and garlic. Dip meat in mixture, then roll in flour. Sauté on both sides in medium skillet in cooking oil, 6 to 8 pieces at a time, 2 or 3 minutes to desired doneness.
Serve with hot barbecue sauce.

BEEF RICE CASSEROLE 4 SERVINGS

1-pound top round steak, boneless or
    chuck blade steak
Salt and pepper to taste
½ cup flour
¼ cup cooking oil
1 cup rice
¼ teaspoon salt

¼ teaspoon pepper
1 clove garlic, minced
1 can (10½ ounces) condensed consommé
1 small onion, thinly sliced
1 can (4 ounces) mushrooms,
    stems and pieces (optional)

Preheat oven to 325°. Cut meat into strips ¼ inch thick. Season meat with salt and pepper to taste and coat with flour. Brown in cooking oil in medium skillet. Wash rice and place in 2-quart greased casserole. Add ¼ teaspoon salt, ¼ teaspoon pepper, garlic, and mushrooms. Arrange meat on top of rice. Add consommé and 1 cup water. Arrange onion slices over meat. Cover and bake approximately 1 hour, or until meat is tender.

BEEF DILL ROLLS 4 TO 6 SERVINGS

2-pound round tip steak
¼ cup plus 2 tablespoons flour, divided
1½ teaspoons salt
⅛ teaspoon pepper
3 slices bacon, cut in half
3 medium dill pickles,
    cut in half lengthwise

3 tablespoons cooking oil
1 medium onion, chopped
½ cup dill pickle juice
½ cup tomato juice
2 teaspoons Worcestershire sauce
2 tablespoons chopped parsley

Cut meat into 6 long, narrow pieces, ½ inch thick. Combine ¼ cup flour, salt, and pepper. Pound seasoned flour into the steak. Place bacon on top of each piece of meat and roll around pickle half, meat on the outside. Fasten with wooden picks or tie with string. In a medium size skillet, brown meat rolls in cooking oil. Pour off drippings. Add onion, ½ cup water, and pickle juice. Cover tightly and simmer 1 to 2 hours, or until tender.

STEAK AND BACON ROLLS 6 TO 8 SERVINGS

3½-pound round tip steak
6 to 8 slices bacon
    (enough to cover steak slices)
2 onions, sliced ½ inch thick
3 tablespoons cooking oil

Salt and pepper to taste
1 teaspoon garlic powder
1½ tablespoons flour
1½ cups beef broth

Preheat oven to 325°. Cut meat into ¼ inch thick strips slightly wider than a slice of bacon. Cut onion slices in half. Place a slice of bacon on each strip of meat. Place halved onion slice on top of bacon. Roll meat so onion is on inside and steak on outside. Heat oil in large skillet. Season meat with salt, pepper, and garlic powder. Brown in cooking oil. Remove meat to 2-quart casserole. Discard all but 1½ tablespoons oil from skillet. Add flour, stir to make smooth paste. Add beef broth and simmer until slightly thickened. Correct seasoning and pour sauce over meat. Bake 1½ hours, or until tender.

For a change, use long strips of beef for kabobs instead of cubes. Thread them onto the skewer in an S-shape with small pieces of vegetable, or what have you, in the curves.

BAKED BURGUNDY STRIPS 8 SERVINGS

2½-pound round tip steak, boneless or
    flank steak
2 tablespoons flour
1 teaspoon seasoned salt
1 teaspoon salt
½ teaspoon pepper
1 teaspoon nutmeg

½ teaspoon garlic powder
2 tablespoons butter or margarine
1 medium onion, minced
1 cup red Burgundy wine
1½ cups beef broth (or more if needed)
1 can (4 ounces) mushrooms

Preheat oven to 350°. Cut meat into 12 strips, 2 inches thick and 4 inches wide. Combine flour with seasonings and coat meat. In medium skillet, sauté meat in butter. With slotted spoon, remove to 3-quart casserole. Sauté onion in skillet until soft but not browned. Add additional butter if necessary. Add to meat, add Burgundy and beef bouillon to cover. Bake covered 1 hour. Add mushrooms and bake 20 minutes more, or until meat is tender.
NOTE: *Halfway through cooking time, potatoes, carrots, and parsnips may be added.*

PEPPERS AND STEAK 4 SERVINGS

1-pound loin sirloin steak, boneless
2 green bell peppers, cut in thin strips
1 can (4 ounces) mushrooms, drained
1 teaspoon oregano
1 clove garlic, crushed with
    1 teaspoon salt

¼ cup cooking oil
¼ teaspoon pepper
¼ cup dry sherry

Cut meat into strips ½ inch thick and 2 inches wide. Sauté peppers, mushrooms, oregano, and garlic in cooking oil in medium skillet. Remove from skillet, add meat and simmer until tender, about 10 minutes. Drain off oil. Return pepper mixture to skillet, cover, and simmer 15 minutes. Add sherry and simmer 5 minutes longer.

JERKY FLANK STEAK APPROXIMATELY 75 PIECES

1½-pound flank steak
½ teaspoon seasoned salt
⅛ teaspoon garlic powder
⅛ teaspoon pepper
1 teaspoon monosodium glutamate

1 teaspoon onion powder
¼ cup Worcestershire sauce
¼ cup soy sauce
2 tablespoons liquid smoke (optional)

Trim off fat. Semifreeze meat and slice with the grain, making strips approximately 2 inches long and ½ inch thick. Place meat in shallow baking dish. Combine all other ingredients and pour over meat. Marinate overnight. Preheat oven to 125°. Lay strips of marinated meat in single layer on oven rack with a baking sheet or foil underneath to catch drippings. Leave oven door open a crack and bake 8 to 12 hours, or until meat is chewy. Test by tasting occasionally.
Serve as appetizer or snack. Store on pantry shelf.

Money-saver: Buy beef in large pieces and cut into strips or cubes yourself instead of paying a butcher to do it. It is easiest to slice when half frozen.

Ground Beef

Cowboy didn't
use much
ground beef
'till he got to town

THEN as NOW
His grilling and broiling—
dry-heat method
His simmering
in a dutch oven—
moist-heat method

Ground beef doesn't go 'way back, far as I know. We ate a lot of beef on th' move, an' we used bigger chunks. After we got on to it, we took to ground beef th' way we did to bunkhouse bridge (poker). Plain ground beef with jist th' right amount of fat ground up with th' lean can be cooked by dry-heat or moist-heat methods—same as any beef.

Formed in a big mound, ground beef can be baked same as a roast. Formed into patties, it can be broiled in a pan outdoors over th' fire. Grilled in th' open is my fav'rite, and I don't care if they call it hamburger or Sals'bury Steak, as long as they don't burn it up. When you come right down to it, that's th' only way you can ruin a piece of beef. (You can always add water and cook it on out, simmered slow an' easy 'til beef is tender.)

Moist-cookin' works great with ground beef, too. Those mixed dishes go down real fine, 'specially if plenty of beef is in 'em. In th' old days we always put in what we had, for as many as we could, for as long as possible. Shore hated th' slim pickin's of an ol' bean outfit.

Almost like instant grass (ground feed poured into a cattle feeder) is what is knowed today as skillet dinners. They even come sweet 'n sour. I tried some and decided it was kinda like gettin' my jam mixed up with my chili. Not bad, tho.

Yep, ground beef can be cooked a passle of ways. Roughest part could be cullin' all those recipes an' follerin' all th' directions. Still, it's jist like takin' a step at a time when yore easin' an ol' pony thru th' brush or down a mountainside.

COWMAN'S BARBECUED BURGERS

(When a cowboy gits roped an' tied by a woman an' settles down with a ranch, he's a cowman. This roundup recipe shows how th' wimmen folk has spruced up brandin'-time chuck and cowboy language to boot.)

Brown six pounds of ground beef in a dutch oven. Pour off fat. Add three large onions, chopped fine; three teaspoons salt; and two teaspoons pepper. Stir and cook until the onions get soft and golden. Add two cups sliced mushrooms, two cans mushroom soup, two cans tomato soup, four tablespoons chili powder, two tablespoons prepared mustard, and four crushed beef bouillon cubes. Simmer over coals for about an hour, stirring often.

Scoop out the centers of twenty-four big sourdough buns or hard rolls and spoon the beef mixture into buns.

TINY TACO MEATBALLS 5 DOZEN

1 pound lean ground beef
½ onion, chopped
1 egg, slightly beaten

½ package (1¼ ounces) Taco Mix
Salt, pepper and garlic powder to taste

Mix all ingredients together and form into tiny meatballs. Put on foil-lined baking pan and place about 4 inches under broiler. Broil until brown and sizzling, turning to brown on all sides. (Or bake 10 to 15 minutes in 400° oven.) Serve on toothpicks.

STEAK TARTARE 30 HORS D'OEUVRE

2 pounds fresh lean loin tenderloin,
    double ground
2 egg yolks, beaten
2½ cups minced onion

2 tablespoons Worcestershire sauce
4 anchovies, mashed (optional)
½ cup capers, drained (optional)
Salt and pepper to taste

Mix together all ingredients and chill thoroughly. Mound on serving dish, garnish with parsley sprigs, and serve with party rye bread as an hors d'oeuvre.
NOTE: *Meat must be very fresh to be eaten raw.*

To crush garlic easily, slice, place in a round wooden bowl, sprinkle with salt, and mash with a fork, using a circular motion. But remember, the bowl will probably retain the odor of garlic, so don't use a bowl that is also used to serve fruit or candy.

BEEF BALLS IN WINE 4 DOZEN

2 pounds lean ground beef
1 envelope (¾ ounce) mushroom gravy,
    dissolved in ¼ cup boiling water
1 egg, beaten
¼ cup butter or margarine
¼ cup flour
2 beef bouillon cubes, dissolved in
    ½ cup boiling water

1 cup rosé wine
2 sprigs parsley
2 tablespoons catsup
¼ teaspoon thyme
1 clove garlic, minced

Preheat oven to 325°. Combine mushroom gravy with meat and egg. Shape mixture into balls (1 tablespoon each) and place on lightly oiled baking sheet. Bake 20 minutes. Melt butter in a medium size skillet and blend with flour. Add bouillon and wine gradually, stirring well after each addition. Add parsley, catsup, thyme, and garlic and simmer, stirring constantly, until thickened. Lower heat, cover, and simmer 15 minutes. Remove parsley and discard. Using a slotted spoon, transfer beef balls to skillet and stir into sauce. Turn into serving dish and garnish with snipped parsley.

Try to handle ground beef as little as possible in order to preserve juiciness. Mix just enough to distribute other ingredients evenly—don't play cement mixer. Use a light touch.

STUFFED GRAPE LEAVES 36 DOLMAS

½ pound lean ground beef
½ pound ground veal
1 jar (16 ounces) grape leaves
⅓ cup chopped dill
6 mint leaves, chopped
2 medium onions, chopped
⅔ cup cooked rice
Salt and pepper to taste

2 carrots, sliced
1 medium onion, sliced
3½ cups beef broth, divided
5 tablespoons flour
¼ cup butter or margarine
1 egg yolk, beaten
1 teaspoon lemon juice

Bring 2 quarts of water to boil. Drop grape leaves into pot, turn off heat, and allow leaves to soak 1 minute. Pour off hot water and replace immediately with cold water. Remove leaves from water and separate gently. Drain on absorbent paper. In a large bowl, mix together beef, veal, dill, mint, chopped onion, rice, salt, and pepper. Fill 36 grape leaves with meat mixture, rolling to enclose completely. Place carrot and onion slices on bottom of large saucepan. Cover with 4 grape leaves and arrange stuffed leaves, seamed side down, on top. Pour 2 cups beef broth over rolls and bring to a boil. Lower heat and simmer, covered, 35 minutes. Drain and remove to chafing dish and keep warm. In a medium saucepan, over low heat, blend flour into melted butter and stir in remaining beef broth gradually to make smooth sauce. Beat in egg yolk and season mixture with lemon juice, salt and pepper to taste. Pour sauce over stuffed grape leaves and heat through.

 Use a melon-ball scraper for making uniform cocktail balls. For hamburgers, use an ice cream scoop.

BURGUNDY MEATBALLS 3 DOZEN

1½ pounds lean ground beef
½ cup corn-flake crumbs
1 small onion, grated
1 teaspoon cornstarch
1 teaspoon salt
¼ teaspoon allspice

1 egg, beaten
1 tablespoon Worcestershire sauce
¼ cup catsup
1 tablespoon sweet pickle relish
1 can (5⅓ ounces) evaporated milk
Burgundy Sauce (see recipe below)

Preheat oven to 400°. Combine all ingredients and shape into small balls. Bake on lightly oiled baking sheet 10 to 15 minutes. Keep warm in chafing dish with Burgundy Sauce poured over.

BURGUNDY SAUCE

2¼ tablespoons cornstarch
2 beef bouillon cubes
¾ cup red Burgundy wine

½ teaspoon salt
⅛ teaspoon pepper

Combine all ingredients with 1 cup water and simmer, stirring constantly, over medium heat until thick. Pour over meatballs in chafing dish.

Too much salt? There are several solutions. Increase the quantity of gravy, but for Heaven's sake, don't add more salt. If you can't do that, add a few pinches of brown sugar. It will mask the saltiness without sweetening the gravy. No brown sugar? Add a few thin slices of potato and cook in gravy until translucent. No potatoes? Throw out the gravy and start again!

STUFFED MUSHROOMS 15 TO 20 HORS D'OEUVRE

½ pound lean ground beef
2 tablespoons chopped onion
3 teaspoons butter or margarine
2 to 3 tablespoons chopped
*   mushroom stems*
Salt and pepper to taste
2 tablespoons chopped parsley

4 tablespoons coarsely chopped
*   walnuts*
4 tablespoons bourbon
2 eggs, lightly beaten
⅓ cup bread crumbs
15 to 20 large mushroom caps

Preheat oven to 375°. In a medium size skillet, lightly sauté onion in butter until soft but not browned. Add beef and mushroom stems. Brown thoroughly, add salt and pepper, and remove from heat. Stir in parsley, walnuts, and bourbon. Stir in beaten eggs, then add bread crumbs. Pile into mushroom caps which have been placed in an oiled baking dish. Bake, uncovered, 20 minutes.

HEARTY BEEF SOUP 6 SERVINGS

1 pound lean ground beef
3 large onions, sliced
1 tablespoon butter or margarine
1 clove garlic, minced
3 cups beef stock (see page 202)
1 can (16 ounces) stewed tomatoes
1 cup diced potatoes
1 cup diced celery

1 cup diced green beans
1 cup diced carrots
1 cup dry red wine
2 tablespoons chopped parsley
½ teaspoon basil
¼ teaspoon thyme
Salt and pepper to taste

In a large soup kettle, sauté onion in butter until soft but not browned. Add meat and garlic and cook until meat is brown. Drain off fat. Add all remaining ingredients. Bring soup to a boil, lower heat, and simmer 1 hour.
VARIATION: *Substitute cubed leftover roast for ground beef.*

MEATBALL SOUP 8 SERVINGS

½ pound lean ground beef
1 large can (28 ounces)
*   solid-pack tomatoes*
1 clove garlic, chopped
2 onions, chopped, divided
2 green chili peppers, seeded and
*   chopped, divided*
1 tablespoon cooking oil

1 teaspoon chili powder
½ teaspoon ground oregano, divided
Salt and pepper to taste
Pinch of cayenne
½ pound lean ground sausage meat
1 cup cornmeal
2 eggs, beaten

In a large pot, combine tomatoes and 2 quarts water. Simmer covered while preparing other ingredients. In a small skillet, sauté garlic, ½ the onion, and ½ the chilies in cooking oil. Add chili powder and ½ cup liquid from soup pot. Stir until smooth and add to soup. Season with ¼ teaspoon oregano, salt, pepper, and cayenne. Continue to simmer. In a large bowl, combine ground beef, sausage, remaining onion, chilies, and oregano. Add salt to taste, cornmeal, and eggs. Mix together and form into meatballs about the size of cherry tomatoes. Drop meatballs into soup and continue to simmer 1 hour.
VARIATIONS: *Add 1 cup thin noodles or alphabets to soup.*

CURED BEEF SAUSAGE 8 PATTIES

2 pounds lean ground beef
2 teaspoons sausage seasoning
2 teaspoons salt
1 tablespoon brown sugar

2 teaspoons instant meat tenderizer,
    dissolved in 2 tablespoons water
Cooking oil

Mix all ingredients, except cooking oil, thoroughly. Let set 2 hours in cool place. (This is the secret of fine flavor.) Form into ¼-inch patties and sauté in skillet with a minimal amount of cooking oil. Or wrap and store in refrigerator or freezer for cooking at a future date.
NOTE: *Do not store in refrigerator for more than 2 or 3 days. Freeze for longer storage.*

BEEF PANCAKES APPROXIMATELY 12

½ pound lean ground beef
3 egg yolks, lightly beaten
1 tablespoon minced parsley
1 tablespoon grated onion
¼ teaspoon seasoned salt

½ teaspoon pepper
½ teaspoon vinegar
½ teaspoon baking powder
3 egg whites, stiffly beaten
Cooking oil

Preheat oven to 350°. Mix together all ingredients except egg whites and cooking oil, then fold in beaten whites. Bake by tablespoonfuls a few minutes on lightly oiled hot griddle. When puffed up, turn and brown other side. Serve at once with mushroom or beef gravy, or Taco Sauce. Good as a main dish or, if cooked in smaller spoonfuls, as an hors d'oeuvre.
VARIATIONS: *Add one or more of the following: 2 tablespoons finely chopped green bell pepper; 2 tablespoons finely chopped celery; 2 tablespoons finely chopped green onion; 2 tablespoons diced green chilies.*

BASIC HAMBURGER 4 SERVINGS

1 pound lean ground beef
1 teaspoon salt
¼ teaspoon pepper

1 tablespoon minced onion
½ teaspoon sugar

Mix all ingredients together and form into 4 patties. Pan fry (with 1 tablespoon cooking oil if meat is very lean), broil, or grill to desired doneness.
Serve on buttered bun with a wide choice of garnishes such as catsup, mustard, relish, or tomato or onion slices. Or serve with barbecue sauce or gravy.

Do not flatten patties with spatula, knife, or an encyclopedia during cooking. You'll end up with a dry, juiceless hamburger and a tasty encyclopedia.

To avoid soggy hamburger rolls, toast rolls lightly under the broiler and spread with a thin layer of butter before serving.

HAMBURGERS–SPECIAL
SEASONINGS AND TOPPINGS 8 SERVINGS

2 pounds lean ground beef   ¼ teaspoon pepper
2 teaspoons salt

Combine meat with salt and pepper. Add additional seasoning as desired. Form into 8 patties. Pan fry (with 2 tablespoons cooking oil if meat is very lean), broil, or grill. Add generous helping of topping, if desired.

Italian style

Add ½ cup chopped onion and ½ teaspoon oregano or ¼ teaspoon basil and ¼ teaspoon oregano. When hamburger is almost done, top with slices of mozzarella cheese and pizza sauce and cook until cheese melts.

Mexican style

Add ½ cup chopped onion. Top with mixture of cooked kidney beans, chopped green bell pepper, chopped onion, and sliced ripe olives.

Hawaiian style

Omit salt and season meat with ½ teaspoon ground ginger and 2 tablespoons soy sauce. Garnish with pineapple chunks and flaked coconut.

Oriental style

Omit salt and pepper. Season meat with 2½ tablespoons soy sauce or Worcestershire sauce, 1 tablespoon chopped onion, few drops pressed garlic, and freshly ground pepper to taste. Mix well, cover tightly, and refrigerate several hours. Serve topped with ginger-flavored chutney or bottled sparerib sauce.

East Indian style

Season with 1 teaspoon curry. Garnish with banana slices, chutney, and 4 tablespoons flaked coconut.

French style

Baste meat with dry red wine during cooking. Top with sautéed mushroom slices, minced parsley, and pimiento strips.

Guacamole Topping

Mash 1 large ripe avocado. Stir in 1½ teaspoons lemon juice, 1½ teaspoons grated onion, ¼ teaspoon salt, and 6 drops hot pepper sauce. Spoon onto meat and top with tomato slices.

Blue Cheese and Sour Cream Topping

Mix ⅓ cup crumbled blue cheese with ¾ cup dairy sour cream and 2 tablespoons thinly sliced green onion. Place green bell pepper ring on each hamburger and fill center with cheese mixture. Top with additional sliced green onion, if desired.

Olive Topping

Combine ⅓ cup halved stuffed green olives, ⅓ cup halved pitted ripe olives, 3 tablespoons mayonnaise, and 3 tablespoons dairy sour cream. Mix lightly.

Creamy Mustard Topping

Combine ¼ cup prepared mustard, ½ cup mayonnaise, and 1 tablespoon very thinly sliced onion. Mix well.

Cheddar Cheese Topping

Melt slice of cheese on hamburger, add pickle strip, a dash of catsup, and some chopped parsley.

Do you have trouble thickening sauces smoothly? Soften some butter; mound an equal amount of flour on a piece of waxed paper. Knead together with fingers and add to sauce. This is an easy lump-free way to thicken liquids.

Have condiments such as catsup, mustard, relish, or anything else at room temperature before using on hamburgers. You wouldn't put ice-cold sauce on hot roast beef, would you?

PIZZA TWO 12-INCH PIZZAS

2 pounds lean ground beef
1 can (6 ounces) tomato paste
1 can (8 ounces) tomato sauce
1 tablespoon oregano
1 teaspoon basil
1 teaspoon salt

2 cloves garlic, mashed
Dash of pepper
Pizza Dough (see recipe below)
1 can (4 ounces) sliced mushrooms
3½ cups grated mozzarella cheese
⅔ cup grated Parmesan cheese

Preheat oven to 400°. Brown meat in skillet, and pour off fat. Set aside. Mix tomato paste, tomato sauce, and seasonings and spread mixture on Pizza Dough. Cover with meat and mushrooms. Sprinkle with mozzarella and Parmesan cheese. Bake 25 minutes.

PIZZA DOUGH

1 package dry yeast
4 tablespoons olive oil, divided
1 teaspoon sugar

1 teaspoon salt
4 cups flour
2 tablespoons cooking oil

Dissolve yeast in 1½ cups warm water. Stir in 2 tablespoons oil. Mix together sugar, salt, and flour and sift into bowl. Add yeast mixture and knead until smooth. Put into greased bowl, cover with clean towel, and let rise in warm place until double in bulk, about 2 hours. Oil two 12-inch pie pans or one 11- x 15-inch baking sheet with 2 tablespoons cooking oil. Punch dough down. Roll to fit pans. Let stand 10 minutes before filling.

VARIATION: *Chopped onion, sliced Italian sweet sausage, anchovy fillets, diced bacon, and chopped green bell pepper are among the many things that can be added to pizza filling.*

NOTE: *If time is a higher priority than budget, use a packaged pizza dough mix.*

GROUND BEEF AND ONION PIE 6 SERVINGS

1 pound lean ground beef
1 cup plus 3 tablespoons biscuit mix,
   divided
⅓ cup light cream
2 medium onions, chopped
1 teaspoon salt

¼ teaspoon pepper
½ teaspoon monosodium glutamate
2 eggs, lightly beaten
1 cup small-curd cottage cheese
Paprika

Mix 1 cup biscuit mix with cream, using a fork. Knead gently 10 times on surface lightly dusted with 1 tablespoon biscuit mix. Roll dough to fit 9-inch pie plate. Ease dough into plate and flute edges. Preheat oven to 375°. Sauté beef and onion together until brown. Drain off fat. Add salt, pepper, monosodium glutamate, and 2 tablespoons biscuit mix. Spread in dough-lined pie pan. Blend eggs with cottage cheese. Pour over meat. Sprinkle with paprika. Bake 30 minutes. Cut into wedges.

When afternoon guests linger for cocktails and you can't run out to the store, spicy meatballs save the day. Add ¼ teaspoon ginger to 1 pound ground beef along with your usual spices. Shape into tiny meatballs, brown quickly, and serve for cocktails with your favorite dip. Make them up in advance, cook, store in the freezer, and you'll never be caught unprepared.

MEAT TARTS 18 SMALL PIES

FILLING

2 pounds lean ground beef
1 tablespoon flour
2 large onions, chopped
3 tablespoons chopped parsley or
   1 tablespoon dried parsley flakes

6 green onions, chopped
Few drops Tabasco sauce
Salt to taste
Pastry (see recipe below)

Sprinkle meat with flour, brown in large skillet. Add onion and sauté until onion is soft but not browned. Drain off fat. Add other ingredients. Simmer about 10 minutes. Cool before placing in dough.

PASTRY

4 cups flour
2 teaspoons baking powder
½ cup shortening, melted

2 eggs
1 cup milk (approximately)

Sift flour and baking powder together. Add shortening, then eggs. Add enough milk to make a stiff dough. Roll very thin on lightly floured board or pastry cloth. Preheat oven to 400°. Cut circles of dough, using a saucer as a pattern. Fill each ½ full with meat mixture. Fold dough over, dampen edges with water and crimp with fork. Prick crust. Place on ungreased baking sheet and bake 15 to 20 minutes, or until golden.

BARBECUE CUPS 4 SERVINGS

¾ pound lean ground beef
½ cup barbecue sauce
1 tablespoon instant minced onion

Salt and pepper to taste
1 can refrigerated flaky biscuits
¼ cup shredded Cheddar cheese

Preheat oven to 400°. In a large skillet, brown meat, drain off fat. Add barbecue sauce, onion, salt, and pepper. Separate biscuits. Place each biscuit in an ungreased muffin cup, pressing dough up sides to edge of cup. Spoon meat mixture into cups. Bake 10 to 15 minutes or until golden brown. Sprinkle with cheese, return to oven until cheese is melted.

MEAT AND POTATO PIE 2 SERVINGS

¾ pound lean ground beef
1 cup soft bread crumbs
1 egg, beaten
½ cup milk
2 tablespoons minced onion
1 teaspoon salt

⅛ teaspoon pepper
1 teaspoon prepared horseradish
2 teaspoons catsup
2 cups mashed potatoes
½ cup shredded Cheddar cheese

Preheat oven to 350°. Combine meat, crumbs, egg, milk, onion, and seasonings. Spread meat mixture in 8-inch pie plate and bake 30 minutes. Drain off fat. Prepare mashed potatoes and spread over the meat. Sprinkle with cheese and return to oven until cheese melts.

When buying prepackaged ground beef or ground beef on sale, pay close attention to color—it should be bright reddish-pink. Any traces of brownishness means the meat is not fresh. A dull, pale pink color, with lots of white flecks, indicates meat with an excess of fat. Paying for fat is expensive and wasteful. Top-quality ground beef is a good buy because less shrinkage will occur than in poor-quality meat overloaded with fat.

SESAME MEATBALLS 4 SERVINGS

1 pound lean ground beef
1 cup coarsely grated raw potatoes
½ teaspoon salt
¼ teaspoon pepper
1 tablespoon dried parsley flakes
1 small onion, minced

1 teaspoon finely grated lemon peel
1 egg, beaten
5 beef bouillon cubes
2¼ teaspoons cornstarch
2 tablespoons sesame seeds

Mix meat, potato, salt, pepper, parsley, onion, lemon peel, and egg. Form into 12 balls. In a skillet with tightly fitting cover, bring 2½ cups water to a boil and dissolve the bouillon cubes in it. Add meatballs, cover, and simmer 30 minutes. Remove meatballs and thicken broth with cornstarch dissolved in 1 tablespoon water. Add sesame seeds. Serve gravy over meatballs.

Do your meatballs suffer from an annoying tendency to fall apart at the seams during cooking? Try plunging them—momentarily!—into rapidly boiling water before cooking. They'll keep their shape—and the hot water seals in the flavor.

109

MEXICAN MEATBALLS
WITH CHILI SAUCE 6 SERVINGS

1 pound lean ground beef
1 pound lean ground pork
3 slices fresh white bread
¼ cup milk
2 teaspoons salt

¼ teaspoon pepper
1 teaspoon chili powder
½ teaspoon oregano
2 eggs, slightly beaten
Chili Sauce (see recipe below)

Soak bread in milk and mash slices with fork. Add beef, pork, and remaining ingredients and mix well with hands. Shape mixture into 1½-inch meatballs. Place on lightly oiled baking sheet and set aside.

CHILI SAUCE

½ cup finely chopped onion
1 clove garlic, crushed
2 tablespoons olive oil
1 tablespoon chili powder

1 teaspoon salt
¼ teaspoon oregano
¼ teaspoon ground cumin
1 can (10½ ounces) tomato purée

Preheat oven to 400°. Sauté onion and garlic in olive oil until soft but not browned. Add remaining ingredients and mix well. Bring to a boil, stirring. Lower heat and simmer, covered, 15 minutes. While sauce is simmering, place meatballs in oven and bake 15 minutes. Add 1½ cups water to sauce. Return to boil. Drop browned meatballs into sauce. Simmer, covered, 25 minutes, stirring occasionally.

A cardinal rule: Read everything before doing anything. Get acquainted with a recipe before you start cooking. Read it thoroughly, make sure you have all ingredients (or valid substitutions), all utensils and enough time.

GREEN BEAN AND MEATBALL
CASSEROLE 4 SERVINGS

1 pound lean ground beef
4 slices bacon
¼ cup fine bread crumbs
1 egg, beaten
Pepper to taste
1 cup dairy sour cream, divided
¼ cup dry vermouth
1 envelope (1⅜ ounces) dry onion soup mix

1 can (10¾ ounces) condensed cream of mushroom soup
1 can (4 ounces) mushrooms, drained and diced
½ teaspoon oregano
1 package (10 ounces) frozen green beans, cooked and drained

Fry bacon in medium size skillet. Remove and drain on absorbent paper. Crumble bacon and set aside. Reserve half the drippings in skillet. Combine bread crumbs, egg, pepper, and ½ cup sour cream. Mix well and add to meat, mixing thoroughly. Shape into small meatballs and brown in reserved bacon drippings. Drain meatballs on absorbent paper. Discard fat in skillet. Pour vermouth into skillet over high heat and scrape up particles. Preheat oven to 350°. Pour vermouth and drippings into a large bowl and combine with dry onion soup mix, mushroom soup, mushrooms, oregano, cooked beans, and cooked meatballs. Toss gently and spoon into 2-quart casserole. Cover and bake 15 minutes.
Garnish with grated cheese, if desired.

SOUR CREAM MEATBALLS 4 SERVINGS

1 pound lean ground beef
1 egg, beaten
1 cup soft bread crumbs
1 tablespoon minced onion
1 teaspoon salt
Pepper and garlic powder to taste
½ teaspoon prepared horseradish

¼ teaspoon nutmeg
¼ teaspoon allspice
1 tablespoon Worcestershire sauce
Few drops Tabasco sauce
3 tablespoons cooking oil
Sour Cream Sauce (see recipe below)

Combine meat with egg, bread crumbs, onion, and seasonings. Shape into walnut-sized meatballs. Sauté in cooking oil in large skillet until golden on all sides. Drain and serve with Sour Cream Sauce.

SOUR CREAM SAUCE

3 tablespoons minced onion
2 cups dairy sour cream

1 tablespoon Worcestershire sauce
1 can (2 ounces) sliced mushrooms

Remove meatballs from skillet, add minced onion, and sauté 3 or 4 minutes. Combine sour cream, Worcestershire, and mushrooms. Add to skillet, simmer until warmed through; do not boil.
Meatballs may be served with sauce over hot noodles or combined with sauce and cooked noodles, placed in casserole, and heated in warm oven.

Does raw ground meat stick to your fingers when you're making meatballs or hamburgers? Good news for sticky fingers—just dip hands in cold water first and the meat won't stick.

ITALIAN MEAT LOAF 4 TO 6 SERVINGS

*average
#5 2   8-15-77*

1½ pounds lean ground beef
1 egg, beaten
½ cup cracker crumbs or dry bread
*   crumbs*
½ cup minced onion
2 cans (8 ounces each) tomato sauce
*   with cheese, divided*

½ teaspoon oregano
1 teaspoon salt
⅛ teaspoon pepper
2 cups shredded mozzarella cheese

Preheat oven to 350°. Combine egg, cracker crumbs, onion, ⅓ cup tomato sauce, oregano, salt, and pepper. Mix well and add to meat. Mix thoroughly and shape into flat rectangle about 10 x 12 inches on waxed paper. Sprinkle cheese evenly over meat. Roll up like a jelly roll and press ends of roll to seal. Place on rack in shallow baking dish. Bake 1 hour. Drain off excess fat. Pour on remaining tomato sauce and bake an additional 15 minutes.
Garnish with asparagus spears.

CURRIED MEAT LOAF 8 SERVINGS

2 pounds lean ground beef
½-cup fine cracker crumbs
1 can (5⅓ ounces) evaporated milk
¼ cup finely chopped green bell pepper
⅓ cup minced onion
⅓ cup chili sauce

2 teaspoons salt
¼ teaspoon pepper
1 can (8¾ ounces) crushed pineapple,
    drained
½ teaspoon curry powder

Preheat oven to 325°. Mix together all ingredients except pineapple and curry. Shape into a 10- x 5-inch loaf and place on rack in open roasting pan. Combine pineapple and curry and spread over top of loaf. Bake 1½ hours.

APPLE FILLED MEAT LOAF 8 TO 10 SERVINGS

2½ pounds lean ground beef
1½ cups packaged dry herbed stuffing
1 can (1 pound 4 ounces) unsweetened
    apples, drained and chopped
3 eggs, beaten

2 teaspoons salt
2 tablespoons prepared mustard
1 large onion, minced
3 tablespoons prepared horseradish
¾ cup catsup

Preheat oven to 350°. In a mixing bowl, combine all ingredients. Mix thoroughly. Shape into 1 or 2 loaves. Place on rack in broiler pan. Bake 1 to 1½ hours.

CORN STUFFED MEAT LOAF 4 SERVINGS

1 pound lean ground beef
1 potato, grated
Salt and pepper to taste
¼ teaspoon sage
2 tablespoons tomato juice

1 can (16 ounces) cream-style corn
1 onion, thinly sliced
1 can (16 ounces) whole tomatoes,
    drained

Preheat oven to 350°. Combine meat, potato, salt, pepper, sage, and tomato juice. Spread ½ meat mixture in oiled baking dish. Add, in layers, corn, onion, and tomatoes. Season with salt and pepper. Cover with remaining meat mixture and bake 1 hour.

BANANA MEAT LOAF 6 TO 8 SERVINGS

2 pounds lean ground beef
2 tablespoons chopped onion
2 teaspoons salt
½ teaspoon pepper

2 cups soft bread crumbs
2 teaspoons Worcestershire sauce
1½ cups mashed ripe bananas
    (about 4 bananas)

Preheat oven to 350°. Mix beef, onion, salt, pepper, crumbs, and Worcestershire. Add mashed bananas and blend well. Pack in 8- x 4-inch loaf pan or shape into loaf and place on a broiler pan. Bake about 1 hour.

BEEF AND POTATO ROLL 8 SERVINGS

1½ pounds lean ground beef
1 cup soft bread crumbs
1½ tablespoons instant minced onion
½ cup dry white wine
1½ teaspoons salt
1 egg, beaten
¼ teaspoon Italian herb seasoning

¼ teaspoon pepper
1 package (12 ounces) frozen hashed
    brown potatoes, thawed
⅓ cup grated Parmesan cheese
¼ cup chopped parsley
1 teaspoon onion powder
Tomato Sauce (see recipe below)

Preheat oven to 375°. Mix crumbs, onion, wine, salt, egg, herb seasoning, and pepper, and let stand a minute to moisten crumbs. Add meat, and mix with a fork until well blended. Shape into a flat 10-inch square on a sheet of waxed paper. Mix potatoes with cheese, parsley, and onion powder. Arrange in an even layer over meat, leaving 1 inch uncovered on two opposite sides. Roll up, starting with one side where meat is not covered with potatoes, using paper to lift meat. Place seam side down in shallow, lightly greased roasting pan. Bake in moderately hot oven about 35 minutes. Spoon Tomato Sauce over meat, and bake 5 to 10 minutes longer. Remove to serving platter, slice, and serve.

TOMATO SAUCE

¼ cup dry white wine
1 teaspoon prepared mustard

1 can (8 ounces) tomato sauce

Combine and blend well. Spoon over meat as directed.

Put a strip or two of partially cooked bacon in the bottom of a meat loaf pan to prevent meat loaf from sticking; the bacon flavor won't transfer. Better yet, bake the loaf on a rack in a small roasting pan and forget about sticking. Place the bacon, uncooked, over the top and now the bacon flavor will transfer—so much the better.

CHILI RELLENO BAKE 6 SERVINGS

1½ pounds lean ground beef
2 cans (4 ounces each) green chilies
½ cup shredded sharp Cheddar cheese
½ cup chopped onion
½ teaspoon salt

Dash of pepper
1½ cups milk
¼ cup flour
4 eggs, beaten
Dash of Worcestershire sauce

Cut chili peppers lengthwise, remove seeds. Spread half of the chilies in a 10- x 6- x 1½-inch baking dish. Sprinkle with cheese. Brown meat with onion. Drain off fat. Season with salt and pepper. Spread meat mixture over chilies in the baking dish and arrange remaining chilies on top. Preheat oven to 350°. Combine milk, flour, and eggs. Add Worcestershire. Pour over meat-chili layers and bake 45 to 50 minutes, or until knife inserted in center comes out clean. Let stand 10 minutes before serving.

MOCK ENCHILADAS 6 SERVINGS

1 pound lean ground beef
⅓ cup chopped onion
1 tablespoon cooking oil
1 teaspoon salt
¼ teaspoon pepper

1 can (16 ounces) chili con carne with
   beans
1 can (6 ounces) tomato sauce
1 package (6 ounces) corn chips
1¼ cups diced or grated Cheddar cheese

Preheat oven to 350°. Sauté onion in cooking oil until soft but not browned. Set aside. Brown meat in large skillet. Drain off fat. Add onion and season with salt and pepper. Add chili con carne and tomato sauce. Place layer of corn chips in oiled 2-quart baking dish. Alternate layers of chili con carne mixture, corn chips, and cheese. Bake about 10 minutes.

For a larger quantity:

5 pounds lean ground beef
1½ cups chopped onion
3 cloves garlic, minced
2 tablespoons chili powder
2 teaspoons oregano
2 teaspoons seasoned salt
3 cans (6 ounces each) tomato paste

2 cans (8 ounces each) tomato sauce
2 quarts cooked pinto or kidney beans
Salt to taste
3 packages (6 ounces each) corn chips
2 pounds Cheddar cheese, diced or
   grated

Preheat oven to 350°. Sauté onion and garlic in cooking oil until soft but not browned. Set aside. Brown meat in very large skillet. Drain off fat. Add onion, garlic, chili powder, oregano, seasoned salt, tomato paste, tomato sauce, cooked beans, and salt. Oil large casserole, or 2 or 3 smaller ones, layer as above with corn chips, chili con carne mix, and cheese. Bake about 30 minutes for a large casserole, less for smaller ones.

LASAGNA 12 SERVINGS

2 pounds lean ground beef
1 medium onion, minced
1 clove garlic, minced
2 teaspoons dried parsley flakes
2 teaspoons basil
2 teaspoons oregano
2 teaspoons salt
1 can (20 ounces) stewed tomatoes
1 can (6 ounces) tomato paste
7 to 8 ounces lasagna noodles

2 cartons (15 ounces each) ricotta
   cheese or cottage cheese
2 eggs, beaten
2 teaspoons salt
½ teaspoon pepper
2 tablespoons dried parsley flakes
½ cup grated Parmesan cheese
1 pound mozzarella cheese,
   thinly sliced

Brown meat in large skillet. Drain off fat. Add next 8 ingredients. Simmer, uncovered, stirring occasionally, until thickened, about 1 hour. Cook noodles in boiling salted water until tender. Drain and rinse in cold water. Preheat oven to 375°. Meanwhile combine ricotta cheese with next five ingredients. Place half the noodles in 13- x 9- x 2-inch baking dish. Spread half the cheese mixture over noodles. Add half the meat mixture and half the sliced mozzarella. Repeat layers. Bake 30 minutes.

MEXICAN BEEF CASSEROLE 8 SERVINGS

2 pounds lean ground beef
1 medium onion, chopped
1 can (10¾ ounces) condensed cream of
    mushroom soup
1 can (10¾ ounces) condensed cream of
    chicken soup

8 to 10 corn tortillas (see page 206)
1 can (7 ounces) chopped green chilies
1 pound Cheddar cheese, grated

Sauté ground beef until brown. Drain off fat. Add onion and cook until tender. Add soups and ½ soup can of water. Preheat oven to 325°. Line bottom of baking dish with 4 tortillas broken into pieces. Cover with ½ meat mixture, then ½ of the chilies, and ½ of the cheese. Use rest of tortillas for next layer, then meat, chilies, and cheese. Bake until hot and bubbling, about 30 to 45 minutes.

QUICK CHILI-BURGER CASSEROLE 6 SERVINGS

1 pound lean ground beef
1 cup elbow macaroni
1 can (10½ ounces) condensed
    chili-beef soup

1 can (10¾ ounces) condensed tomato
    soup
1 teaspoon salt
3 or 4 slices sharp Cheddar cheese

Cook macaroni and drain. Preheat oven to 350°. Brown meat, drain off fat and add soups, ½ soup can of water, salt, and macaroni. Cook, stirring, 5 to 7 minutes, or until bubbly. Place in a medium size casserole with sliced cheese on top. Bake just until cheese melts.

CASHEW NUT CASSEROLE 8 TO 10 SERVINGS

2 pounds lean ground beef
2 or 3 large onions, chopped
2 tablespoons butter or margarine
2 teaspoons salt
1 package (8 ounces) egg noodles
2 cans (10¾ ounces each) condensed
    cream of mushroom soup

1 can (13 ounces) evaporated milk
1 can (4 ounces) mushrooms (optional)
½ cup grated sharp Cheddar cheese
1 can (3 ounces) chow mein noodles
½ pound cashew nuts

Sauté onion in butter until soft but not browned and drain. Add meat and brown. Add salt, drain off fat, and set aside. Cook noodles and drain. Add mushroom soup, milk, and mushrooms, and mix together. Preheat oven to 325°. Combine meat with soup and noodle mixture. Place in 3-quart casserole, and top with grated cheese. Bake 15 minutes. Remove from oven. Reduce oven setting to 275°. Mix chow mein noodles with cashew nuts and sprinkle on top of casserole. Return to oven and bake an additional 15 minutes.

MEAT ROLL CASSEROLE 6 SERVINGS

1 pound lean ground beef
½ cup cracker crumbs
¼ cup milk
½ medium onion, finely minced
2 tablespoons minced parsley
2 teaspoons Worcestershire sauce
1 teaspoon salt
¼ teaspoon pepper
1 egg, beaten
6 slices boiled ham, ⅛ to ¼ inch thick

18 whole cloves
3 tablespoons butter or margarine
⅔ cup light brown sugar
½ cup orange juice
2 teaspoons prepared mustard
1 can (20 ounces) apricot halves,
    drained
1 can (8 ounces) peach slices, drained
1 cup pineapple chunks, drained
½ cup green grapes or other fruit

Preheat oven to 350°. Soak cracker crumbs in milk a few minutes, then combine with onion, parsley, Worcestershire, salt, pepper, and egg. Blend with beef. Spread some of this mixture on each ham slice and roll up like a jelly roll. Place, seamed side down, in ungreased baking dish. Insert 3 cloves along center of each roll. Melt butter in small saucepan and stir in brown sugar and orange juice. Simmer until sugar melts, then stir in mustard. Pour mixture over ham rolls and bake 45 minutes, basting frequently. Arrange fruit on top of rolls and return to oven until well heated, about 10 minutes.

PINEAPPLE BEEF RINGS 4 TO 5 SERVINGS

1 pound lean ground beef
1 egg, beaten
1¼ teaspoons salt
⅛ teaspoon pepper
⅛ teaspoon sage
1 teaspoon curry

½ cup bread crumbs
1 cup milk
3 tablespoons chopped onion
¼ teaspoon dry mustard
8 to 10 slices canned pineapple,
    drained

Preheat oven to 350°. Combine all ingredients except pineapple. Divide into 8 or 10 equal parts, shape each like a doughnut, and arrange on individual pineapple slices. Place on rack in baking pan and bake 45 minutes.
Garnish with parsley.

LAYERED CASSEROLE 8 SERVINGS

1½ pounds lean ground beef
2 teaspoons salt
2 teaspoons sugar
1 can (16 ounces) tomatoes
1 can (8 ounces) tomato sauce
2 cloves garlic, crushed or ½ teaspoon
    garlic powder
Pepper to taste

1 package (5 ounces) egg noodles,
    cooked and drained
1 cup dairy sour cream
1 package (3 ounces) cream cheese,
    softened
6 green onions with tops, chopped
1 cup grated Cheddar cheese

Preheat oven to 325°. Cook meat in large skillet until browned. Drain off fat. Add salt, sugar, tomatoes, tomato sauce, garlic, and pepper and simmer over low heat 5 to 10 minutes. Combine noodles with sour cream, cream cheese, and green onion. Arrange meat mixture and noodle mixture in alternate layers in a 2-quart casserole. Top with grated cheese and bake 25 minutes.

BEEF CASSEROLE
WITH WATER CHESTNUTS 8 SERVINGS

1½ pounds lean ground beef
1 medium onion, chopped
1 clove garlic, pressed
1 teaspoon salt
1 teaspoon pepper
1 can (4½ ounces) chopped ripe olives
1 can (5 ounces) water chestnuts, sliced

4 to 5 ounces thin noodles
*   or small shell macaroni*
1 can (4 ounces) mushrooms, drained
1 can (10¾ ounces) condensed cream of
*   chicken soup*
¼ cup dry red wine (optional)
2 cups dairy sour cream

Sauté meat with onion and garlic. Drain off fat. Add salt, pepper, olives, and water chestnuts, and heat together. Cook noodles and drain. Preheat oven to 350°. In a large bowl, combine noodles, meat mixture, mushrooms, soup, ½ soup can water, wine, and sour cream. Pour into 2-quart casserole and bake 30 minutes.

Remember—ground beef is extremely perishable. If possible, have the butcher grind it for you on the day you plan to use it, or, better yet, grind it yourself just before using.

TAMALE PIE 6 SERVINGS

1 pound lean ground beef
¼ cup chopped onion
1 cup diced celery
1 clove garlic, minced
1 tablespoon cooking oil
¾ cup cornmeal
1 can (28 ounces) tomatoes

1 can (16 ounces) whole kernel corn,
*   undrained*
1 can (4 ounces) chopped ripe olives
1 tablespoon salt
1 tablespoon chili powder
1 teaspoon Worcestershire sauce
⅓ cup grated Cheddar cheese

Sauté onion, celery, and garlic in oil until soft but not browned. Drain and reserve. Brown meat in skillet, drain and reserve. Combine cornmeal with ¾ cup juice drained from tomatoes. Preheat oven to 375°. Heat remaining tomatoes in saucepan, stir in moistened cornmeal and cook over low heat 5 minutes, stirring frequently. Add corn, olives, salt, chili powder, Worcestershire, onion mixture and meat. Blend well. If mixture is too dry, moisten with a small amount of tomato juice or water. Butter a 2-quart casserole and pour in meat mixture. Sprinkle with grated cheese and bake, uncovered, 30 minutes.

ONION BISCUIT CASSEROLE 6 SERVINGS

1 pound lean ground beef
1 onion, chopped
1 tablespoon cooking oil
Salt and pepper to taste
1 can (16 ounces) cut green beans,
    drained

1 can (16 ounces) whole-kernel corn,
    drained
1 can (10½ ounces) condensed tomato
    soup
Onion Biscuits (see recipe below)

Sauté onion in cooking oil in medium size skillet until soft but not browned. Add meat and seasoning and brown lightly. Drain off fat. Add vegetables and soup to skillet. Mix well and heat to boiling. Pour into oiled 1½-quart casserole. Top with Onion Biscuits.

ONION BISCUITS

¾ cup chopped onion
1 tablespoon cooking oil
1¼ cups biscuit mix

1 teaspoon celery seed
1 egg, beaten
6 tablespoons milk

Preheat oven to 450°. Sauté onion in cooking oil until soft but not browned. Drain. Mix all ingredients together at once. Turn onto floured surface and knead a few minutes. Roll ½ inch thick and cut with a doughnut cutter. Place doughnuts around edge of casserole. Arrange doughnut centers in middle of casserole. Be certain meat mixture is hot before placing biscuits on top. Bake 10 to 15 minutes or until biscuits are golden brown.

BEEF JAMBALAYA 6 TO 8 SERVINGS

1 pound lean ground beef
3 tablespoons cooking oil
2 large green bell peppers, chopped
1 cup chopped onion
1 clove garlic, mashed
1 can (16 ounces) stewed tomatoes
1 can (8 ounces) tomato sauce
¼ teaspoon paprika

½ teaspoon chili powder
½ teaspoon Worcestershire sauce
Few drops Tabasco sauce
Salt and pepper to taste
1 package (1 pound) frozen shrimp,
    cooked
2 cups cooked rice

Place cooking oil in dutch oven or heavy skillet and sauté green peppers, onion, and garlic until soft but not browned. Add ground beef and cook until brown. Drain off excess fat. Add remaining ingredients, except shrimp and rice, cover, and simmer gently about 20 minutes. Add shrimp and rice and simmer until thoroughly heated.
VARIATION: *This mixture can also be used for stuffing green peppers. To make stuffed peppers, cut off tops of peppers and discard stem. Remove seeds and white membrane. Parboil peppers, drain, and fill with Jambalaya. Top with bread crumbs, place upright in an oiled casserole. Pour 1 cup tomato juice into casserole and bake 20 to 30 minutes, until peppers are tender. If necessary, just before serving place under broiler briefly to brown crumbs. This should fill between 8 and 10 peppers.*

opposite: BEEF AND POTATO ROLL
page 120: FRANKS AND BURGERS
page 121: BEEF BURGER SPECIAL

CAJUN CHOW MEIN 6 TO 8 SERVINGS

1½ pounds lean ground beef
1 cup chopped onion
1 cup chopped celery
1 cup diced green bell pepper
1 can (4 ounces) sliced mushrooms

1 can (16 ounces) tomatoes
2 teaspoons salt
½ teaspoon pepper
1 cup rice

Sauté meat in large skillet. Drain off fat. Add remaining ingredients. Cover and bring to a boil. Reduce heat and simmer 35 minutes, or until rice is tender. It may be necessary to add a little tomato juice if mixture becomes too dry.

MACARONI AND BEEF SKILLET SUPPER 6 SERVINGS

2 pounds lean ground beef
1 cup elbow macaroni
1 cup diced onion
1 clove garlic, mashed
1 can (8 ounces) tomato sauce
1 cup catsup
1 can (8 ounces) mushroom stems
    and pieces, undrained

2 tablespoons Worcestershire sauce
1 teaspoon salt
½ teaspoon Italian seasoning
¼ teaspoon monosodium glutamate
Dash of black pepper

Cook macaroni according to directions on package. Drain and set aside. Sauté ground beef, onion, and garlic in large skillet until meat is brown and onion transparent. Drain off fat. Add remaining ingredients, except macaroni. Bring mixture to a boil and simmer gently about 5 minutes. Add cooked macaroni and simmer 5 more minutes.
Serve with grated cheese, if desired.
VARIATION: *Substitute spaghetti for macaroni.*

PICADILLO 4 SERVINGS

1 pound lean ground beef
1 large onion, thinly sliced
2 cloves garlic, minced
3 small tomatoes, peeled and chopped
1 tart apple, peeled and chopped
    (optional)
½ cup raisins, soaked in warm water
    and drained
¼ to ½ cup stuffed green olives,
    quartered

½ cup dry red or white wine
Salt and pepper to taste
Pinch of cinnamon (optional)
Pinch of cloves (optional)
1 green bell pepper, cut in strips
¼ cup slivered almonds, sautéed
    in butter or margarine (optional)

Sauté meat in large skillet until browned, stirring frequently. Drain off fat. Add onion and garlic and cook until soft but not browned. Add tomatoes, apple, raisins, olives, wine, and seasonings. Simmer over low heat about 20 minutes. Add green pepper during last 5 minutes of cooking.
Sprinkle with almonds and serve over hot rice.

opposite: VEALBALLS IN SPICY SAUCE

CHILI CON CARNE 4 TO 6 SERVINGS

1 pound lean ground beef
1 cup chopped onion
¼ cup diced green bell pepper
1 can (15 ounces) kidney beans
1¾ cups tomatoes

1½ tablespoons chili powder
1½ teaspoons salt
¼ teaspoon pepper
1 tablespoon vinegar

Sauté meat, onion, and green pepper in a large skillet. Drain off fat. Add remaining ingredients and simmer 15 minutes.

GROUND BEEF KONA STYLE 4 TO 6 SERVINGS

2 pounds lean ground beef
1 package Chinese long rice °
2 cloves garlic, thinly sliced
1 slice ginger root
2 tablespoons peanut oil
1 cup soy sauce, divided

½ pound green beans, cut French style
1 can (4 ounces) button mushrooms,
    drained
4 green onions, sliced diagonally
¾ cup coarsely chopped celery
    (optional)

Soak long rice in water 15 minutes, then cook in boiling water 10 minutes. Drain and set aside. In skillet, sauté garlic and ginger root in 2 tablespoons oil 3 minutes. Add meat and brown. Drain off excess fat. Add ¾ cup soy sauce and beans. Cover and simmer until beans are almost tender. Add long rice, mushrooms, green onion, and celery. Mix well, cutting through mixture 2 or 3 times with knife and fork to shorten length of long rice. Add remaining soy sauce, cover, and simmer 5 minutes.

° Chinese long rice, or peastarch noodles, can be purchased in Chinese food stores. If not available, you may substitute 2 ounces bean thread noodles or 4 ounces cellophane noodles.

An amazing number of people, not to mention cookbooks, labor under the mis-conception that ground beef needs to be browned in fat or oil. This is an added expense and bad for your health to boot. Most of the time the dish ends up so greasy that the fat has to be skimmed off anyway. Who needs it? Even lean ground beef contains enough fat to brown itself, as long as you stir constantly to prevent sticking to the bottom of the skillet. If you're still skeptical, use a nonstick pan.

TACO SPOONBURGERS 6 TO 8 SERVINGS

2 pounds lean ground beef
2 teaspoons Worcestershire sauce
2 teaspoons soy sauce
¾ cup catsup

2 tablespoons Taco sauce
1 teaspoon garlic powder
Salt and pepper to taste
1 can (4 ounces) green chilies

Sauté meat with onion. Drain off fat and add remaining ingredients. Simmer 30 minutes. Serve on toasted hamburger buns, garnished with Parmesan cheese or, serve in taco shells garnished with Cheddar cheese. If desired, place briefly in moderate oven to melt cheese.

EMPANADAS 15 TURNOVERS

2½ cups flour
1 teaspoon salt
½ cup butter or margarine

1 egg, beaten
Milk
Filling (see recipe below)

Mix flour with salt. Cut in butter until dough forms very fine particles. Add egg and ½ cup ice water. Stir until dough cleans bowl. Knead into small ball. Preheat oven to 375°. Cut dough into about 15 pieces. On a lightly floured board, roll out each piece to a 4-inch circle. Or roll half of the dough and then cut into circles using a small saucer as a guide. Top each circle with a heaping tablespoon of filling. Fold over and press edges together with fork. Prick top. Brush with milk. Place on lightly oiled baking sheet and bake 12 to 15 minutes, or until lightly browned.

FILLING

1 pound lean ground beef
1 large onon, diced
1 can (4 ounces) green chili peppers,
*   diced*

1 clove garlic, mashed
1 can (4 ounces) chopped black olives
3 tablespoons dry onion soup mix
1 tablespoon flour

Brown beef in a skillet, add onion, and cook until onion is soft but not browned. Drain off fat. Add remaining ingredients, sprinkling flour over all and adding just enough water to hold filling together. Simmer 10 minutes and place on circle of dough.

VARIATION: *To make Burritos, cut filling recipe in half, butter about 12 flour tortillas (see page 206) on one side, fill with meat mixture, close ends, and place in foil-lined baking dish. Preheat oven to 400° and bake about 20 minutes, or until brown and crisp.*

MEXICAN STUFFED PEPPERS 12 SERVINGS

½ pound lean ground beef
1 teaspoon chopped onion
2 cloves garlic, chopped
½ cup seedless raisins
½ cup slivered almonds
1 can (8 ounces) tomato sauce
Salt and pepper to taste

8 green bell peppers
1 cup tomato juice
⅓ pound walnuts, blanched and
*   chopped*
4 tablespoons chopped parsley
3 pimientos, thinly sliced
1 cup heavy cream, whipped

Sauté beef with onion and garlic until meat is browned. Drain off fat. Add raisins, almonds, tomato sauce, salt, and pepper. Simmer about 10 minutes. Cut stem from each pepper. Remove seeds and membrane. Parboil peppers about 5 minutes. Preheat oven to 350°. Stuff with filling and place upright in shallow baking dish. Pour tomato juice around peppers and bake 15 minutes. Stir walnuts, parsley, and pimiento into whipped cream. Spoon over filled peppers just before serving.

Buy top-quality ground beef in quantity when you spot a sale. (Obviously, don't let your eyes get bigger than your stomach. Only buy what you will use within the recommended storage time for your freezer.) Make lots of individual seasoned patties and freeze in small plastic bags. They'll always be there when you need them, ready to use.

TACOS 16 TO 18 SERVINGS

2 pounds lean ground beef
1 teaspoon salt
½ teaspoon pepper
1 teaspoon garlic powder
3 tablespoons chili powder
⅛ teaspoon cayenne
3 dozen corn tortillas·(see page 206)

Cooking oil
1 head lettuce, shredded
3 large onions, diced
3 tomatoes, diced
½ pound Longhorn cheese, grated
Taco Sauce or hot sauce

Blend meat with salt, pepper, garlic powder, chili powder, and cayenne and brown in heavy skillet, stirring frequently. Drain off fat. In separate skillet, heat tortillas in cooking oil. Drain on absorbent paper. Fill each tortilla with meat, lettuce, onion and tomato. Top with cheese. Fold and serve with Taco Sauce.

ENCHILADAS 6 TO 8 SERVINGS

MEAT FILLING

2 pounds lean ground beef
1 large onion, chopped
1 can (4 ounces) diced green chilies
    (optional)

1 clove garlic, minced
1 teaspoon salt
2 teaspoons oregano (optional)
Dash of pepper

Sauté all ingredients in heavy skillet until onion is transparent and meat lightly browned. Drain off fat into a bowl and reserve for sauce. Set filling aside.

SAUCE

4 tablespoons flour
4 tablespoons drippings from meat
1 small onion, chopped
1 can (4 ounces) chopped green chilies
2 teaspoons chili powder

2 teaspoons oregano
2 tablespoons vinegar
½ teaspoon salt
Dash of pepper
2 cans (8 ounces each) tomato sauce

Stir flour into drippings and gradually add 2 cups of water. Add remainder of ingredients and simmer about 30 minutes. Additional water may be added during simmering if needed.

NOTE: *As a substitute for homemade sauce use 2 cans (16 ounces each) Enchilada Sauce.*

TO COMPLETE ENCHILADAS:

12 corn tortillas (see page 206)
Cooking oil

½ pound Cheddar cheese, grated

Preheat oven to 350°. Dip tortillas quickly in hot cooking oil, and then dip in sauce, one at a time. Do not allow them to brown or become crisp. Place large spoonful of meat filling in each tortilla. Sprinkle with cheese and roll up. Place filled tortillas side by side in a 3-quart oiled casserole and pour sauce over. Top with remaining cheese. Place in oven and bake 25 to 30 minutes.

Completed casserole can be covered, frozen, and used at a later date.

CANNELLONI 6 TO 8 SERVINGS

TOMATO SAUCE

1½ cups chopped onion
1 clove garlic, minced
¼ cup olive oil or cooking oil
1 can (28 ounces) peeled tomatoes
1 can (15 ounces) tomato sauce or 1 can
* (6 ounces) tomato paste plus 1 cup*
* water*

1½ teaspoons salt
¼ teaspoon pepper
1 teaspoon sugar
1 teaspoon oregano
1 teaspoon basil
1 teaspoon dried parsley flakes

In a large sauce pan, sauté onion and garlic in oil until onion is soft but not browned. Add remaining ingredients. Bring to boil while stirring. Lower heat and simmer, covered, about 1 hour.

BEEF-CHEESE FILLING

1½ pounds lean ground beef
1 cup chopped onion
1 clove garlic, minced
2 tablespoons butter or margarine
1 teaspoon salt
¼ teaspoon pepper

½ teaspoon oregano
2 eggs, beaten
¼ cup dry red wine
½ pound ricotta cheese or cottage cheese
1 cup grated mozzarella cheese,
¼ cup grated Parmesan cheese

Sauté onion and garlic in butter in large skillet until onion is soft but not browned. Drain and add meat. Cook over low heat, stirring until meat has lost red color. Drain. Add salt, pepper, oregano, eggs, wine, and cheeses. Blend thoroughly and set aside.

TO COMPLETE CANNELLONI:

14 large pasta tubes °
¾ pound mozzarella cheese, sliced

½ cup grated Parmesan cheese

Boil and drain pasta as directed on package. Preheat oven to 350°. Spoon filling into 14 tubes. Pour ½ tomato sauce in 2½-quart baking dish. Arranged stuffed pasta in one layer. Pour on remaining sauce. Cover with thin slices of mozzarella cheese. Top with Parmesan cheese and bake 25 to 30 minutes.

° Buy 1 package (8 ounces) manicotti or cannelloni tubes or roll tubes from 4-inch squares of crêpe dough (see page 193) or egg noodle dough.

When cooking pasta, add a little cooking oil to the water. The pasta will stand apart and glisten. But don't overcook—there's nothing worse than gluey, pasty, mushy pasta. It should be cooked "al dente"—firm but tender.

CREOLE CABBAGE ROLLS 6 SERVINGS

1 pound lean ground beef
1 cabbage, about 4 pounds
1 cup cooked rice
¾ cup chopped onion, divided
¼ cup minced parsley
Seasoned salt and pepper to taste
2 to 3 drops Tabasco sauce
1 egg, beaten
1 clove garlic, crushed

½ cup chopped green bell pepper
    (optional)
2 tablespoons butter or margarine
1 can (16 ounces) tomatoes
1 tablespoon honey
1 bouillon cube, dissolved in ½ cup
    boiling water
¼ cup lemon juice

Wash and core cabbage and place in lightly salted boiling water. Remove outer leaves as they loosen. Reserve 12 large leaves, chop remainder of head and reserve. Mix meat, rice, ¼ cup onion, parsley, 1 teaspoon salt, pepper, Tabasco, and egg. Divide mixture among the cabbage leaves and roll into packages. Place in a shallow casserole, seamed side down. Preheat oven to 350°. Sauté garlic, ½ cup onion, and green pepper in butter. Add ½ teaspoon salt and remaining ingredients except chopped cabbage. Simmer gently about 10 minutes, then spoon over cabbage rolls. Cover and bake about 30 minutes. Serve with cabbage in sour cream (see recipe below).

CABBAGE IN SOUR CREAM

2 tablespoons butter or margarine
Reserved chopped cabbage
2 tablespoons sugar
1 tablespoon caraway seeds

Salt and pepper to taste
1 egg, beaten
1 cup dairy sour cream
3 tablespoons lemon juice

In a large skillet, melt butter, add cabbage, and cook covered over low heat until tender. Add seasonings. Mix together egg, sour cream, and lemon juice. Add to cabbage and simmer until thoroughly heated.

STUFFED CHILIES 6 SERVINGS

1 pound lean ground beef
12 large green chilies with stems
    (fresh, canned, or frozen)
1 teaspoon salt, divided
1 clove garlic, crushed
1½ cups cornmeal

2 tablespoons flour
12 strips Cheddar cheese
3 eggs, beaten
1 tablespoon bacon drippings
1 tablespoon cooking oil

Peel chilies. Open small slit below stems and remove seeds. Brown meat and drain. Add ½ teaspoon salt and garlic. Cool slightly. Combine cornmeal, flour, and remaining salt, and set aside on wax paper. Fill each chili with meat and one strip of cheese. Roll in beaten egg and then in the cornmeal mixture. Sauté to crisp golden brown on both sides in combination of bacon drippings and oil. Drain on paper towels and serve.

STUFFED ONIONS 6 SERVINGS

¾ pound lean ground beef
6 large onions
½ cup chopped mushrooms
½ teaspoon chili powder, divided
½ teaspoon salt

Dash of pepper
Dash of sugar
½ cup shredded Cheddar cheese
1 can (10¾ ounces) condensed Cheddar
  cheese soup

Cut off ends of unpeeled onions and boil in water to cover until almost tender, 25 to 30 minutes. Cool, slip off skins and remove centers, leaving ½- to ¾-inch shell. Chop pulp removed from onions. Combine chopped onion, meat, and mushrooms in medium size skillet and cook until meat is lightly browned, stirring now and then to keep crumbly. Drain off fat. Stir in ¼ teaspoon chili powder, salt, pepper, sugar, and cheese. Fill onion shells with mixture. Preheat oven to 350°. Arrange onions in a deep casserole and add about 3 tablespoons water to prevent scorching. Bake uncovered 25 minutes or until tender. Remove to serving platter. Mix soup, with an equal amount of water and remaining chili powder. Heat in saucepan and pour over stuffed onions.

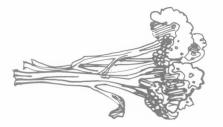

BEEF STRUDEL 4 TO 6 SERVINGS

1 pound lean ground beef
4 strudel leaves (room temperature)
2 onions, finely chopped
2 tablespoons butter or margarine
¾ cup bread crumbs

2 tablespoons chopped fresh dill
Salt and pepper to taste
2 egg yolks, beaten
1 cup dairy sour cream
¼ cup butter, melted

Preheat oven to 350°. Place strudel leaves between damp towels for later use. In a medium size skillet, sauté onion in butter until soft but not browned. Drain and set aside. Brown meat in skillet, drain thoroughly and combine with onion. In a separate bowl mix bread crumbs, dill, salt, pepper, egg yolks, and sour cream. Add to meat and blend. Place meat on waxed paper 14 inches long and shape meat into 12-inch rectangle. Remove 2 strudel leaves from between towels, place them, one on top of the other, on a separate damp towel. Brush top leaf with melted butter. Put 2 more strudel leaves on top of first 2 and brush top with butter. Roll meat from waxed paper on to leaves, ¼ inch from edge of dough. Fold long edge over meat and turn up edges at top and bottom. Raise cloth at long end and roll strudel over like a jelly roll. Brush entire surface with melted butter and place in ungreased pan. Bake 20 mintues or until golden. Turn over and bake an additional 20 minutes.
Serve with Béarnaise Sauce (page 202) seasoned with dill instead of with tarragon.
VARIATION: *Divide meat into eight 3-inch rectangles. Fold single strudel leaf in half and brush with melted butter. Fold in half again, brush with butter, and place meat on dough. Turn strudel up at top and bottom and roll. Brush entire surface with butter and bake as large strudel. This variation requires 8 strudel leaves and ½ cup melted butter.*

129

Veal

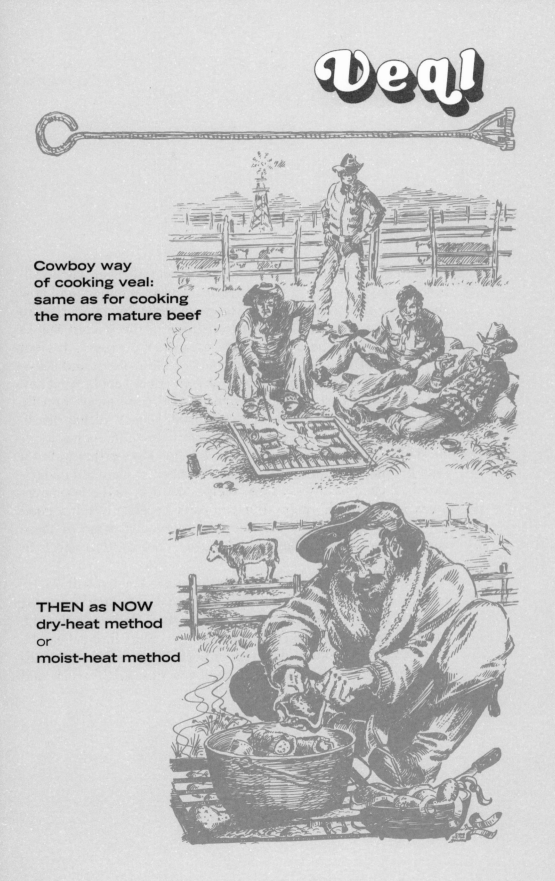

Cowboy way
of cooking veal:
same as for cooking
the more mature beef

THEN as NOW
dry-heat method
or
moist-heat method

131

Back in th' days before "grass fat" an' "pen fed" beef wuz available, veal was jist about th' best eatin'. And I c'n understand how those countries with no room to grow grain for convertin' to mature beef still eat veal. But to us here in the United States, veal is gettin' to be as outa date as a neck-tie party. It's not avail'ble in all butcher shops, an' people is eatin' it less and less—reason bein' a combination of high cost and poor keepin' qual'ties.

Some of th' best tastin' ways to fix veal come over from th' old world: Weiner Schnitzel, Veal Parmigiana, Veal Paprikash, and a whole herd of others. I had to copy down th' names to git th' spellin' right. (One ol' cowpoke I know, swears that unless a man c'n spell a word at least three ways he jist plain ain't edge'-cated.) I can't hardly say these recipes neither, an' I shore never knew of 'em on th' range. But you can't necessar'ly tell a good cow by th' brand she's awearin, an' so even if some of these names is new to me I have to admit th' proof of th' brand is in th' eatin'.

If you can't buy veal, don't let it throw ya. You c'n still use th' recipes. Some of those fancy "gormay" cooks may flat out insist on usin' milk-fed veal, from calves less than three months old, but to my way of thinkin', most any recipe callin' for veal can be made from our modern-day, tender beef. I'll cross-breed th' old-world recipes with new-world beef any day in th' week and twict on Sundays.

MAKE-DO VEAL BIRDS

Take some thin slices of veal from th' round an' trim into pieces about th' size of yore hand. Sprinkle salt and pepper on each slice and wrap around a skinny peeled potato (or use a fat spud sliced longways into slim lengths). Hog tie ever bird with string or fasten with edges together with slivers of wood whittled off a green bush.

Brown th' birds in bacon drippin's in a dutch oven. Add two cups water, put lid on, and let simmer over th' coals until done. Thicken th' gravy with some flour and it's "Come and git it" time. You c'n dude up these birds if you dip 'em in an egg beat up with a tablespoon milk, roll 'em in bread crumbs, deep fry 'em, and finish cooking like before.

Veal is the meat of the calf. The best veal available comes from exclusively milk-fed animals, under fourteen weeks of age, and is grayish in color. A pink or reddish cast to the meat means that the animal was older and was given solid food. It will not be quite as tender as milk-fed veal. Veal is naturally lean and usually benefits from the addition of fat or liquid in the cooking process. Although it should always be served well-done (internal temperature 175°), avoid overcooking which will toughen meat.

VEAL ROASTING CHART		
Cut	Weight	Oven Temperature 325° Minutes per Pound
Leg	5 to 8 pounds	35 minutes
Loin	4 to 6 pounds	35 to 40 minutes
Rolled Shoulder	3 to 5 pounds	40 to 45 minutes
Stuffed Breast	3 to 4 pounds	40 to 45 minutes
Shoulder	4 to 6 pounds	35 to 40 minutes

Primal Cut	Meat Board Recommended Name for Retail Veal Cut	Commonly Used Names for Retail Cut	Recommended Cooking Methods
Shoulder	Shoulder Arm Roast	Shoulder Roast; Round Bone Roast	Braise, Roast
	Shoulder Arm Steak	Round Bone Steak; Shoulder Steak; Shoulder Chop, Round Bone; Round Bone Chops	Braise, Panfry
	Shoulder Blade Roast	Shoulder Roast; Blade Roast	Braise, Roast
	Shoulder Blade Steak	Shoulder Steak; Shoulder Chops	Braise, Panfry
	Shoulder Roast Boneless	Rolled Shoulder; Shoulder Boneless; Rolled Roast	Braise, Roast
	Veal for Stew	Stew Veal; Veal Stew (Large pieces); Veal Stew (small pieces); Veal Stew Boneless	Braise, Cook in Liquid

Primal Cut	Meat Board Recommended Name for Retail Veal Cut	Commonly Used Names for Retail Cut	Recommended Cooking Methods
Fore Shank	Shank Cross Cuts	Veal Shank; Cross Cut Shank	Braise, Cook in Liquid
Breast	Breast	Breast of Veal; Veal Breast	Braise, Roast
	Breast Riblets	Riblets	Braise, Cook in Liquid
Rib	Rib Roast	Rib Roast; Rib Veal Roast	Roast
	Rib Chops	Chops; Rib Chop; Rib Veal Chop	Braise, Panfry
	Rib Chops Boneless	Chops; Boneless Chops	Braise, Panfry
	Rib Crown Roast	Crown Roast; Crown Rib Roast	Roast
Loin	Loin Roast	Loin Roast	Roast
	Loin Roast Boneless	Rolled Loin Roast; Boneless Loin Roast	Roast
	Loin Kidney Chops	Kidney Chops; Kidney Veal Chops	Braise, Panfry
	Loin Chops	Chops; Loin Chops; Loin Veal Chops	Braise, Panfry
	Loin Top Loin Chops	Chops; Boneless Veal Chops	Braise, Panfry
Leg	Leg Sirloin Roast	Sirloin Roast	Roast
	Leg Sirloin Steak	Steak; Sirloin Steak; Sirloin Chop	Braise, Panfry
	Leg Sirloin Roast Boneless	Rolled Double Sirloin Roast; Boneless Sirloin Roast	Roast
	Leg Round Roast	Leg Roast; Leg of Veal	Braise, Roast
	Leg Round Steak	Veal Scallopini; Veal Steak; Steakettes	Braise, Panfry
	Leg Rump Roast	Rump Roast; Rump of Veal	Braise, Roast
	Leg Rump Roast Boneless	Rolled Rump Roast; Roast Boneless; Rump of Veal Boneless	Braise, Roast
	Leg Heel Roast	Heel Roast	Braise
	Cubed Steak	Cubed Steak; Cubed Veal Steak	Braise, Panfry
	Cubes for Kabobs	Kabobs; Stew; City Chicken	Braise
	Cutlets	Cutlets	Braise, Panfry

Round (Leg)

③④ Round Roast

② Boneless Rump Roast

② Rump Roast

Cutlets (Thin Slices)

① ③ ④ Cutlets

① ③ ④ Rolled Cutlets

③④ Round Steak

Sirloin

Cubed Steak

① Sirloin Chop

① Boneless Sirloin Roast

① Sirloin Roast

Loin

① Top Loin Chop

① Loin Chop

① Kidney Chop

① Loin Roast

Rib

④ Boneless Rib Chop

④ Rib Chop

④ Crown Roast

④ Rib Roast

Shoulder

③ Arm Roast

②③ Boneless Shoulder Roast

② Blade Roast

② Blade Steak

③ Arm Steak

(Large Pieces)

(Small Pieces)

①②③ for Stew

Veal Chart

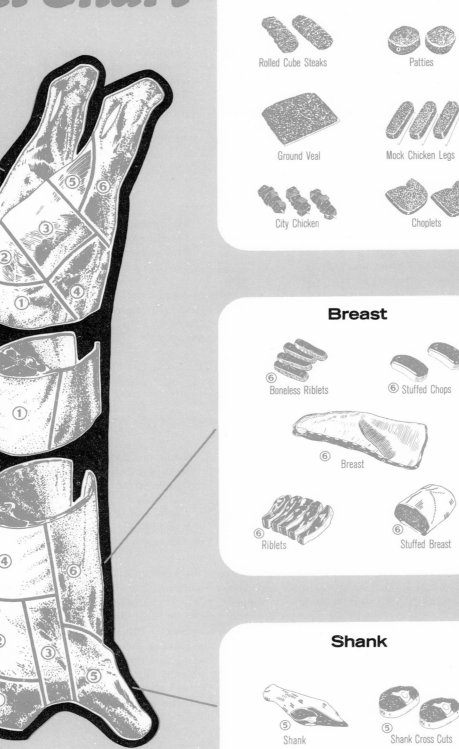

Veal for Grinding or Cubing

Rolled Cube Steaks

Patties

Ground Veal

Mock Chicken Legs

City Chicken

Choplets

Breast

⑥ Boneless Riblets

⑥ Stuffed Chops

⑥ Breast

⑥ Riblets

⑥ Stuffed Breast

Shank

⑤ Shank

⑤ Shank Cross Cuts

ormation courtesy of National Live Stock and Meat Board.

VEALBALLS IN SPICY SAUCE 40 TO 50 MEATBALLS

SAUCE

½ cup wine vinegar
4 tablespoons lemon juice
2 cans (6 ounces each) tomato paste
2 tablespoons Worcestershire sauce
½ cup dark brown sugar, firmly packed

2 teaspoons dry mustard
2 teaspoons salt
½ teaspoon chili powder
2 medium onions, minced

In a saucepan, blend all ingredients together with ¼ cup of water. Bring to a boil, stirring occasionally. Remove from heat and allow to stand at room temperature several hours so flavors can blend. Pour into chafing dish.

VEALBALLS

2 pounds ground veal
4 anchovy fillets, drained and finely
   chopped
½ clove garlic, mashed

2 teaspoons prepared mustard
Freshly ground white pepper to taste
6 tablespoons butter or margarine
1 teaspoon cooking oil

Mix all ingredients except butter and cooking oil and form into small balls. In large skillet, sauté balls in combined butter and oil, shaking pan vigorously to brown on all sides. Drain and add meatballs to chafing dish with sauce.
Sprinkle generously with paprika. Serve with toothpicks.

STUFFED ROAST BREAST OF VEAL 6 SERVINGS

3-pound veal breast
1 cup dried prunes, pitted
1 large apple, peeled, cored, and diced
4 cups seasoned croutons
1 teaspoon salt
½ teaspoon ground cinnamon
¼ teaspoon mace

¼ teaspoon ground ginger
Dash of ground cloves
2 tablespoons butter or margarine,
   melted
1 cube beef bouillon
2 tablespoons sugar

Preheat oven to 350°. Cut pocket in breast for stuffing. Combine prunes with ¾ cup water in small saucepan. Cover and simmer 3 minutes. Drain liquid into cup and reserve. Dice prunes. Combine prunes and apple with croutons, salt, and spices in large bowl. Drizzle melted butter over top and toss gently. Sprinkle salt lightly in pocket of veal, then stuff with prune mixture. Fasten with skewers. Place in roasting pan. Dissolve bouillon cube in 1 cup hot water, pour into roasting pan, and cover. Bake 2 hours, basting with pan drippings several times. Uncover and continue to roast 15 minutes, or until meat is tender. While meat cooks, combine ¼ cup of prune liquid and sugar in saucepan. Heat to boiling, stirring constantly, and simmer 5 minutes. Fifteen minutes before veal is done, brush with part of sauce. Continue roasting, brushing once or twice with remaining prune sauce, until veal is richly glazed.

Beware of overcooking veal—it dries out easily, and overcooking will make it tough. If you smell something ghastly in the kitchen but you can't see what it is through the smoke, you've overcooked the veal!

POT ROASTED BREAST OF VEAL 6 TO 8 SERVINGS

4-pound veal breast
Salt and pepper to taste
Stuffing (see recipe below)
2 tablespoons butter or margarine
1 carrot, sliced

1 small onion, sliced
1 bay leaf
Pinch of thyme
¾ cup dry white wine

Cut pocket in breast. Season meat inside and out with salt and pepper. Fill pocket with stuffing and secure with skewers. Brown in butter in a large heavy kettle. Add 1½ cups water and remaining ingredients. Bring to boil, cover, and simmer 1½ to 2 hours, or until very tender, adding more water if necessary. Slice meat, pour pan liquid over top or serve separately.

STUFFING

½ cup chopped onion
2 tablespoons butter or margarine
1 can (4 ounces) mushroom stems and
*   pieces, drained*

2 tablespoons chopped parsley
1 cup soft bread crumbs
1 egg, slightly beaten

Sauté onion in butter, until soft but not browned. Add mushrooms, stir in parsley and bread crumbs, add beaten egg, and mix well. Simmer until thoroughly warm.

POT ROASTED VEAL RUMP 6 TO 8 SERVINGS

4-pound veal leg rump roast
3 tablespoons butter or margarine
Salt and freshly ground pepper to taste
1 carrot, sliced
2 small onions, sliced
3 sprigs parsley

Pinch of thyme
1 small bay leaf
2 cups chicken broth
2 tablespoons flour
1 can (4 ounces) sliced mushrooms

Brown meat on all sides in butter in large, heavy kettle. Season with salt and pepper. Add remaining ingredients, except flour and mushrooms, and bring to boil. Cover, lower heat, and simmer, turning several times and basting with liquid, 2½ hours or until fork-tender. Remove meat to platter and keep warm. Strain liquid, skim off fat, and thicken with the flour mixed with a little cold water. Add mushrooms and simmer 5 minutes. Correct seasoning and serve with meat.

ROAST LEG OF VEAL 6 SERVINGS

4-pound veal leg roast, boned and
*   larded*
Salt and pepper to taste
4 strips bacon
1 medium onion, sliced
1 carrot, chopped
1 teaspoon thyme

1 bay leaf, crumbled
2 cloves garlic, slivered
4 tablespoons butter or margarine,
*   melted*
1 cup vermouth
Flour

Preheat oven to 375°. Rub roast with salt and pepper and cover with bacon. Place in roasting pan and add onion, carrot, thyme, bay leaf, and garlic. Roast uncovered 2 hours or until meat thermometer reads 165°. Combine melted butter with vermouth and baste frequently during cooking. Remove meat from oven and allow to stand 10 minutes before serving. Strain pan juices and thicken with flour to make gravy.

VEAL ROAST SMITANE 8 SERVINGS

5- to 6-pound veal leg rump roast
  boneless
2 cups dairy sour cream
1 envelope (1⅜ ounces) dry onion soup
  mix

1 teaspoon salt
Freshly ground pepper to taste
3 tablespoons butter or margarine
¼ cup finely snipped fresh dill or 2
  tablespoons dill weed

Blend sour cream and soup mix and let stand at room temperature while browning meat. Rub roast with salt and pepper, Brown slowly and thoroughly in butter in dutch oven or skillet that can be used in oven. Spread top and sides of meat with sour cream mixture. Sprinkle with dill. Cover and simmer over very low heat 2¼ to 3 hours, or roast in skillet in 325° oven, uncovered, the same amount of time.

COLD VEAL ROAST 6 SERVINGS

4-pound veal leg rump roast
Flour
½ cup olive oil
1 stalk celery, chopped
1 medium onion, chopped
2 cups chicken broth
½ cup white wine

1 can (7 ounces) chunk-style tuna,
  undrained
8 anchovy fillets, drained
½ cup mayonnaise
3 tablespoons lemon juice
4 cups cold cooked rice

Wipe veal with damp paper towels and coat lightly with flour. In dutch oven, brown veal in hot olive oil, on all sides. Add celery and onion. Sauté until onion is soft but not browned. Add chicken broth, wine, tuna, and anchovy fillets. Bring to boil. Lower heat and simmer, covered, 2 to 2½ hours or until fork-tender, turning veal occasionally. Remove veal, reserving liquid. Cool veal quickly and refrigerate, covered, overnight. Purée reserved liquid in food mill or electric blender. Refrigerate, covered, overnight. Next day, remove fat from purée. Add mayonnaise and lemon juice and mix well.
To serve: Spoon cold rice onto serving platter. Slice veal and arrange over rice. Top with purée mixture and garnish with capers.

BREADED VEAL AND TOMATO 8 TO 10 SERVINGS

12 veal cutlets (3 pounds)
3 eggs
¼ cup milk
3 tablespoons Parmesan cheese
1 tablespoon chopped parsley
¾ cup flour
1 teaspoon salt
½ teaspoon white pepper
4 tablespoons olive oil

4 tablespoons butter or margarine
1 tablespoon finely chopped shallots
1 clove garlic, finely chopped
3 cups cooked rice seasoned with
  saffron
6 medium tomatoes, peeled, seeded,
  and coarsely chopped or 1 can
  (1 pound 13 ounces) peeled
  tomatoes, drained

Pound cutlets thin. Beat together eggs, milk, Parmesan cheese, and parsley. In a separate bowl, combine flour with salt and pepper. Dip veal slices, one at a time, into flour mixture and then into egg mixture. Place in refrigerator 30 minutes. Combine olive oil and butter in large skillet and sauté meat until golden brown on both sides. Remove from pan and keep warm. Sauté shallots and garlic in the same oil and butter until soft but not browned. Drain off oil, add tomatoes and cook 3 to 4 minutes. Place veal slices on bed of saffron rice. Pour tomatoes over and serve at once.

To make veal extra tender, soak it overnight in milk in the refrigerator.

WIENER SCHNITZEL 4 SERVINGS

4 veal cutlets (1 pound)
3 tablespoons lemon juice
Salt and freshly ground pepper to taste
1 egg, beaten with 1 tablespoon water

¼ cup flour
½ cup dry bread crumbs
2 tablespoons butter or margarine
1 tablespoon olive oil

Wipe cutlets with damp cloth and pound thin. Sprinkle with lemon juice and marinate in glass dish about 10 minutes. Pat dry and season with salt and pepper. Dip in egg, then in flour. Shake off excess, then dip in bread crumbs. Shake off excess and refrigerate 30 minutes. Heat butter and olive oil in heavy skillet and brown cutlets over medium heat, about 3 minutes on each side, or until golden brown.
Garnish with lemon wedges and anchovy fillets.

VEAL A L'ORANGE 6 SERVINGS

6 veal cutlets (1½ pounds)
¼ cup butter or margarine

Salt and pepper to taste

SAUCE

2 tablespoons finely chopped shallots
   or onion
Juice of 1 lemon
Juice of 1 orange
¼ cup orange-flavored liqueur
2 teaspoons grated lemon rind
2 teaspoons grated orange rind

1 cup milk
2 tablespoons flour
1 cup chicken stock
1 can (8 ounces) mushrooms, chopped
¼ cup dairy sour cream
Salt and pepper to taste

Pound cutlets until very thin. Season with salt and pepper. Sauté in butter until lightly browned on both sides. Preheat oven to 300°. Arrange cutlets in shallow baking dish. Cover and bake about 20 minutes. Meanwhile, add shallots to skillet juices and sauté until soft but not browned. Stir in lemon and orange juices, liqueur, and lemon and orange rind. Simmer over low heat, stirring to remove all the brown bits from bottom of pan. Combine milk and flour and add to pan. Cook, stirring, over low heat until sauce is smooth and thick. Add chicken stock and mushrooms. Remove from heat and stir in sour cream. Season with salt and pepper and pour sauce over the veal just before serving.

VEAL ROLLS MARSALA 6 SERVINGS

6 veal cutlets (1½ pounds)
6 thin slices boiled ham (about ¼ pound)
½ pound mozzarella cheese, sliced
¼ cup butter or margarine

1 tablespoon flour
Dash of pepper
½ cup Marsala wine

Pound veal very thin. Place 1 slice ham and 1 slice cheese on each veal cutlet. Roll up and secure with wooden picks. Heat butter in large skillet over medium heat. Lightly brown veal rolls on all sides. Reduce heat to low, cover skillet, and simmer 15 minutes, or until veal is fork-tender. Remove from heat. Transfer veal rolls to platter and keep warm. Combine flour and pepper with ¼ cup water to make a smooth paste. Stir into drippings. Simmer, stirring, 3 minutes. Add wine, simmer, stirring, 1 minute. Pour sauce over veal rolls.
Garnish with chopped parsley.

141

VEAL PARMIGIANA 8 TO 10 SERVINGS

12 veal cutlets (3 pounds)
1 cup dry bread crumbs
½ cup grated Parmesan cheese
2 eggs, slightly beaten
1 cup chopped onion
1 clove garlic, mashed
4 tablespoons olive oil, divided
1 can (16 ounces) stewed tomatoes
2 cans (8 ounces each) tomato sauce

1½ teaspoons basil
½ teaspoon thyme
½ teaspoon onion powder
½ teaspoon salt
¼ teaspoon pepper
2 tablespoons butter or margarine
½ pound mozzarella cheese, sliced
½ cup grated Parmesan cheese

Mix bread crumbs and Parmesan cheese. Dip veal slices in beaten egg and coat well with crumb mixture. Place in refrigerator and chill 30 minutes while preparing sauce. Sauté onion and garlic in 2 tablespoons olive oil in skillet until soft but not browned. Add tomato sauce, basil, thyme, onion powder, salt, and pepper. Cover and simmer 15 minutes. Preheat oven to 350°. Heat 2 tablespoons olive oil with butter in separate skillet until mixture foams. Add veal slices, a few at a time, and brown on both sides. Arrange veal in large shallow baking dish and cover with sliced mozzarella and sauce. Sprinkle with Parmesan cheese. Bake 15 to 20 minutes, or until sauce bubbles and cheese melts.

SWISS VEAL 6 SERVINGS

6 veal cutlets (1½ pounds)
Salt and pepper to taste
3½ tablespoons butter or margarine, divided
1 tablespoon minced shallots
1 teaspoon tarragon
¾ cup dry white wine

1½ cups brown gravy
Dash of hot pepper sauce
18 thin tomato slices
18 thin avocado slices
Grated Parmesan cheese
6 slices Swiss cheese
1 can (8 ounces) tomato sauce

Pound veal very thin. Season with salt and pepper. Melt butter in large skillet, add meat, and sauté lightly on both sides. Remove cutlets and keep warm. Add more butter to skillet if necessary, and sauté shallots with tarragon until soft but not browned. Add wine and simmer until liquid is reduced by half. Stir in gravy, 1 tablespoon butter, and several drops hot pepper sauce. Preheat oven to 350°. Place cutlets in shallow baking dish and top each one with three overlapping slices each of tomato and avocado. Pour wine sauce over cutlets, sprinkle with Parmesan cheese, and top each with a slice of Swiss cheese. Bake 15 minutes or until meat is tender. Heat tomato sauce in small saucepan. Just before serving meat, top each cutlet with 2 or 3 tablespoons tomato sauce.

VEAL PAPRIKASH 4 TO 6 SERVINGS

1½-pound veal leg round steak
3 slices bacon, diced
1 medium onion, chopped
½ cup tomato sauce

1 tablespoon paprika
½ teaspoon salt
1 cup dairy sour cream

Cut meat into ¾-inch cubes. Fry bacon and onion in medium skillet until bacon is crisp and onion soft but not browned. Remove, drain, and set aside. Brown veal on all sides in bacon fat in same skillet. Drain off fat. Add sautéed onion, crumbled bacon, tomato sauce, paprika, and salt. Simmer 20 minutes or until meat is tender. Add sour cream and simmer 5 minutes. Serve over hot noodles.

VEAL SPINACH ROLLS 6 SERVINGS

6 veal cutlets (1½ pounds)
2 slices bacon, diced
¼ cup chopped onion
2 cups chopped raw spinach or 2
    packages (10 ounces each) frozen
    spinach, thawed
¾ cup cooked rice

½ teaspoon salt
⅛ teaspoon pepper
¼ teaspoon garlic powder
⅛ teaspoon marjoram
⅛ teaspoon nutmeg
2 tablespoons cooking oil
1 can (8 ounces) tomato sauce

Pound meat to ¼ inch thickness. Fry bacon with onion until bacon is crisp and onion soft but not browned. Add spinach, rice, salt, pepper, garlic powder, marjoram, and nutmeg. Cook over low heat, stirring, until spinach is slightly wilted, or, if using frozen spinach, until just warm. Place about 2 tablespoons spinach mixture on each piece of meat. Roll and fasten with wooden picks. Brown meat rolls slowly in cooking oil in large skillet. Pour off drippings. Add tomato sauce and ¼ cup water to veal in skillet. Cover tightly and simmer about 30 minutes, or until tender.

VEAL FRICASSEE WITH CHIVE DUMPLINGS 6 TO 8 SERVINGS

2-pound veal shoulder roast boneless
¼ cup flour
1 teaspoon salt
⅛ teaspoon pepper
1 teaspoon thyme
½ teaspoon poultry seasoning
3 tablespoons cooking oil
1 onion, sliced
½ cup sliced celery

1 cup dry vermouth
1 can (10¾ ounces) chicken broth
1 package (9 ounces) frozen Italian
    green beans, thawed
1 can (4 ounces) sliced mushrooms,
    undrained
3 tablespoons diced pimiento
Chive Dumplings (see recipe below)

Cut meat into 1½-inch cubes. Combine flour, salt, pepper, thyme, and poultry seasoning. Mix well and coat veal cubes in flour mixture. Heat cooking oil in large dutch oven. Brown veal on all sides, remove and set aside. Add onion and celery to dutch oven and sauté, stirring, about 5 minutes, or until onion is soft but not browned. Add vermouth and stir to scrape up particles. Return meat to dutch oven. Add chicken broth, beans, mushrooms, and pimiento. Bring to boil. Reduce heat and cook, covered, 5 minutes. Add Chive Dumplings and continue as directed below.

CHIVE DUMPLINGS 18 DUMPLINGS

1½ cups flour
2 teaspoons baking powder
¼ teaspoon salt
2 tablespoons chopped chives

1 tablespoon butter or margarine,
    melted
1 egg, beaten
⅓ to ½ cup milk

Into medium bowl, sift flour, baking powder, and salt. Stir in chives. With fork, stir in butter and egg. Add ⅓ cup milk or, if mixture seems dry, a little more milk. Drop dumplings on simmering meat. Cook, tightly covered (do not lift lid), 25 minutes, or until dumplings are thoroughly cooked.

 Most of your favorite chicken casserole recipes are just as delicious if veal is substituted for chicken. But don't use recipes that call for chicken still on the bone, unless you can figure out how to make sautéed veal wings.

VEAL AND PEPPERS 4 TO 6 SERVINGS

1½-pound veal for stew
2 tablespoons olive oil
3 tablespoons butter or margarine
1 large onion, sliced
4 large green bell peppers,
    cut in strips

⅔ cup dry white wine
1 can (16 ounces) stewed tomatoes
Salt and pepper to taste

Brown veal in combination of olive oil and butter in large skillet. Remove and set aside. Sauté onion and green pepper in remaining oil and buter until soft but not browned. Remove and reserve. Drain off fat. Add wine to skillet and scrape up particles. Return meat, onion, and pepper to skillet. Add tomatoes and season with salt and pepper. Cover and simmer 20 minutes, or until meat is tender.

VEAL RAGOUT 6 SERVINGS

1½-pound veal shoulder roast boneless
½ cup diced onion
4 tablespoons butter or margarine,
    divided
½ teaspoon salt
⅛ teaspoon pepper
2¼ cups chicken broth, divided

½ cup diced carrots
1 stalk celery, sliced
½ medium green bell pepper,
    cut in thin strips
½ pound mushrooms, sliced
Fresh parsley
2 tablespoons flour

Cut meat into 1-inch cubes. Sauté onion in dutch oven, in 2 tablespoons butter until soft but not browned. Add meat and sauté. Sprinkle with salt and pepper. Add 2 cups chicken broth, carrots, celery, green pepper, mushrooms, and 1 sprig parsley. Simmer, covered, for about 25 minutes, or until veal is almost tender. In small saucepan, heat remaining butter and stir in flour until smooth. Stir in remaining chicken broth gradually. Add to veal and simmer until sauce is thickened.
Garnish with chopped parsley and serve over rice.

MEXICAN VEAL WITH ALMONDS 6 SERVINGS

3-pound veal shoulder blade roast
4 cloves garlic, chopped
2 medium onions, divided
Salt and pepper to taste
⅛ teaspoon thyme

3 tablespoons butter or margarine
½ cup ground walnuts
1 can (13 ounces) evaporated milk
4 tablespoons ground almonds
2 tablespoons flour

Cut veal in half, place in dutch oven, and cover with 1½ quarts of water. Add garlic, one whole onion, salt, pepper, and thyme. Simmer 1 hour. Remove from heat, cool, and cut meat in thin slices. Reserve broth. In a large skillet, melt butter and sauté remaining onion, chopped fine, until soft but not browned. Add walnuts, milk, salt, pepper, and broth in which meat was cooked. Add sliced meat and simmer 30 minutes.
Remove meat to warm serving platter and sprinkle with almonds. Thicken remaining liquid with flour and serve as gravy.

When purchasing veal, look for white meat with a slight greenish tinge, and white satiny fat that smells of milk. This means that the animal has been almost exclusively milk-fed. Meat with a reddish color indicates solid feeding; this veal will not be as tender as milk-fed veal.

VEAL CHOPS IN WINE 4 SERVINGS

4 veal chops
Salt and pepper to taste
¼ cup cooking oil
1 clove garlic, sliced
½ cup dry white wine or dry sherry

1 beef bouillon cube, dissolved in ½ cup
    boiling water
4 small white onions
6 carrots, cut in small chunks
4 small potatoes, halved

Sprinkle meat on both sides wtih salt and pepper. Heat cooking oil with garlic in large skillet. Add veal and brown on both sides. Remove garlic, add wine and dissolved bouillon cube. Simmer, covered, 10 minutes. Arrange vegetables around and over meat. Correct seasoning. Cover and continue to simmer 30 minutes, or until vegetables are tender. Add additional wine if more liquid is needed.

 Veal steaks or chops can be broiled if marinated first. Try a garlic-flavored marinade and broil 4 or 5 inches from heat, brushing occasionally with marinade.

VEALBALLS WITH CAPER SAUCE 6 TO 8 SERVINGS

1½ pounds ground veal
½ pound lean ground pork
2 tablespoons butter or margarine
1 cup finely chopped onion
1 cup packaged herbed stuffing
1 teaspoon grated lemon peel
1 teaspoon anchovy paste
1 teaspoon salt

½ teaspoon pepper
2 teaspoons Worcestershire sauce
¼ cup chopped parsley
2 eggs, beaten
3 cans (10½ ounces each) condensed
    beef bouillon
1 cup dry white wine

SAUCE

¼ cup butter or margarine
¼ cup flour
¼ cup capers, drained

½ teaspoon anchovy paste
2 tablespoons chopped parsley

Combine ground veal with ground pork. Heat 2 tablespoons butter in small skillet. Sauté onion until soft but not browned. Drain. In large bowl, combine onion with meat, stuffing, lemon peel, anchovy paste, salt, pepper, Worcestershire, parsley, and eggs. Mix well with moistened hands and shape into balls 2 inches in diameter. In large kettle, bring bouillon and wine to a boil. Drop meatballs, one by one, into boiling liquid. Be certain liquid does not stop boiling while adding meatballs. Lower heat and simmer, covered, 20 minutes. With slotted spoon, remove meatballs from cooking liquid. Keep warm. Strain liquid, reserving 3 cups. To make sauce, melt ¼ cup butter in large saucepan, remove from heat. Add flour, stirring to make smooth mixture. Return to heat, and gradually stir in reserved liquid and bring to boil, stirring constantly. Add capers. Combine anchovy paste with small amount of liquid from kettle and add to sauce. Add meatballs. Cover kettle, return mixture to boil. Remove from heat. Stir in parsley.
Serve over hot noodles.

Many people are gun-shy about buying veal because the price per pound is fairly high. Remember, though, veal cutlet is economical because it is pounded very thin and a little goes a long way. Several servings per pound means a lower cost per portion.

SOUR CREAM VEAL LOAF 6 TO 8 SERVINGS

1½ pounds ground veal
½ pound lean ground pork
1 medium onion, minced
2 carrots, grated
1½ teaspoons salt

⅛ teaspoon pepper
½ cup dairy sour cream
½ cup dry vermouth
Flour

Preheat oven to 350°. Combine all ingredients except vermouth and flour. Mix thoroughly and pack into a 9- x 5-inch loaf pan. Bake 1½ hours. Remove loaf from pan and place pan over moderate heat. Add vermouth and scrape up particles. Thicken with flour, simmer 5 minutes, and serve over loaf.

OSSO BUCCO 4 SERVINGS

4 veal shank cross cuts
½ cup flour
1 teaspoon salt
¼ teaspoon pepper
2 tablespoons bacon drippings
1 tablespoon olive oil
1 cup coarsely chopped onion
1 cup coarsely chopped carrots
1 cup coarsely chopped celery

2 cloves garlic, crushed
1 cup peeled and coarsely chopped
    tomatoes
1 cup dry white wine
1 teaspoon basil
1 teaspoon thyme
1 bay leaf
3 tablespoons chopped parsley

Combine flour, salt, and pepper. Coat veal shanks, shaking off excess flour. Heat bacon drippings and olive oil in dutch oven. Sauté veal shanks, turning until all sides are nicely browned. Remove from pot and set aside. Add onion, carrot, celery, and garlic and cook slowly about 5 minutes. Add tomatoes, wine, basil, thyme, and bay leaf. Mix well and bring to a boil. Return veal shanks to pot and simmer, covered, about 2 hours. Just before serving, add parsley.

VEAL SHANK STEW 6 SERVINGS

6 veal shank cross cuts
5 tablespoons cooking oil
1 cup chopped onion
½ cup diced celery
½ cup diced carrot
1 can (10½ ounces) condensed onion
    soup or condensed beef broth

½ teaspoon salt
¼ teaspoon pepper
Flour
1 teaspoon grated lemon rind
1 teaspoon lemon juice
1 tablespoon tomato paste
2 tablespoons chopped parsley

Brown shank pieces in cooking oil in dutch oven or heavy kettle. Remove pieces as they brown. Pour off all but 2 tablespoons oil. Add onion, celery, and carrot. Sauté until tender but not browned. Return shanks to pan. Add onion soup, 1 cup water, salt, and pepper. Simmer, covered, 1½ to 2 hours, or until meat is tender. Thicken gravy with flour blended to a smooth paste with cold water. Stir in lemon rind, lemon juice, tomato paste, and parsley. Heat through. Pour over meat.

After breading veal cutlets or chops, refrigerate for 30 minutes before cooking. Breading will stick to meat more securely and not fall off during cooking.

VEAL DIVIDEND SUPREME 6 SERVINGS

3 cups diced cold roast veal
12 small onions
3 large carrots, sliced
1 bay leaf
Few sprigs parsley
1 cup dry white wine
2 cans (14 ounces each) chicken broth
4 green onions, trimmed and chopped
1 clove garlic, minced

2 stalks celery, sliced
1 pound mushrooms, sliced
6 tablespoons butter or margarine
½ cup flour
¼ teaspoon thyme
2 tablespoons lemon juice
2 egg yolks
1 cup cream
Salt and pepper to taste

Combine onion, carrots, bay leaf, parsley, wine, and chicken broth in large saucepan. Heat to boiling. Simmer 20 minutes, remove from heat. Strain liquid into medium size bowl. Reserve vegetables separately, discarding bay leaf and parsley. In a skillet, sauté green onion, garlic, celery, and mushrooms in butter until soft but not browned. Sprinkle flour and thyme over top. Stir in lemon juice and reserved liquid from vegetables. Cook slowly, stirring constantly, 10 minutes. Stir reserved vegetables and veal into sauce, heat to boiling, and simmer 5 minutes. Beat egg yolks with cream in small bowl, stir in about 1 cup hot sauce, then stir egg mixture into rest of sauce. Heat slowly, stirring constantly, until hot. Season with salt and pepper.
Serve over hot rice.

VEAL TIMBALES 4 SERVINGS

2 cups finely chopped cooked veal
1 egg, beaten
1 cup milk
1 cup soft bread crumbs

1 tablespoon minced parsley
1 teaspoon minced onion
Salt and pepper to taste
Tomato Sauce (see recipe below)

Preheat oven to 350°. Blend egg into milk. Add remaining ingredients except tomato sauce. Divide into 6 well-buttered baking cups. Set cups in pan of hot water and bake 30 minutes, or until firm. Unmold onto individual serving plates and cover with Tomato Sauce.

TOMATO SAUCE

1 tablespoon butter
1 tablespoon flour
1 cup tomato juice

½ teaspoon basil
Salt and pepper to taste

Melt butter in saucepan, stir in flour, add tomato juice, and seasonings. Simmer, stirring, until thickened.

VEAL SALAD 4 SERVINGS

1 cup diced cold cooked veal
1 hard-cooked egg, chopped
1 cup cooked peas, carrots, or green
    beans

Salt and pepper to taste
3 tablespoons mayonnaise
½ cup chopped stuffed green olives

Mix meat, egg, and vegetables. Season with salt and pepper. Add mayonnaise and chopped olives.
Chill and serve on crisp lettuce garnished with cherry tomatoes.

Variety Beef

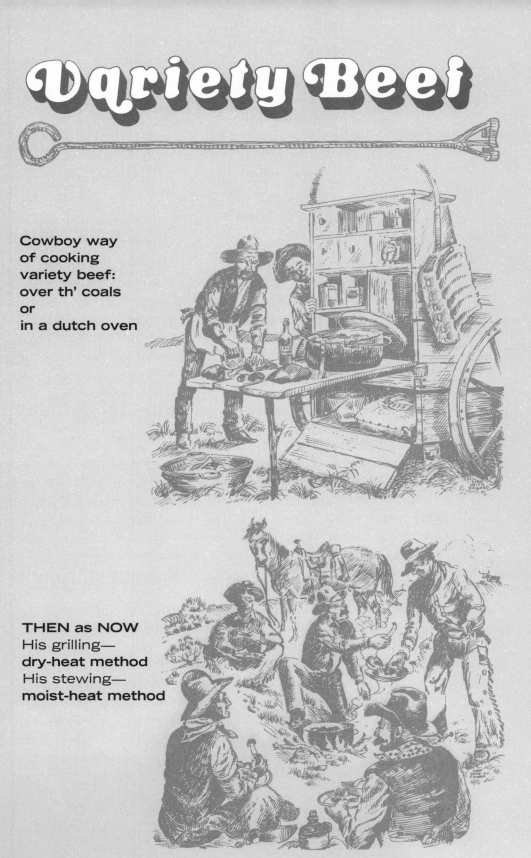

Cowboy way
of cooking
variety beef:
over th' coals
or
in a dutch oven

THEN as NOW
His grilling—
dry-heat method
His stewing—
moist-heat method

149

What is variety beef? I figger if it's beef and ya can eat it but you don't rightly know what else to call it, say "variety." And it has variety, that's for shore. There's liver, tongue, sweetbreads, kidneys, tripe, brains, even th' bony chunks of meat like short ribs, oxtails, and beef shanks, not to mention our ol' brandin'-time delicacy, Mountain Oysters (calf fries). Whether you call these beef parts delicacies or not is up to you, but we shore ate 'em and liked 'em, and I see 'em served up in th' fanciest eatin' houses.

On trail rides or at the ranches, these perishib'l variety meats was come by only at butcherin' time. We worked real hard an' at th' end of a tuff day it wuz mighty fine to set down to a Son-of-a-Bitch Stew that'd been simmerin' over th' coals for hours and hours in a dutch oven. This stew wuz called by lots of other names, but famous wherever there wuz cows and cowboys.

Nowadays most variety beef c'n be bought at any butcher's and at most any time of th' year an' cooked more ways than a bronco c'n buck.

Liver, heart, and kidneys can all be broiled or pan broiled. So can brains and sweetbreads if you par boil and drain 'em first. If you want to use moist-heat methods to cook 'em, all variety beef takes kindly to steamin', fryin', and boilin'. Tongue is best braised or boiled. Oxtails usual'y wind up in th' soup or stew.

Short ribs from a choice beef c'n be broiled. Less tender ribs can be throwed in a dutch oven to simmer with some "skunk eggs" (onions) and other vegetables. Ribs c'n be seasoned Sweet 'n Sour, done up Russian style, and cooked other ways.

SON-OF-A-BITCH STEW

This recipe uses most of th' innards from a fresh butchered calf. Like most stew recipes, th' exact amounts of what's in it ain't all that big of a deal.

Cut th' marrow gut into one-inch pieces and brown it in a quarter-inch of bacon drippin's in a big dutch oven. Cut the heart, sweetbreads, both kidneys, and a pound of lean beef into one-and-a-half-inch chunks and toss 'em in th' pot with th' marrow gut. Cover meat with water an' cook over th' coals for maybe half an hour. Add a fourth of th' liver cut up, two chopped onions, four garlic cloves, and salt and pepper to taste. Cook real slow all day, addin' more water if th' stew gets too thick. Two hours before servin' add th' brains to th' pot.

Variety meats, also known as specialty cuts, are an exciting treat for an adventurous cook. Generally low in cost and high in nutrition, they should play an important part in menu planning. Included in the category of variety meats are all edible internal organs and very bony cuts, such as oxtails and ribs. Be certain to use most variety meats within 24 hours of purchase as they are highly perishable. In a pinch, they may be kept as long as 48 hours.

Brains

Calf brains are more flavorful and delicate in texture than beef brains. Allow 1 pound, or 2 calf brains, for 4 servings.

To prepare for cooking:

1. Soak in cold water 1 hour (soak beef brains 4 hours).
2. Remove membrane and veins.
3. Soak beef brains again to whiten.
4. Simmer in salted acidulated water (1 teaspoon salt, 1 tablespoon vinegar to each quart) 15 to 20 minutes. Simmer beef brain 20 to 25 minutes.
5. Drain and plunge into very cold water to cool.
6. Drain and dry.

Heart

Heart meat is firm and rather dry. Obviously a highly exercised muscle, it usually requires slow, moist heat in order to make it tender. Heart may also be ground and used as a substitute for ground beef. A 4- or 5-pound beef heart will serve 6. Allow 1 calf heart per individual serving.

To prepare for cooking:

1. Wash thoroughly.
2. Remove veins, arteries, fat, and blood clots.

Kidneys

Veal kidneys are the most tender. Large beef kidneys are stronger in flavor and need slow, moist heat in order to make them tender. Veal kidneys should be cooked over moderate heat to a medium-rare stage; beware of overcooking. One veal kidney serves 1 or 2; one beef kidney will serve 3 to 4.

To prepare for broiling:

1. Split lengthwise without completely separating halves.
2. Brush cut side with melted fat, if desired.
3. Thread skewers along edges to prevent curling.

To prepare for other types of cooking:

1. Remove membranes (sautéing one minute in cooking oil makes this easier).
2. Soak 2 hours in cold salted water.
3. Drain and wipe dry.
4. Remove off-flavors and off-odors by blanching briefly in acidulated water, or by sautéing briefly over fairly high heat.
5. Drain and wipe dry, or cool.

Liver

Liver is a famously abundant source of iron and vitamins A and B. Tender calf and baby beef liver may be broiled or cooked quickly in a minimum of fat. Liver from more mature animals may require braising. One pound serves 4.

To prepare for cooking:

1. Wipe with damp cloth.
2. Remove outer skin and veins.

Oxtail

Oxtail, though not one of the meatiest beef cuts, is nevertheless very tasty. It lends itself well to braising, stuffing, and to the famous oxtail soup which is the pride of gourmet restaurants and fine cooks. Oxtail is usually skinned, unless it is to be stuffed. One pound serves 2.

To prepare for stuffing:

1. Soak whole, with skin on, in cold water.
2. Remove bone carefully, without damaging skin.

To prepare for cooking by another method:

1. Remove skin, if not already removed.
2. Cut into uniform chunks, unless otherwise specified.

Sweetbreads

Sweetbreads include the longish thymus or "throat" gland, and the rounded, more desirable pancreas or "heart" gland. They come in pairs (one of each type) usually from the calf, but occasionally from beef.

Sweetbreads are soft and white and need firming before cooking. Allow 1 pound, or 2 pairs, per 4 persons.

To prepare for cooking:

1. Soak in cold water until white. Drain.
2. Place in cold salted water to cover.
3. Heat to just under boiling, stirring frequently with a wooden spoon.
4. Drain and firm by plunging into cold water.
5. Drain and remove connective and covering tissues.

Testes

Calf testes, also known as fries or Rocky Mountain Oysters, are the gonads of young male animals. They may be substituted in recipes calling for sweetbreads. Allow 2 or 3 per person.

To prepare for cooking:

1. Simmer briefly in water to cover.
2. Drain and plunge into cold water until cool enough to handle.
3. Remove skin.
4. Soak in cold water 2 to 3 hours.

Tongue

Tongue is a popular variety meat, often served cold as luncheon meat as well as hot for dinner. Beef tongue is sold fresh, smoked, or pickled; calf tongue is only sold fresh. The best buy is a beef tongue weighing less than 3 pounds. If pickled tongue is very salty, it may be soaked in cold water to cover several hours or overnight.

To prepare for cooking:

1. Scrub well.
2. If smoked or pickled, blanch if desired, simmering 10 minutes.
3. Drain.
4. Remove skin, roots, small bones, and gristle after cooking. Tongue should be cool enough to handle, but not cold or it will be difficult to skin.

Tripe

Tripe is the edible portion of beef stomach. It is sold fresh, blanched, or pickled, partially precooked or uncooked. There are several different types of tripe, including the fat part of the belly, or "gras double," and honeycomb tripe, from the second part of the stomach. It should have a firm but pliant texture when cooked, but will lose this texture if cooked over high heat. One pound will serve 2 to 3 people.

To prepare for cooking:

1. Wash in several changes of cold water.
2. If not partially precooked, simmer 3 to 3½ hours in salted acidulated water.
3. If blanched or pickled, simmer 1 to 1½ hours in salted water.
4. Drain and cut into pieces for cooking.

Short Ribs

Allow about 1 pound per serving. Cooking time for ribs cut 2 x 2 x 4 inches is 1½ to 2½ hours. Brown ribs on both sides in heavy utensil or under broiler. Pour off drippings at intervals. No cooking oil is needed to brown most short ribs.
Season with salt and pepper, as desired.
Add a small amount of water.
Cover tightly and simmer until tender.
Ribs may also be baked in a slow oven, 325°, without water, until tender.
Make sauce or gravy from pan liquid, if desired.

Outdoor Cooking:

Parboil short ribs about 1 hour, or until tender. Grill until brown on an open fire, with or without brushing with sauce or marinade.
Or:
Sprinkle with meat tenderizer and allow to stand about 30 minutes before grilling. It will take about 1 hour to cook on grill.
Or:
Marinate ribs from 3 hours to overnight. Grill 1 to 1½ hours. Brush ribs with sauce or marinade during cooking.
Turn occasionally to assure even cooking.

opposite: CORNED BEEF AND CABBAGE
page 156: SIRLOIN STEAK
page 157: LIVER AND ONIONS

SWEET 'N SOUR SHORT RIBS 4 SERVINGS

3 to 4 pounds chuck short ribs
Salt and pepper to taste
½ cup catsup
¼ cup vinegar
3 tablespoons brown sugar
½ teaspoon dry mustard
½ teaspoon salt

1 medium onion, sliced diagonally
1 green bell pepper, cut in 1-inch
   squares
1 can (13¾ ounces) pineapple tidbits,
   drained (reserve juice)
3 tablespoons cornstarch

Preheat oven to 325°. Brown short ribs in their own fat in dutch oven or large heavy skillet. Pour off drippings. Season with salt and pepper to taste and place in covered pan. Bake about 2 hours. Pour off excess fat. Combine catsup, vinegar, brown sugar, mustard, ½ teaspoon salt, and ¼ cup water. Pour over ribs. Return to oven for 30 minutes. Add onion and green pepper and bake 30 minutes longer. Remove ribs to serving dish. Mix reserved pineapple juice with cornstarch. Add cornstarch mixture and tidbits to sauce in roasting pan. Cook 10 minutes, or until sauce thickens and pineapple is heated through. Pour over ribs and serve immediately.

BARBECUED SHORT RIBS 2 SERVINGS

2 pounds lean chuck short ribs
Salt, pepper, and paprika to taste
1 tablespoon cooking oil
1 large onion, sliced
¼ cup catsup

2 tablespoons vinegar
1 teaspoon Worcestershire sauce
⅛ teaspoon chili powder
¼ teaspoon celery seed

Cut ribs into serving pieces. Season with salt, pepper, and paprika. Heat cooking oil in pressure cooker. Brown ribs with onion. Combine remaining ingredients with 1 cup of water and add to ribs. Put lid on pressure cooker. Bring pressure up to 15 pounds and cook 20 to 25 minutes. Or: Cover and bake in 350° oven 1½ to 2 hours, or until well done, basting occasionally.

RUSSIAN RIBS 4 TO 6 SERVINGS

4 to 5 pounds lean chuck short ribs
1 cup sliced onion
2 to 3 cloves garlic, crushed
2 tablespoon butter or margarine
1 teaspoon salt

1 teaspoon thyme
1 bay leaf
½ teaspoon pepper
1 cup vodka
½ cup condensed beef broth

Sauté onion and garlic in butter until golden. Add salt, thyme, bay leaf, and pepper. Stir in vodka and beef broth. Heat to steaming. Set aside. Cut ribs in serving-size pieces. Place in one layer in shallow pan and pour marinade over ribs. Cover and refrigerate at least 4 hours or overnight. Turn ribs once or twice. Preheat oven to 350°. Place ribs, bone side down, well spaced, in shallow roasting pan. Pour marinade over. Bake 1½ to 2 hours, basting often.

opposite: SHORT RIBS

HAWAIIAN SHORT RIBS 4 SERVINGS

3 to 4 pounds chuck short ribs
1 can (30 ounces) sliced pineapple
¼ cup soy sauce

1½ teaspoons ground ginger
1 tablespoon brown sugar
8 maraschino cherries

Cut ribs into service-size pieces. Preheat oven to 350°. Place on rack in pan and brown in oven 1 to 1½ hours. Cool and trim off excess fat. Drain juice from pineapple and add enough water to make 2 cups. Mix with soy sauce, ginger, and brown sugar. Place browned ribs in dutch oven, pour sauce over and simmer 2 hours, covered, adding more water if necessary. Remove ribs to hot platter. Brown pineapple slices slightly under broiler. Surround ribs with pineapple slices. Put cherry in center of each slice.

RANCH RIBS 6 SERVINGS

5 to 6 pounds chuck short ribs
⅓ cup soy sauce
¼ cup honey

⅓ cup Burgundy or claret wine
1 medium onion, sliced

SAUCE

1 small onion, chopped
3 tablespoons butter or margarine
1 cup catsup
1 cup chili sauce
Freshly ground pepper to taste
2 tablespoons liquid smoke

2 tablespoons Worcestershire sauce
2 tablespoons brown sugar
2 tablespoons lemon juice
4 tablespoons honey
1 clove garlic, minced
3 to 4 tablespoons dry red wine

Preheat oven to 300°. Trim outside fat from ribs and arrange in one layer in a large, shallow baking pan. Mix soy sauce, honey, and wine and pour over ribs. Place onion slices on top. Cover pan with foil. Bake 1 hour. Remove from oven. Drain and discard liquid. While ribs are baking, sauté onion in butter until soft but not browned. Combine with all remaining sauce ingredients and simmer 10 to 15 minutes. Pour ½ of the sauce over cooked ribs, cover, and continue baking 45 minutes. Uncover. Add remaining sauce and continue to bake, uncovered, 30 minutes.

BOILED TONGUE

Fresh:

Wash tongue thoroughly and place in large kettle. Cover with salted water (1 teaspoon salt for each quart of water). If desired, add an onion cut in quarters, a sprig of parsley, 1 or 2 bay leaves, several peppercorns or cloves, a stalk of celery, or, for variety, ¼ cup brown sugar, 1 small orange cut in half, 1 tablespoon whole allspice or pickling spice, 1 hot pepper from pickling spice. Simmer until tongue is tender (3 to 4 hours or about 1 hour per pound). When tender, plunge into cold water, remove skin, and trim root ends. To serve cold, cool in cooking liquid after skinning.

Smoked:

Soak tongue overnight in cold water. Drain and cover with fresh cold water. Bring to a boil and discard water. Cover with hot water and cook as for fresh tongue.

Quick Method:

Pressure cooker—40 minutes at 10 pounds pressure. Reduce pressure gradually.

 When serving tongue cold, trim, peel, and allow to cool in its own broth for added flavor. Peeling cold tongue is next to impossible.

CRANBERRY BEEF TONGUE 6 TO 8 SERVINGS

1 tongue
1 cup brown sugar
1 cup cooked cranberries

¼ cup butter or margarine
1 tablespoon whole cloves
1 lemon, sliced

Simmer tongue in water to cover 3½ hours. Skin and slice. Mix 1 cup cooking liquid from tongue with remaining ingredients in 2-quart saucepan. Add tongue slices and simmer about 15 minutes.

SWEET AND SOUR TONGUE 6 SERVINGS

1 tongue, cooked (see basic directions,
    page 154)
1 small onion, sliced
¼ cup butter or margarine
1 tablespoon flour
¼ cup dry red wine
2 tablespoons wine vinegar
2 tablespoons chopped parsley

½ cup pickle relish
2 tablespoons catsup
⅛ teaspoon thyme
⅛ teaspoon sage
½ cup sweet pickle juice
1 clove garlic, mashed
1 bouillon cube, dissolved in 2
    tablespoons boiling water

Cut tongue in small cubes. Sauté onion in butter until soft but not browned. Stir in flour and add remaining ingredients, except tongue. Simmer 30 minutes. Add tongue and cook 15 to 20 minutes more.

TONGUE IN WHITE WINE 6 SERVINGS

3-pound tongue
Salt and pepper to taste
3 onions, halved
2 cloves garlic, minced
½ cup vinegar

1 bay leaf
1 can (16 ounces) stewed tomatoes
½ cup soy sauce
1 cup dry white wine

Boil tongue until skin can be peeled off easily. Peel and trim. Rub skinned and trimmed tongue with salt and pepper and place in deep pot with tight-fitting lid. Add remaining ingredients and water to cover tongue. Cover pan tightly and cook over low heat, turning occasionally, until tongue is fork-tender. Add additional water if needed. When tender, remove tongue from pan in one piece and discard bay leaf. Put remaining ingredients through food mill and strain. Return liquid to pan and cook over low heat until thickened. Pour over thinly sliced tongue and serve.

ROYAL TONGUE SALAD 4 TO 6 SERVINGS

2 cups cooked tongue (see basic directions, page 154)
1 cup diced celery
1 cup bing cherries, pitted

4 hard-cooked eggs, sliced
½ cup pecans
1 teaspoon salt

Cut tongue in narrow strips and combine with celery, cherries, eggs, pecans, and salt. Chill thoroughly. Serve on a bed of salad greens with mayonnaise on the side.

BEEF HEART POT ROAST 6 TO 8 SERVINGS

1 beef heart
1 cup sour milk *
Bread stuffing (see recipe below)
2½ tablespoons flour
2 tablespoons cooking oil
12 small white onions
1 cup chopped celery
Bouquet garni
2 whole cloves

8 peppercorns
Salt to taste
18 small potatoes
18 small turnips or 6 large turnips, cut in chunks
18 mushrooms, stems removed
1 can (15 ounces) baby carrots
Flour

Wash heart and remove veins and arteries. Soak 1 hour in sour milk to increase tenderness. Drain. Stuff cavity with bread stuffing (do not pack). Sew opening securely. Rub heart with flour and sear in 2 tablespoons cooking oil. Transfer to dutch oven. Add onions, celery, bouquet garni, cloves, peppercorns, and salt. Cover with cold water, bring to boil, and simmer 3 hours. After about 2½ hours add potatoes and turnips. Continue cooking until tender. Fifteen minutes before serving, add carrots and mushrooms. Arrange heart and vegetables on a warm platter. Thicken gravy (1 tablespoon flour to 1 cup liquid) and pour over all.

STUFFING

1 cup dry bread crumbs
½ cup chopped onion
1 tablespoon chopped parsley
1 clove garlic, mashed

3 tablespoons chopped green bell pepper
1 egg, beaten
Milk to moisten

Combine all ingredients and blend together.

* To make sour milk: Add 1 tablespoon vinegar or lemon juice to 1 cup milk.

BEEF HEART ITALIENNE 6 TO 8 SERVINGS

1 beef heart
3 tablespoons cooking oil
½ cup chopped onion
1 clove garlic, minced
1½ teaspoons salt
⅛ teaspoon pepper

2 tablespoons chopped pimiento
1 can (6 ounces) tomato paste
1 can (1 pound 14 ounces) tomatoes
1 package (8 ounces) spaghetti, cooked
½ cup shredded Cheddar cheese

Trim coarse·fibers from top and inside of heart. Wash heart well, drain, and cut into 1-inch cubes. Heat cooking oil in large skillet. Add meat, onion, and garlic and sauté until browned. Add salt, pepper, pimiento, tomato paste, and tomatoes. Cover and simmer 2 hours or until meat is tender and mixture is thickened.
Serve over hot spaghetti and top with cheese.

DUTCH OVEN BEEF HEART 4 TO 6 SERVINGS

1 beef heart
½ pound mushrooms, sliced
½ cup butter or margarine, divided
1 cup flour
1 teaspoon garlic powder
½ teaspoon basil

½ teaspoon rosemary
½ teaspoon thyme
2 cups red Burgundy wine
1 envelope (1⅜ ounces) dry
*   onion soup mix*

Preheat oven to 275°. Slice heart, remove fat and ligaments. Combine flour, garlic powder, and herbs and dredge heart in flour mixture. Reduce unused seasoned flour. Sauté mushrooms in half the butter in dutch oven, remove, and reserve. Add remaining butter to dutch oven and brown heart. Mix unused seasoned flour with enough water to make paste. Add with wine, sautéed mushrooms, soup mix, and enough water to barely cover meat. Cover dutch oven tightly. Bake 5 to 6 hours. Serve in pan gravy.

Brains may be substituted in all recipes calling for sweetbreads.

Sweetbreads or brains, broken into small pieces, are delicious in scrambled eggs.

SCRAMBLED EGGS AND BRAINS 6 TO 8 SERVINGS

2 calf brains
1 tablespoon vinegar
6 eggs
½ cup milk

¾ teaspoon salt
¼ teaspoon pepper
3 tablespoons bacon drippings

Soak brains in cold water 1 hour. Remove membrane and veins. Wash brains and cook in salted aciduated water (see page 39) for 18 to 20 minutes. Drain and plunge into cold water to cool. Drain again and separate brains into small pieces. Beat eggs, add milk, salt, and pepper. Sauté brains lightly in bacon drippings. Add egg mixture and cook slowly, stirring constantly, until eggs are set but still moist. Serve immediately.

BRAIN AND MUSHROOM STEW 4 SERVINGS

2 calf brains
⅓ pound fresh mushrooms, sliced

3 tablespoons butter or margarine
Red Wine Sauce (see recipe below)

Soak brains in cold water one hour. Remove membrane and veins. Wash brains and cook in salted acidulated water (see page 39) for 18 to 20 minutes. Drain. Rinse in cold running water, drain, and cut into small pieces. Place in flameproof casserole. Sauté mushrooms in butter about 5 minutes. Drain and add to brains. Pour hot wine sauce over mixture and set over very low heat until heated. Serve immediately.

RED WINE SAUCE

2 tablespoons chopped carrot
2 tablespoons chopped celery
2 tablespoons chopped onion
4 tablespoons butter or margarine,
    divided
1 small piece bay leaf

Pinch of thyme
1½ cups dry red wine
1½ cups beef stock (see page 202),
    divided
Sliver of garlic (optional)
1 teaspoon flour

Sauté vegetables in 2 tablespoons butter. Add bay leaf, thyme, wine, ½ cup beef stock, and garlic. Cook over high heat until reduced one half. Add remaining beef stock and simmer 15 to 20 minutes. Strain into aonther pan and thicken with flour and remaining butter kneaded together.

Brains are fairly bland in flavor, so be sure to pep them up with lively seasoning.

LIVER LOAF 6 SERVINGS

1½ pounds beef liver, sliced
2 tablespoons cooking oil
¼ cup chopped onion
¼ cup chopped celery
¼ pound pork sausage meat

1 teaspoon salt
1 cup soft bread crumbs or cooked rice
1 egg, beaten
⅔ cup milk
Spanish Sauce (see recipe below)

Preheat oven to 350°. Wipe liver with damp cloth and remove skin and veins. Sauté lightly in cooking oil, remove and chop fine. Sauté onion and celery in same skillet and add to liver. Add sausage, salt, bread crumbs, egg, and enough milk to moisten mixture well. Pack firmly into a loaf pan and bake 1½ to 2 hours. Serve with Spanish Sauce.

SPANISH SAUCE

2 tablespoons chopped onion
2 tablespoons cooking oil
1 tablespoon flour
1 can (16 ounces) tomatoes

½ cup chopped celery
¼ cup chopped green bell pepper
Salt and pepper to taste

Sauté onion in cooking oil. Blend in flour, add tomatoes, celery, and green pepper. Season and cook 20 minutes, or until sauce is thick.

 Liver will toughen if overcooked or cooked over excessively high heat. Either calf's liver or beef liver may be used in a given recipe by simply adjusting cooking time. Beef liver is less tender than calf's liver and therefore should cook longer. Test for doneness by pricking with a fork.

LIVER AND ONIONS 4 SERVINGS

1 pound calf's liver, thinly sliced
2 tablespoons flour
Salt and pepper to taste
2 tablespoons cooking oil

Paprika
6 slices bacon
2 onions, sliced

Wipe liver with damp cloth and remove skin and veins. Mix flour with salt and pepper and dredge liver in seasoned flour. Sauté liver quickly in cooking oil on both sides to desired doneness (2 minutes on each side for rare, 4 minutes for well·done). Do not overcook. Remove to warm platter and sprinkle with paprika. Cook bacon until crisp. Drain, reserving fat, and place on top of cooked liver. Sauté onion in reserved bacon fat. Drain and add to platter. Serve immediately.

DEVILED LIVER 4 SERVINGS

1 pound beef liver, sliced
1½ teaspoons salt
½ teaspoon pepper
1 teaspoon dry mustard
⅛ teaspoon cayenne
⅛ teaspoon paprika

3 tablespoons melted butter or margarine
2 teaspoons vinegar
2 teaspoons Worcestershire sauce
2 egg yolks
¾ cup dry bread crumbs
½ cup bacon drippings or cooking oil

Wipe liver with damp cloth and remove skin and veins. Combine salt, pepper, dry mustard, cayenne, paprika, butter, vinegar, Worcestershire, and egg yolks. Mix well. Dip liver slices into mixture, then into bread crumbs. Pan fry in bacon drippings, turning frequently until meat is browned and tender, about 20 minutes.

Cook liver sliced rather than whole. Browning improves flavor.

SWISS LIVER 4 TO 5 SERVINGS

1¼ pounds beef liver, sliced
3 tablespoons butter or margarine
2 tablespoons minced onion
1 can (4 ounces) sliced mushrooms
¾ teaspoon salt
¾ teaspoon sugar
¼ teaspoon tarragon

⅛ teaspoon pepper
Dash of nutmeg
1 cup thinly sliced celery
½ cup dry red wine
3 tablespoons chopped parsley
1½ tablespoons flour
½ cup dairy sour cream

Heat butter in large skillet, add onion and sauté until soft but not browned. Wipe liver with damp cloth and remove skin and veins. Cut in thin strips, add to skillet, and brown, turning often. Drain mushrooms, reserving liquid. Add mushrooms to liver and brown lightly. Add salt, sugar, tarragon, pepper, nutmeg, celery, reserved mushroom liquid, wine, and parsley. Cook, covered, 5 minutes. Mix flour to smooth paste with ¼ cup of water, blend into hot mixture. Cook, stirring constantly, until gravy thickens and comes to boil. Remove from heat, blend in sour cream. Serve over hot rice.

STEAK AND KIDNEY PIE 4 TO 6 SERVINGS

1 beef kidney (about 1¼ pounds)
1 pound round steak, ½ to ¾ inch thick
1 small onion, quartered
¼ cup cooking oil
2 teaspoons salt

Dash of pepper
¼ teaspoon savory
2 medium size potatoes, cut into
    ½-inch cubes
Pastry for 1-crust pie

Remove outer membrane of kidney. Split kidney open and remove all fat and white veins. Soak in cold water 2 hours. Drain. Cut kidney and steak into ¾-inch cubes. Sauté kidney, steak, and onion in cooking oil in large skillet, stirring frequently. Sprinkle with salt, pepper, and savory. Add potatoes and enough water to cover. Simmer until meat is tender, about 30 to 40 minutes. Add more water if needed. Preheat oven to 425°. Remove meat and vegetables to a 2-quart casserole. Thicken gravy with a little flour, if desired, and pour mixture over meat. Place pastry crust on top, cutting several slits to allow steam to escape. Bake about 20 minutes, or until crust is golden.

KIDNEY STEW 4 TO 6 SERVINGS

2 beef kidneys
¼ cup butter or margarine
⅓ cup flour
¼ cup Madeira wine
1 can (10½ ounces) condensed beef broth
3 carrots, thinly sliced
Salt, pepper, and garlic powder to taste

1 package (10½ ounces) frozen peas,
    thawed
1 can (4 ounces) mushrooms
1 can (16 ounces) small onions
1 package (8 ounces) wide noodles,
    cooked

Remove outer membrane of kidney. Clean well and cut into small cubes. Preheat oven to 350°. Sauté kidneys in butter in skillet. Stir in flour, blend well. Place in 2-quart casserole. Add wine to skillet and scrape up particles. Pour over kidneys. Add beef broth, carrots, salt, pepper, and garlic powder to casserole. Cover and bake 45 minutes. Add peas, mushrooms, and onion and bake uncovered 30 minutes longer.

 Do not overcook kidneys; they should remain slightly pink in the center. Boiling kidneys in a sauce will harden them. Never flambé kidneys for longer than 1 minute or they will toughen.

To keep kidneys from curling while broiling, slice in half lengthwise almost all the way through and secure edges with skewers.

SPANISH TRIPE 8 TO 10 SERVINGS

3 pounds precooked tripe
1 large onion, minced
2 cloves garlic
2 tablespoons cooking oil
2½ cups tomato purée
½ cup tomato sauce

1 bay leaf
1 teaspoon oregano
2 chili peppers or ⅛ teaspoon
    Tabasco sauce
Salt and pepper to taste

Wash tripe thoroughly and cut into long, very narrow strips. Sauté onion and garlic in cooking oil until soft but not browned. Add remaining ingredients and simmer, covered, about 30 minutes. Add drained tripe and simmer, uncovered, until tender, about 30 minutes.

NOTE: *If tripe is not precooked, see page 154 for directions and preparation.*

MENUDO (TRIPE) 8 TO 10 SERVINGS

3 pounds precooked tripe
2 cloves garlic
Salt to taste

2 cans (1 pound 13 ounces each)
white hominy
Dash of chili powder

Wash tripe thoroughly and remove all fat. Cut into 1½-inch to 2-inch squares. Bring enough water to cover tripe to boil, add tripe, garlic, and salt. Cover and simmer about 2 hours or until tender. Add hominy and cook ½ hour longer. Add chili powder just before serving.
Garnish with ½ cup chopped onion, chopped parsley, and lemon wedges.
NOTE: *If tripe is not precooked, see page 154 for directions and preparation.*

SWEETBREAD CASSEROLE 4 SERVINGS

2 pairs sweetbreads
1 can (10¾ ounces) condensed cream of
mushroom soup
½ soup can milk or water
⅛ teaspoon pepper
¼ teaspoon marjoram

1 package (10 ounces) frozen
French-style green beans, thawed
1 can (4 ounces) water chestnuts,
drained and sliced
⅓ cup cracker crumbs
¼ teaspoon thyme

Prepare and cook sweetbreads according to directions on page153.Preheat oven to 375°. Slice sweetbreads about ½ inch thick. Blend soup and milk until smooth. Stir in pepper and marjoram. In greased 1½-quart casserole, alternate layers of sweetbreads, green beans, water chestnuts, and soup mixture. Top with cracker crumbs and sprinkle with thyme. Bake, uncovered, 20 minutes.

If you plan to use sweetbreads whole, weight them down after preliminary preparation with a plate and refrigerate several hours.

SWEETBREADS ON TOAST 2 SERVINGS

1 pair sweetbreads
3 or 4 peppercorns
2 tablespoons butter or margarine

1 teaspoon dried onion flakes
½ pound fresh mushrooms, sliced
½ cup red or white dry wine

Prepare and cook sweetbreads according to directions on page 153. Slice into bite size pieces. Melt butter in saucepan, add onion flakes and mushrooms. Cook about 5 minutes, add sweetbreads and wine, and simmer until nearly dry.
Garnish with parsley and serve on toast.

MELT (SPLEEN) CASSEROLE 5 TO 6 SERVINGS

¾ pound beef melt
⅔ cup rice
¼ cup butter or margarine
½ cup sliced celery

¼ cup minced onion
¼ cup chopped green bell pepper
1 cup canned tomatoes
1 teaspoon salt

Cook rice according to package directions. Reserve. Simmer melt 10 minutes in a small amount of water. Drain and chop coarsely. Preheat oven to 350°. Melt butter in large skillet, add melt, celery, onion, and green pepper and sauté until lightly browned. Stir in reserved rice, tomatoes, and salt. Turn into a medium size casserole. Cover, and bake 30 minutes. Uncover and continue to bake 10 minutes longer.

ROCKY MOUNTAIN OYSTERS (CALF TESTES) 6 SERVINGS

12 medium-sized Mountain Oysters
1 egg, beaten
1 cup light cream

3 cups crushed cracker crumbs
4 tablespoons butter or margarine

Wash oysters well and simmer briefly in water to cover. Remove all loose skin or membrane. Split so they will lie flat. Soak in cold water 2 to 3 hours. Dip in mixture of egg and cream. Roll in cracker crumbs. Sauté quickly in butter at high heat until crisp. **VARIATION:** *Mix together in a bag: 1 cup flour; 1 teaspoon salt; ½ teaspoon pepper. Shake oysters in flour mix until thoroughly coated, then sauté in butter.*

OXTAIL SOUP 8 SERVINGS

2 pounds oxtails
2 tablespoons cooking oil
1 tablespoon salt
½ cup chopped onion

1 cup sliced carrot
¾ cup sliced celery
½ cup sauerkraut, drained
1 cup cooked tomatoes

Cut meat into 2-inch pieces. In skillet, brown oxtails in cooking oil. Remove to large kettle or dutch oven and add 2 quarts of water and salt. Cover and simmer 3½ hours. Remove meat from bones and return meat to soup stock. Add vegetables. Cover and simmer 30 minutes. Skim off fat and serve.

OXTAIL RAGOUT 6 TO 8 SERVINGS

4 pounds oxtails
1 cup chopped onion
4 tablespoons cooking oil, divided
½ cup flour
3 beef bouillon cubes, dissolved in
    1 cup boiling water
¼ teaspoon pepper

1 teaspoon garlic powder
1 teaspoon thyme
1 bay leaf
2 tablespoons tomato paste
1 cup cubed potatoes
1 cup sliced carrots

Cut meat into serving-size pieces. Sauté onion in 2 tablespoons cooking oil in kettle until soft but not browned. Remove onion with slotted spoon and reserve. Shake oxtails with flour in bag until well coated. Shake off excess flour. Add 2 tablespoons oil to kettle, heat, and brown oxtails quickly on all sides. Return onion to kettle. Add 7 cups water, dissolved bouillon cubes, pepper, garlic powder, thyme, bay leaf, and tomato paste. Bring to boil over medium heat, lower heat, cover, and simmer, stirring occasionally, 3½ to 4 hours, or until meat is tender. If thicker ragout is desired, mix a small amount of flour and water to a smooth paste, stir into ragout, and cook until bubbly and thickened. Remove bay leaf. Cook potatoes and carrots separately in boiling, salted water until tender, add to ragout just before serving.
Garnish serving dish with hot peas.

Be certain all variety meats are very fresh. Use them promptly—most are extremely perishable.

OVEN BAKED OXTAILS
WITH BARBECUE SAUCE 4 SERVINGS

2 pounds oxtails
¼ cup chopped onion
2 tablespoons butter or margarine
½ teaspoon salt
½ teaspoon cayenne
2 tablespoons brown sugar

1 cup catsup
2 tablespoons vinegar
¼ cup lemon juice
3 tablespoons Worcestershire sauce
½ tablespoon dry mustard
½ cup chopped celery

Preheat oven to 325°. Cut meat into 2-inch pieces. Sauté onion in butter until soft but not browned. Add all remaining ingredients except meat. Simmer about 10 minutes. Place oxtails in roasting pan and cover with sauce. Bake, covered, 2½ to 3 hours, or until meat is tender.

BRAISED OXTAIL 6 SERVINGS

3 pounds oxtails
Flour
3 tablespoons cooking oil
Salt and pepper to taste
1 can (16 ounces) small white onions,
    drained
½ pound mushrooms, sliced

1 clove garlic, minced
6 medium carrots, thickly sliced
1 bay leaf
¼ teaspoon thyme
2 cups dry red wine
Beef stock (see page 202)

Preheat oven to 350°. Cut meat into 2-inch pieces. Dredge oxtails in flour and brown in cooking oil in skillet. Remove oxtails to large casserole and sprinkle with salt and pepper. Sauté onion, mushrooms, and garlic in drippings. Drain and add to casserole with remaining ingredients, using just enough beef stock to cover meat. Bake, covered, 2½ to 3 hours, or until meat is tender.
Garnish with parsley and serve with cornbread.

BRAISED BONES 4 SERVINGS

4 pounds shank cross cuts or chuck
    flat ribs
Salt to taste
2 tablespoons olive oil
2 cloves garlic, minced
1 large carrot, chopped
1 large onion, chopped
1 can (4 ounces) sliced mushrooms

1 can (8 ounces) tomato sauce
1 can (6 ounces) tomato paste
1 can (10½ ounces) condensed chicken
    broth
1 teaspoon basil
¾ teaspoon cinnamon
¼ teaspoon nutmeg
½ cup grated Parmesan cheese

Salt bones and brown a few at a time in olive oil in large skillet. Set aside. Add garlic, carrot, onion, and mushrooms to drippings and sauté until onion is soft but not browned. Add 1 cup water and all remaining ingredients except cheese and browned bones. Simmer about 10 minutes. Add bones and simmer, covered, about 2½ hours. Serve on platter with sauce spooned over bones. Sprinkle with grated cheese and provide lots of extra napkins.

Processed & Prepared

Cowboy way of processing or preparing beef: sun-drying jerky

THEN as NOW
His jerky making—
dry-heat method
His jerky cooking
(after soaking
or pounding)—
moist-heat method

Processed or prepared beef is not considered th' same as fresh beef. It's been dried, pickled, or preserved in some form. There's corned beef, chipped beef, canned beef, and beef wieners, for instance.

'Course, not everybody wearin' a "Stetson" is a cowboy, an' not every hot dawg is a beef wiener, so eye-ball th' label before ya buy any. If hot dawgs is wearin' th' right brand, you can cook 'em dry-method or moist-method—same as ya can fresh beef—grilled, fried, baked, pan broiled, steamed, boiled, tossed in a stew or in a casserole. Ya c'n cook 'em more ways than there are spots on an Appaloosa colt.

Might say processed beef got invented out on th' frontier. Whether you give th' American Indian credit for jerkin' beef from th' buffalo or say jerky comes from Spanish *charque* (dried beef), you'll have to admit cowpokes shore took up the idea of cuttin' fresh beef into strips and dryin' it in th' sun. Without no ice box we ate a lot of jerky. We got awful tired of jerky gravy, jerky stew, jerky with beans, jerky with chili, but when it comes right down to a life-and-death matter how can you beat a saddle sandwich?

JERKY

Cut lean beef into strips about a half-inch thick, an inch wide, an' as long as possible. Trim away all fat, because it'll turn rancid. Sprinkle th' strips with salt or dip in brine made of one cup salt to a half-gallon water. Hang th' strips on lines to dry—in the sun if ya can. And if yore afoot for anythin' else, use a "bob wire" fence. Pepper real good to keep th' flies away and watch out for varmints. Weather decides how long it takes beef to dry— couple of days to a week. It's done when it's shrivil'ld up an' turns black. It's chewey and real good.

You c'n make jerky outdoors on a barbecue grill. Cover it with an ol' window screen if yore fussy, but don't let nuthin' touch th' meat. Keep pieces from touchin' each other an' take 'em in at night if there's critters or if ya don't live in a real dry climate.

You can also dry strips of beef in th' oven. Lay 'em accrost wire oven-racks. Keep oven door open with temperature at lowest settin' so's beef dries, not cooks. Turn it over once and give it eight hours all told dryin' time.

NEW ENGLAND BOILED DINNER 8 SERVINGS

4-pound brisket corned boneless
16 small beets
8 medium potatoes
8 medium carrots

1 large turnip
1 medium head cabbage
Salt and pepper to taste
Butter or margarine

Place meat in large heavy kettle. Cover with water and bring to a boil. Skim off foam and scum as it rises to surface. Reduce heat and simmer, covered, about 3 hours, or until tender. Add additional water during cooking if necessary. Scrub beets, remove all but 1 inch of stem, place in boiling water to cover, and cook until tender, about 30 minutes for small young beets. Drain, cool, slip off skins, and return to pot. Season as desired with salt, pepper, and enough butter to reheat before serving. Peel potatoes, carrots, and turnip. Cut turnip into large pieces, halve potatoes, and carrots if desired. Add to corned beef 30 to 35 minutes before meat is done. Remove outer leaves from cabbage, quarter, remove core, and add to corned beef at the same time as the other vegetables. Carve meat and place in center of large platter. Surround with cooked vegetables and serve with prepared horseradish and mustard pickles.

FRUITED CORNED BEEF 10 TO 12 SERVINGS

5-pound brisket corned boneless
1 jar (10 ounces) apple jelly
1 lemon, rind and juice
1 orange, rind and juice

1 can (1 pound 4 ounces) apricot halves,
   drained
1 can (1 pound 4 ounces) pineapple
   chunks, drained

Place meat in large kettle and cover with water. Simmer, covered, 4 hours, or until tender. Skim off foam and scum as it rises to surface. (Some corned beef is saltier than others, so you may wish to pour off water at the end of an hour, then cover with fresh water and continue cooking.) Preheat oven to 350°. Combine jelly, lemon rind and juice, and orange rind and juice in saucepan. Heat until jelly melts. Remove meat from water. Plack on rack in roasting pan. Arrange apricots and pineapple chunks around meat. Baste meat and fruit with half the jelly glaze. Bake, uncovered, 15 minutes. Baste again with remaining glaze. Bake 15 minutes longer. Remove meat and fruit to heated platter.

GLAZED CORNED BEEF 10 TO 12 SERVINGS

5-pound brisket corned boneless
1 medium onion, quartered
1 stalk celery
1 carrot
1 clove garlic, quartered
1 bay leaf
½ teaspoon rosemary

⅓ cup catsup
2 tablespoons wine vinegar
2 tablespoons honey
2 tablespoons mint jelly
1 tablespoon butter or margarine
1 tablespoon prepared mustard

Place meat in large kettle, cover with cold water, add onion, celery, carrot, garlic, bay leaf, and rosemary. Cover, heat to boiling, then simmer 4 hours, or until meat is tender. Skim top of water several times during cooking. Preheat oven to 350°. Drain meat and place on rack in shallow roasting pan. In a saucepan, combine remaining ingredients and heat to boiling. Pour glaze over meat and bake 20 minutes, basting occasionally until well glazed.

CORNED BEEF HASH WITH EGGS 6 SERVINGS

1 can (15½ ounces) corned beef hash
1 tablespoon minced onion
1 tablespoon minced green bell pepper
2 tablespoons butter or margarine

Dash of Tabasco sauce
Dash of Worcestershire sauce
Salt and pepper to taste
6 eggs

Sauté onion and green pepper in butter in a large skillet until onion is soft but not browned. Add hash and mix well. Season with Tabasco, Worcestershire, salt, and pepper. Cook, stirring constantly, until heated through. Smooth out surface and make six depressions on top of hash. Break one egg into each depression. Season eggs with salt and pepper, cover skillet, and cook over low heat until eggs are set.
Garnish with paprika and serve on toast.
NOTE: *Substitute diced leftover corned beef and diced cooked potatoes for canned hash.*

Many processed meats, such as corned beef, are cured in a salty solution which leaves behind a generous reminder of its presence. Either rinse the meat in cold water several times before cooking, or warn your favorite uncle before he adds his customary blizzard of salt to the "meat 'n taters."

RED FLANNEL HASH 6 SERVINGS

1½ cups cubed cooked corned beef
½ cup minced onion
3 tablespoons butter or margarine
1½ cups diced cooked beets

1½ cups diced boiled potatoes
½ cup evaporated milk
Salt and pepper to taste

In a large skillet, sauté onion in butter until soft but not browned. Add remaining ingredients and mix carefully. Adjust heat during cooking so that crust forms on bottom of skillet but does not burn. Use a spatula to turn crust through hash. When thoroughly hot and new crust has formed, serve immediately.
NOTE: *Substitute 1 can (15½ ounces) corned beef hash for meat and potatoes in recipe.*

CORNED BEEF SALAD 6 SERVINGS

1 can (12 ounces) corned beef, chopped
1 package (3 ounces) lemon-flavored
    gelatin
1 can (10½ ounces) condensed beef
    bouillon
1 to 2 tablespoons vinegar,
    depending on sharpness desired

1 cup mayonnaise
1 cup finely chopped celery
1 cup finely chopped onion
2 tablespoons chopped green bell
    pepper
3 hard-cooked eggs, chopped

Dissolve gelatin in beef bouillon heated to boiling. Add vinegar. Cool until slightly thickened and fold in mayonnaise. Add chopped meat, vegetables, and eggs. Chill or oil 2-quart ring mold, pour mixture into mold, and chill 3 to 4 hours, or until firm. Unmold on bed of lettuce, by loosening edges of mold with sharp knife, dipping mold quickly in hot water and inverting on serving platter.

Are you an adventurous, do-it-yourself type? Are you so well organized that you can plan meals two weeks ahead? If so, see Homemade Corned Beef, page 65.

CORNED BEEF RING 6 SERVINGS

2 cups chopped cooked corned beef
2 envelopes unflavored gelatin
1 cup hot tomato juice
Juice of one lemon

¼ cup diced celery
½ cup mayonnaise
¼ cup diced cucumber

Mix gelatin with ¼ cup cold water. Add remaining ingredients, and mix. Chill or oil 2-quart ring mold, pour mixture into mold, and chill 3 to 4 hours, or until firm. Unmold on bed of lettuce, by loosening edges of mold with sharp knife, dipping mold quickly in hot water and inverting on serving platter.

HEARTY SPLIT PEA SOUP 6 SERVINGS

1 pound all-beef frankfurters, sliced
2 cans (10¾ ounces each) split pea soup
2 soup cans milk

Salt and pepper to taste
1 cup seasoned croutons

Heat soup with milk and stir until smooth. Add sliced frankfurters and simmer. Add croutons to soup just before serving.

VARIATION: *Substitute 1 jar (5 ounces) dried beef, torn into bite-size pieces, in place of frankfurters.*

NEW ENGLAND BEANS AND FRANKS 6 SERVINGS

1 pound all-beef frankfurters
2 cups dried pea beans or
    Great Northern beans
2 onions, one halved, one sliced thin
2 teaspoons salt, divided

½ teaspoon ginger
½ teaspoon dry mustard
¼ teaspoon pepper
¾ cup maple syrup or dark molasses
½ pound lean salt pork, cubed

Bring 1 quart water to a boil in a large kettle. Drop beans in water and boil 2 minutes. Turn off heat and soak beans 1 hour. If necessary, add additional water to cover beans by at least 2 inches. Add halved onion and bring to a boil, lower heat, and simmer 1 hour, or until beans are tender. Add additional water during cooking if necessary. Drain beans over bowl, reserving liquid. Remove onion and discard. Add ½ teaspoon salt. In a separate bowl, combine 1½ teaspoons salt, ginger, mustard, pepper, and maple syrup. Mix well and add to beans, blending carefully until beans are well-coated. Preheat oven to 275°. Cover bottom of a 2½-quart casserole with salt pork and sliced onion. Add seasoned beans and 3 cups of reserved liquid. Cover casserole and bake 6 hours, adding additional liquid if necessary. Correct seasoning and cover top of beans with frankfurters cut into thirds. Return to oven uncovered and bake 1 hour.

NOTE: *Reheated leftover beans will require additional liquid since beans will absorb liquid when stored in either refrigerator or freezer.*

 Do your frankfurters explode during cooking? Pierce them with a fork first to prevent hot dog shrapnel from covering the kitchen walls. Don't cook in boiling water; franks should simmer.

FRANKFURTER CORN CASSEROLE 4 TO 6 SERVINGS

1 pound all-beef frankfurters,
    cut in 1½-inch slices
2 cups peeled and very thinly sliced
    potatoes

1 can (16 ounces) cream-style corn
1 onion, sliced
½ teaspoon salt
1 green bell pepper, cut in rings

Preheat oven to 350°. Layer frankfurters, potatoes, corn, and onion in a 2-quart casserole. Sprinkle with salt. Cover with green pepper rings. Bake, covered, 35 to 40 minutes. Uncover during last 15 minutes of cooking.

SOUTH SEAS SANDWICH 6 SERVINGS

8 to 10 all-beef frankfurters, finely
    chopped
3 tablespoons chopped green bell
    pepper
¼ cup chopped cucumber
2 tablespoons slivered almonds, toasted

¼ cup mayonnaise
1 teaspoon lemon juice
½ teaspoon Worcestershire sauce
2 tablespoons catsup
6 frankfurter rolls, split

Preheat oven to 400°. Combine frankfurters, green pepper, cucumber, almonds, mayonnaise, lemon juice, Worcestershire, and catsup. Mix well. Spread mixture between split buns, allowing about ⅓ cup for each. Wrap each bun in foil and bake 10 minutes.

FRANKFURTERS SUPREME 8 SERVINGS

2 cups chopped, all-beef frankfurters
2 hard-cooked eggs, chopped
½ cup grated Cheddar cheese
2 tablespoons pickle relish
¼ cup chili sauce

½ teaspoon garlic powder
1 teaspoon prepared mustard
Salt to taste
8 frankfurter rolls, split

Preheat oven to 400°. Combine all ingredients except rolls. Mix together and fill split rolls generously. Wrap in six 8-inch squares of aluminum foil and secure ends in a tight twist. Place on baking sheet and bake 15 to 20 minutes.
VARIATION: *Freeze before baking (if frankfurters have not been frozen previously) and bake 30 minutes before serving.*

PICNIC SPECIAL 6 SERVINGS

6 all-beef frankfurters, cooked and
    sliced
1 package (8 ounces) macaroni, cooked
½ cup diced green bell peppers
½ cup diced celery

½ cup mayonnaise
Salt and pepper to taste
2 tomatoes, cut in wedges
3 hard-cooked eggs, cut in wedges

Combine cooked frankfurters with cooked macaroni. Add green peppers, celery, mayonnaise, salt, and pepper. Mix well and place in serving dish. Surround with tomato and egg wedges and chill thoroughly before serving.
Garnish with parsley sprigs.

177

BEEF DIP 3 CUPS

1 package (3 ounces) dried chipped beef
4 teaspoons vinegar
2 teaspoons Worcestershire sauce
1 package (8 ounces) cream cheese,
    softened

½ teaspoon onion powder or garlic
    powder
½ cup mayonnaise
Salt to taste

Tear beef into tiny pieces and mix all ingredients in electric mixer. Serve with crinkled potato chips or crackers.

VARIATION: Use 2 cups dairy sour cream and ½ cup of cottage cheese instead of the cream cheese and mayonnaise.

CHIPPED BEEF ROLL UPS 6 SERVINGS

1 package (3 ounces) dried chipped beef
1 package (8 ounces) cream cheese,
    softened

½ teaspoon prepared horseradish
¼ teaspoon garlic powder

Blend cheese, horseradish, and garlic powder. Spread on beef. Roll up and serve with toothpicks.

CREAMED CHIPPED BEEF 4 SERVINGS

1 jar (5 ounces) dried chipped beef
4 tablespoons butter or margarine
1 small onion, diced
4 tablespoons flour
2 cups light cream

1 tablespoon lemon juice
2 tablespoons dry sherry
2 tablespoons minced parsley
⅛ teaspoon paprika
Pepper to taste

Melt butter in a large skillet. Sauté onion until soft but not browned. Add flour and mix to a smooth paste. Gradually add cream, stirring constantly until slightly thickened. Stir in lemon juice, sherry, parsley, paprika, and pepper. Tear dried beef into bite-size pieces and add to sauce. Simmer until meat is thoroughly heated.

Serve immediately on toast points or English muffins for a special Sunday brunch. Or break open baked potatoes and fill with Creamed Chipped Beef for a hearty quick dinner.

CHIPPED BEEF AND CORN 4 SERVINGS

1 jar (5 ounces) dried chipped beef
2 tablespoons chopped onion
½ green bell pepper, chopped
2 tablespoons butter or margarine

1 can (16 ounces) cream-style corn
2 tablespoons chopped pimiento
Salt and pepper to taste

Sauté onion and green pepper in butter in large skillet until soft but not browned. Tear meat into small pieces. Add to onion with other ingredients and simmer 15 minutes. Serve on toast or biscuits, or in pastry shells.

 Dried chipped beef should always be bright red with no brown spots. When refrigerated, it will keep a week in the plastic vacuum pack. If purchased in a sealed glass jar, it will keep indefinitely on the pantry shelf. This is a very helpful emergency item to have on hand if you have unexpected company. You can always prepare creamed chipped beef in a hurry.

CREAMY RICE AND CHIPPED BEEF 4 SERVINGS

1 jar (5 ounces) dried chipped beef
½ cup finely chopped onion
1 tablespoon butter or margarine
1 can (10¾ ounces) condensed cream of
    celery soup or condensed cream of
    mushroom soup

½ cup milk
1 package (10 ounces) frozen green
    peas, thawed
1 beef bouillon cube, dissolved in
    2 cups boiling water
1⅓ cups instant rice

Sauté onion in butter in large skillet until soft but not browned. Tear beef into small pieces and add to skillet with soup, milk, and peas. Add dissolved bouillon cube to meat mixture. Bring to a boil over medium heat. Stir in rice, cover, and reduce heat. Simmer 10 minutes, or until most of the liquid is absorbed.

If chipped beef is too salty, immerse it in boiling water for a few seconds. Then rinse thoroughly.

BUSY DAY STEW 2 SERVINGS

1 can (15½ ounces) beef stew
¼ cup diagonally sliced celery
¼ teaspoon curry powder

1 small clove garlic, minced
1 tablespoon butter or margarine

In medium size skillet, sauté celery, curry powder, and garlic in butter until celery is tender but not browned. Add beef stew. Simmer, stirring occasionally, until thoroughly heated.

BISCUIT COVERED STEW 6 SERVINGS

2 cans (15½ ounces each) beef stew
1 can (16 ounces) whole-kernel corn,
    drained
Salt and pepper to taste
¼ teaspoon basil

¼ teaspoon thyme
1 clove garlic, minced
1 can (8 ounces) refrigerator biscuits
2 tablespoons butter or margarine,
    melted

Preheat oven to 400°. Mix together beef stew, corn, salt, pepper, basil, thyme, and garlic. Place in an ungreased 3-quart casserole. Top with biscuits, brush with melted butter, and bake, uncovered, 15 to 20 minutes, or until biscuits are golden.

Many processed meats are sold ready-to-serve, but not all of them. Be sure to read the label. You may even discover a few additional interesting bits of information, such as ingredients, calorie content, or how to win a cowboy if you submit your favorite recipe.

To prevent beef bacon from curling when pan broiling, press fat out with a broad knife during cooking.

POT ROAST STEW WITH NOODLES 4 SERVINGS

1 can (2 pounds) pot roast
6 slices bacon
3 tablespoons brandy
1 cup dry red wine
2 cans (10½ ounces each) condensed
    consommé
2 cans (4 ounces each) sliced mush-
    rooms

2 bay leaves, crumbled
2 tablespoons chopped parsley
½ teaspoon thyme
Salt, pepper, and garlic powder to taste
Hot cooked noodles

Cut beef into bite-size pieces. Fry bacon until crisp, drain, and discard drippings. Set bacon aside. Combine beef, brandy, wine, consommé, mushrooms, bay leaves, parsley, thyme, salt, pepper, and garlic powder. Simmer 45 minutes to 1 hour.

Thicken gravy, if desired, and serve with stew over noodles. Sprinkle with crumbled bacon.

PICNIC POT ROAST 4 SERVINGS

1 can (2 pounds) pot roast
Salt and pepper to taste
Garlic powder to taste (optional)
2 medium onions, chopped
½ cup chopped green bell pepper
1 can (16 ounces) tomatoes
⅓ envelope (1⅜ ounces) dry onion soup
    mix

1 can (6 ounces) tomato paste
½ teaspoon basil
½ teaspoon oregano
½ teaspoon chili powder
1 tablespoon dried parsley flakes

Cut meat into bite-size pieces, reserving liquid. Combine with liquid and all other incredients. Simmer 45 minutes to 1 hour.

VARIATION: *Add carrots, green beans, potatoes, or noodles.*
NOTE: *Canned pot roast is an easy way to provide hearty meals when camping out.*

 Easy way to remove meat from a can: open both ends and push meat out. Chances are your luck won't hold out long enough for that fickle key to open the can, so use a regular can opener. P.S. An over-sized reusable extra key is handy to have around for emergencies.

Leftovers

Cowboy way
of cooking
leftovers:
heat 'em up again

THEN as NOW
His cooking—
out of doors or
in the house

It didn't matter if we wuz eatin' on th' trail, at camp, or in town —th' thought of leftovers didn't much cross our minds. Any makin's wuz scarce and we usually ate everthin', so there wasn't much left over to scrape up another main dish. Soup wuz a waste of time, salad wuz outa th' question, and who needs an appetizer when his belly is most always ready an' howlin' for solid food? I act'shully thought a beef spread wuz jist another name for a cow outfit.

We shore liked it when we got in on th' ranch style eatin'— that's all's ya c'n eat from a table loaded up with everthin' in-cludin' desserts. Sometimes on th' trail rides we got so hungry we felt like fallin' to with a saddle blanket or easin' our case of th' "hongries" by chewin' on an ol' tarp.

Now in these days of faster transp'tation and better refrig'ra-tion, we not only have more food, but we c'n think ahead and git in on some of those so-called planned leftovers. A food mix is always good for another set-to, and good beef can be called back for another go-round in a "sooflay," casserole, or meat pie.

I can batch if I have to, but I can't exactly see myself throwin' too wide a loop and stirrin' up what I call fancy little "crow-ketties." Deal me in, tho, for choppin' up beef and mixin' fillin's, even if I wouldn't be too handy at stuffin' peppers or tomatoes. And I'd probably be a danged sight better at fixin' a bedroll than a filled beef roll-up.

I git th' biggest kick out of a dish called chow mein. It's chow all right, even when it's cooked in a Chinese wok instead of a dutch oven.

LONE-STAR HASH

This recipe is named for one state but claimed by other states as original.

Heat two tablespoons bacon drippin's or other fat in a skillet or dutch oven 'til they're sputterin' hot. Dump in two cups diced-up cooked potatoes, two cups chopped cooked roast beef or ground leftover steak, and a chopped onion. Season with salt and pepper. Cook real slow an' easy, turnin' it over and over 'till browned. Add a small amount of water—maybe couple tablespoons—kinda towards th' end of cookin' time. If you want a tetch of spice, toss in a can of green chilies.

BEEF PUFF APPETIZERS 12 TO 16 PUFFS

PUFFS

½ cup butter

1 cup flour

1 envelope (1⅜ ounces) dry onion
     soup mix

4 eggs

Preheat oven to 400°. Combine 1 cup water with butter and heat to boiling. Stir in flour all at once, and stir constantly until mixture leaves sides of pan and forms a ball. Remove from heat. Shake soup mix through a sieve over flour mixture to remove large pieces of onion. Beat in eggs, one at a time. Continue beating until mixture is smooth and velvety. For each bite size puff, put ½ teaspoon of dough on ungreased baking sheet. Bake 12 to 15 minutes, or until dry. Cool. Cut puffs open and spoon in meat filling. (Packaged cream puff mix may be used instead.)

FILLING

2 cups ground cooked beef

¼ cup chopped pickles

Dash of catsup

Dash of Worcestershire sauce

3 tablespoons mayonnaise

Mix all ingredients together and fill cream puffs.

PARTY SANDWICHES 24 SMALL SANDWICHES

2 cups ground cooked beef

3 hard-cooked eggs, chopped fine

2 green onions, chopped

½ teaspoon salt

¼ teaspoon pepper

Dash of cayenne

1 large sweet pickle, finely chopped

3 heaping tablespoons mayonnaise

Combine all ingredients and toss. Chill well and spread on small slices of party rye bread.

Garnish with sliced olives.

VARIATION: Serve as a salad on crisp lettuce.

BEEF AND VEGETABLE APPETIZER 8 TO 12 SERVINGS

2 cups cubed cooked roast beef

Celery sticks

Raw zucchini squash slices

Carrot sticks

½ cup Russian dressing

1 cup dairy sour cream

½ teaspoon Worcestershire sauce

Chill meat and vegetables in refrigerator. Make dip by mixing Russian dressing, sour cream, and Worcestershire together. Chill 1 hour. Arrange meat and vegetables in individual mounds around dip.

Garnish with parsley.

NOTE: Store prepared carrot sticks in container filled with ice water flavored with sugar.

FILLED BEEF ROLLS 3 TO 4 DOZEN

18 to 20 thin slices cooked roast beef
Cucumber Filling or Guacamole Filling
(see recipes below)

Spread either filling on slices of cold roast beef, allowing about 2 teaspoons for each slice. Roll up slices, wrap, and chill.
To serve, cut rolls in halves or thirds. Secure each piece with small wooden toothpick and arrange on platter.

CUCUMBER FILLING

2 packages (3 ounces each)
* cream cheese*
½ cup grated cucumber

¼ cup grated radishes
2 teaspoons onion powder

Soften cream cheese, add grated cucumber, radish, and onion salt. To grate cucumber, scoop out seeds and grate remainder, leaving skin on. Press out liquid in strainer.

GUACAMOLE FILLING

1 medium size avocado
1 tablespoon lime juice
1 tablespoon grated onion
½ teaspoon salt

⅛ teaspoon coriander
4 drops Tabasco sauce
½ teaspoon chili powder
¼ cup chopped tomato

Mash avocado. Add lime juice, onion, salt, coriander, Tabasco, chili powder, and tomato. Combine thoroughly.

SPICY BEEF SALAD 4 SERVINGS

1 cup cubed cooked roast beef
1 cup chopped celery
1 cup grated carrots
1 teaspoon grated onion
½ cup mayonnaise

¼ teaspoon salt
¾ teaspoon prepared mustard
¼ teaspoon prepared horseradish
1 cup packaged shoestring potatoes

Combine meat with celery, carrots, and onion. Mix mayonnaise with salt, mustard, and horseradish. Add to meat mixture. Just before serving, add potatoes.
Spoon into lettuce cups and serve at once while potatoes are still crisp.

SOUR CREAM BEEF SALAD 4 SERVINGS

3 cups cooked steak or roast,
* preferably rare, cut in 1-inch strips*
1 cup dairy sour cream
1 teaspoon salt

½ teaspoon Worcestershire sauce
¼ teaspoon Tabasco sauce
⅛ teaspoon garlic powder
1 slice onion, chopped

Mix sour cream, salt, Worcestershire, Tabasco, and garlic powder. Add meat and onion and chill at least 4 hours or overnight.
Serve on bed of lettuce.

185

COLD MEAT SALAD 6 SERVINGS

*2 cups cooked roast beef, cut in
    2-inch strips*
½ cup seedless raisins
*1½ cups fresh pineapple chunks or 1
    can (15¼ ounces) pineapple
    chunks, packed in own juice*
½ cup chopped celery

*½ small green bell pepper, cut in
    thin strips*
¼ cup sliced stuffed green olives
¼ cup slivered almonds
1 tablespoon chopped pimiento
¼ teaspoon salt
½ cup dairy sour cream

Add ⅓ cup warm water to raisins and soak 15 minutes. Drain. Combine beef, raisins, drained pineapple, celery, green pepper, olives, almonds, pimiento, and salt. Toss lightly. Add sour cream and mix well. Chill 2 to 3 hours.
Serve garnished with coconut.
VARIATIONS: *Add ½ to 1 cup diced tart apple. Flavor with curry to taste.*

Treat leftovers gently—they are best reheated over low heat or in a double boiler, or, if you are lucky enough to own one, in a microwave oven.

STUFFED TOMATOES 6 SERVINGS

*2 cups coarsely ground or chopped
    cooked beef*
6 medium tomatoes
½ teaspoon salt, divided
½ cup minced celery

1 tablespoon minced onion
1 tablespoon lemon juice
½ cup mayonnaise
¾ cup crushed potato chips

Slice off tops of tomatoes, scoop out centers, salt lightly wtih ¼ teaspoon salt, and invert at least 30 minutes to drain. Combine beef, celery, onion, lemon juice, mayonnaise, and ¼ teaspoon salt. Stuff drained tomatoes with meat mixture and top with crushed potato chips.
Chill and serve on shredded lettuce.
NOTE: *Save scooped-out tomato in refrigerator, strain, and add to soups and stews.*

VEGETABLE BEEF SALAD 4 TO 6 SERVINGS

2 cups diced cooked beef
½ cup French dressing
½ cup diced cooked potatoes
½ cup cut cooked green beans
½ cup coarsely grated carrots

¼ cup chopped sweet pickle
2 hard-cooked eggs, diced
Salt to taste
½ cup mayonnaise

Pour French dressing over beef, mix well, and chill 1 hour. Combine remaining ingredients and chill separately. Just before serving, lightly toss marinated beef with vegetable mixture.
Serve on shredded lettuce.

MOLDED BEEF SALAD 6 SERVINGS

3 cups diced cooked beef
1 can (10½ ounces) condensed
    consommé
1 envelope unflavored gelatin,
    softened in ½ cup cold water
2 teaspoons seasoned salt

2 tablespoons Worcestershire sauce
1 cup dairy sour cream
1 cup grated carrots
1 cup diced celery
¼ cup chopped green onions

Heat consommé to boiling and stir in softened gelatin until dissolved. Chill until syrupy. Combine salt, Worcestershire, and sour cream and beat into thickened consommé until fluffy. Fold in remaining ingredients and spoon into 6 individual molds rinsed with cold water. Cover and chill several hours until firm.
Unmold on a bed of lettuce, garnish with sliced hard-cooked eggs and tomato wedges.

Too hot to bother reheating that leftover pot roast? Slice it for delicious cold sandwiches. Spread bread with mustard pickles.

JELLIED BEEF LOAF 4 TO 6 SERVINGS

2 cups finely diced cooked beef
1 envelope unflavored gelatin,
    softened in ½ cup cold water
¾ cup tomato juice
¼ cup vinegar
½ teaspoon salt
¼ cup diced celery

¼ cup chopped pimiento
¼ cup diced green bell pepper
¼ cup minced onion
½ cup mayonnaise
½ cup chopped pecans or walnuts
    (optional)
2 hard-cooked eggs, sliced

Soften gelatin in heated tomato juice, then stir in vinegar and salt. Chill until syrupy. Meanwhile, combine remaining ingredients except egg. Arrange egg slices along bottom and sides of loaf pan rinsed with cold water. Mix gelatin and meat mixture thoroughly. Turn into loaf pan and chill 3 to 4 hours, or until firm.
Slice and serve on shredded lettuce.

ROAST BEEF SANDWICH SUPREME 4 SANDWICHES

12 thin slices cold roast beef
½ cup dairy sour cream
1 tablespoon dry onion soup mix
1 teaspoon prepared horseradish,
    well drained

Salt and pepper to taste
8 slices dark bread
Butter, margarine, or mayonnaise
Lettuce

Mix sour cream, soup mix, horseradish, salt, and pepper. Spread bread slices with butter or mayonnaise. Place 3 slices of beef on each of 4 slices of bread. Spread dressing on each slice of beef and top sandwich with crisp lettuce. Cover with second slice of bread and cut diagonally.
Garnish with pickle.

BARBECUE BEEF SANDWICHES 8 SERVINGS

4 cups diced leftover beef
½ cup butter or margarine
2 large onions, diced
1 large green bell pepper, diced
3 stalks celery, diced
1 bottle (26 ounces) catsup

2 tablespoons Worcestershire sauce
Juice 2 lemons or ⅓ cup dry red wine
1 teaspoon salt
1 teaspoon Tabasco sauce
¼ teaspoon allspice
½ teaspoon garlic powder

In a large skillet, melt butter and sauté onion, bell pepper, and celery until soft but not browned. Add 1 cup of water and all remaining ingredients, except meat. Simmer 30 minutes. (If you are using lemon juice, include squeeezed lemon halves and remove before adding meat.) Add beef and simmer 15 minutes.
Serve on hamburger buns or French rolls.

BEEF SOUFFLE 4 TO 6 SERVINGS

2 cups ground cooked beef
3 eggs, separated
Dry bread crumbs
2 tablespoons butter or margarine
2 tablespoons flour
1½ cups milk

½ teaspoon salt
¼ teaspoon pepper
1 tablespoon minced parsley
1 teaspoon grated onion
1 teaspoon tarragon

Preheat oven to 375°. Separate eggs and allow to stand so egg whites are room temperature when beaten. Butter and crumb a 2-quart soufflé dish and set aside. In a medium size saucepan, melt 2 tablespoons butter, add flour, and make smooth paste. Gradually add milk and cook over low heat until slightly thickened, stirring constantly. Add beef, salt, pepper, parsley, onion, and tarragon and mix well. Beat egg yolks and slowly add to beef mixture. Beat egg whites until stiff, but not dry. Fold gently into beef mixture. Pour into buttered soufflé dish. Bake, uncovered, about 45 minutes, or until firm in the center. Serve immediately.
NOTE: *Do not open oven door during baking.*

BARBECUE TURNOVERS 8 TURNOVERS

1¼ cups finely chopped cooked beef
Pastry for 2-crust pie
3 tablespoons butter or margarine
½ green bell pepper, finely chopped
1 small onion, chopped
3 cloves garlic, minced or pressed
1 tablespoon brown sugar
½ teaspoon salt

¼ teaspoon pepper
½ teaspoon dry mustard
½ cup catsup
2 tablespoons vinegar
2 teaspoons Worcestershire sauce
½ teaspoon Tabasco sauce
1 egg, beaten, plus 1 tablespoon water

Melt butter in a large skillet and sauté green pepper, onion, and garlic until soft, but not browned. Add 1 cup water and all remaining ingredients, except meat, and cook over low heat 15 to 20 minutes. Place meat in mixing bowl and add enough sauce to moisten meat and hold it together. Reserve remainder of sauce. Preheat oven to 400°. Divide pastry in half. On a lightly floured board, roll each half into a 9-inch square about ⅛ inch thick. Cut each into 4 smaller squares and put a mound of meat in the center of each. Brush edges with water, fold into triangle, and seal edges by pressing with fork. Prick each turnover with fork. Brush with egg wash. Place on lightly greased baking sheet and bake 15 to 20 minutes, or until nicely browned.

Serve with hot barbecue sauce (see page 204).

CURRIED BEEF CASSEROLE 4 SERVINGS

2 cups diced cooked beef
1 cup chopped onion
3 tart apples, cored, peeled,
    and chopped
6 tablespoons butter or margarine,
    divided

4 tablespoons flour
1½ tablespoons curry powder
1 can (10½ ounces) condensed
    beef broth
¾ cup gravy
Salt and pepper to taste
1 tablespoon lemon juice

In a medium size skillet, sauté onion and chopped apple in 3 tablespoons butter until onion is soft but not browned. Place in bowl, add beef, and set aside. In a medium saucepan, melt 3 tablespoons butter, add flour and curry powder and mix together until smooth. Gradually add beef broth, and gravy. Heat, stirring, until thickened. Season with salt and pepper. Add lemon juice and beef mixture. Heat through.
Serve over hot rice.

SCALLOPED BEEF CASSEROLE 4 SERVINGS

1 cup chopped cooked roast beef
2 tablespoons butter or margarine
2 tablespoons flour
2 cups hot milk

½ teaspoon salt
⅛ teaspoon pepper
1 cup cracker crumbs
4 hard-cooked eggs, sliced

Preheat oven to 350°. Melt butter in medium size saucepan. Stir in flour and slowly pour in hot milk, stirring constantly over low heat until sauce thickens. Season with salt and pepper. Set aside. In a 2-quart greased casserole, make layers of cracker crumbs, sliced eggs, then meat. Repeat until all ingredients are used, reserving 2 tablespoons of cracker crumbs. Pour sauce over all. Sprinkle top with remaining crumbs and bake 30 minutes.
OPTIONAL: *Include layers of canned asparagus.*

Be kind to your refrigerator—make up your own casserole, using whatever leftovers are on hand. Season imaginatively, and freeze for a lazy day.

UPSIDE DOWN MEAT PIE 6 SERVINGS

2 cups diced cooked beef
5 cups cubed soft bread
½ cup sliced celery
¼ cup finely chopped parsley
⅛ teaspoon thyme
⅛ teaspoon pepper
⅓ cup tomato juice

4½ tablespoons butter or margarine
1 beef bouillon cube
1 package (10 ounces) frozen mixed
    vegetables, cooked
½ cup diced cooked potato
1 cup brown gravy

Preheat oven to 375°. Combine bread cubes, celery, parsley, thyme, and pepper. Heat tomato juice with butter and bouillon cube until cube is dissolved. Pour over bread mixture and toss lightly. Pat two thirds of the bread mixture onto sides and bottom of a well-greased 2-quart casserole. Mix diced meat, vegetables, potato, and gravy. Spoon into casserole and sprinkle top with remaining bread mixture. Bake, uncovered, 35 minutes. Remove from oven and allow to stand 5 minutes. Invert on platter, or serve directly from casserole.

189

BEEF CHOW MEIN 4 SERVINGS

1 cup diced cooked beef
½ cup sliced onion
2 tablespoons cooking oil
1½ cups sliced celery
2 beef bouillon cubes, dissolved in
    ½ cup boiling water
1 can (16 ounces) mixed chop suey
    vegetables

3 tablespoons cornstarch, dissolved in
    3 tablespoons water
1 teaspoon brown sugar
½ teaspoon pepper
2 tablespoons soy sauce, mixed with
    3 tablespoons water

In a medium size saucepan, brown meat and onion in oil. Add celery and dissolved beef cubes. Cover and boil 5 minutes. Add chop suey vegetables. Combine cornstarch with brown sugar, pepper, and soy sauce. Add to meat and cook over low heat until mixture thickens and clears.
Serve over crisp chow mein noodles or hot rice.

YORKSHIRE CASSEROLE 3 TO 6 SERVINGS

6 medium slices cooked roast beef
5 tablespoons beef drippings or
    bacon fat
1 package popover mix
1½ tablespoons butter or margarine

1½ tablespoons flour
1 can (10½ ounces) condensed beef
    consommé
Dash of Worcestershire sauce

Preheat oven to 400°. Melt beef drippings in a 9- x 13-inch roasting pan. Lay beef slices on top of drippings. Prepare popover mix according to package directions and pour evenly over beef slices. Bake, uncovered, 40 minutes. Meanwhile, in saucepan, melt butter and stir in flour. Add consommé slowly, and cook over low heat, stirring constantly, until smooth and fairly thick. Add Worcestershire and keep warm. Serve as gravy with casserole.

LIMA BEAN CASSEROLE 6 SERVINGS

2 cups cubed cooked beef
½ pound link sausages
1 medium onion, sliced
1 tablespoon cooking oil
2 cans (16 ounces each) lima beans
1 can (8 ounces) tomato sauce

⅛ teaspoon garlic powder
1 tablespoon butter or margarine
½ cup coarse dry bread crumbs
2 tablespoons chopped parsley (optional)

Preheat oven to 350°. In a small skillet, brown sausage and set aside. In a separate medium size skillet, sauté onion in cooking oil until soft but not browned. Drain lima beans, reserving ¼ cup of liquid. Add lima beans and cubed beef to cooked onion and spoon into an ungreased 1½-quart casserole. In a saucepan, combine tomato sauce, reserved bean liquid, and garlic powder. Heat to just boiling and pour over beans and beef. Top casserole with sausage and bake, covered, about 45 minutes. Melt butter, add bread crumbs and parsley. Sprinkle over casserole and return, uncovered, to oven until crumbs are golden brown.

Put leftover meat and vegetables in a sectioned tray for instant TV dinners. Wouldn't it be great to have ready-made dinners on hand at all times?

opposite: LEFTOVER ROAST BEEF ROLLS

BEEF AND BEAN CASSEROLE 6 TO 8 SERVINGS

2½ cups diced cooked beef
1 teaspoon salt
⅛ teaspoon pepper
1 tablespoon sugar
2 cans (15½ ounces each) kidney beans
    or 1 can kidney beans and 1 can
    (17 ounces) lima beans

2 carrots, coarsely grated
1 small onion, thinly sliced
1 can (30 ounces) tomatoes
Butter or margarine
Parmesan cheese

Preheat oven to 375°. Put beef in buttered 3-quart casserole. Add salt, pepper, and sugar, and pour vegetables over. Dot with butter. Sprinkle with Parmesan cheese. Cover and bake 25 to 30 minutes. Uncover and bake 20 minutes, or until vegetables are tender.

BEEF CREPES 2 DOZEN

FILLING

2 cups finely chopped cooked beef
½ cup chopped green chilies

¼ cup diced onion
1 cup brown gravy

CREPES

2 eggs
1¼ cups milk
1 tablespoon butter or margarine

¼ teaspoon salt
1 cup sifted flour

SAUCE

½ cup butter or margarine
½ cup flour
½ teaspoon salt
1 cup dairy sour cream
1 egg yolk, beaten

1 cup condensed beef consommé
2 tablespoons chopped parsley
1 tablespoon grated Parmesan cheese
½ cup dry white wine
½ teaspoon nutmeg (optional)

Combine meat, chopped green chilies, onion, and gravy and set aside. Mix crêpe ingredients in blender and let stand 1 hour. Pour 1½ tablespoons batter in a 7-inch, very lightly greased skillet. Cook about 1 minute and turn over. Stack until all crêpes have been made. Fill crêpes wtih meat mixture and roll. Place in shallow ovenproof dish. Set aside. To make sauce, melt butter in saucepan, and blend in flour and salt. Add sour cream, egg yolk, and consommé, stir until smooth. Add parsley, cheese, wine, and ½ teaspoon nutmeg. Pour over crêpes and return to warm oven about 10 minutes or until crêpes, filling, and sauce are all hot. Serve immediately.
NOTE: *Filled crêpes may be made ahead and frozen. Sauce should not be made until ready to serve.*

 Don't leave your favorite casserole dish stranded in the freezer. Line it with heavy-duty aluminum foil, leaving a generous overlap, before filling with a casserole. Freeze food until firm, then lift out of dish. Rewrap securely in freezer wrap, date it, and keep frozen until needed. To cook, unwrap and pop it right back in the dish—you already know it will fit.

opposite: BONELESS BARBECUED ROAST

MOCK MACHACA 6 SERVINGS

2 cups thinly sliced or diced cooked
   roast
¼ cup diced onion
1 small clove garlic, diced
1½ tablespoons cooking oil

2 tablespoons flour
1 tomato, diced
½ cup diced green chilies
Salt and pepper to taste

In a large skillet, sauté meat, onion, and garlic in oil until onion is soft but not browned. Add flour and cook until meat is browned. Add tomato, chilies, salt, and pepper and cook until tomato is limp and mixture is slightly dry. Cover and simmer about 15 minutes. If too dry, add a small amount of tomato juice.

VARIATION: *Fill tortillas with cooked mixture for a party lunch.*

FLAVORED BEEF ENCORE 4 TO 6 SERVINGS

2 cups cubed or thinly sliced cooked
   roast beef
1 tablespoon butter or margarine
1 clove garlic, sliced
2 onions, thinly sliced

½ cup dry white wine or dry vermouth
1 cup condensed beef consommé
½ teaspoon paprika
1 teaspoon tarragon vinegar
1 tablespoon flour

Melt butter in a skillet. Sauté sliced garlic 2 minutes, then discard. Add onion, and sauté until soft but not browned. Add wine and consommé and simmer 15 minutes. Add meat and paprika. Simmer just long enough to heat the meat, about 3 minutes. Just before serving, mix vinegar with flour to make paste and stir into skillet. Heat another 2 minutes, or until slightly thickened.

Complements

Cowboy had few
extras
off th' land
with his beef

THEN as NOW
He took his extras
with him or had 'em
hauled to him

195

Complements? Only compl'mints I ever got was on my hoss! Vittles wasn't very fancy. Beans 'n sowbelly (salt pork), biskits 'n lick (syrup), and coffee black or with canned cow. Even at Christmas, when we was sentimental and thinkin' of home, herbs, spices an' trimmin's was as hard for us to come by as a warm bed when we wuz nightherdin' of a frosty moonlight. Wine, cheeses, fresh fruit? Not on th' frontier, an' not on yore nightshirt. We figgered ourselves lucky if we come up with a l'il booze, an' dried peach jam. C'n you imagine some greenhorn expectin' th' chuck wagon to be carryin' th' latest in sauces an' relishes?

We ate some corn dodger an' hush puppies, but mostly our bread was biskits. I notice folks is latchin' on to our old sourdough agin—an' why not! We shore prefer'ed it to store-boughten light bread.

WILD YEAST SOURDOUGH STARTER

Boil two medium-sized, chopped-up potatoes in three cups water until tender. Drain off two cups of th' potato water an' let it git cool to touch. Mix with two cups flour an' two tablespoons sugar in a crock. Don't use no metal. Cover with a light cloth, stir every day, an' in a couple days or so th' starter'll be bubblin' an' lively enuf to use. Never use it all up. Hold back a cup, add two cups flour and two cups water to keep wild yeast alive an' growin'. (Sourdough starter can be dried or chilled to save, but it works best if ya keep usin' out of it and buildin' it back.)

SOURDOUGH BISCUITS

For breakfast, start th' night before by mixin' half cup of starter with a cup of milk or water an' a cup of flour. Cover an' keep warm if you have to put it in yore bedroll. Sourdough starter doesn't take kindly to bein' too hot or too cold, and it has to be tamed same as any other wild thing. Next mornin' pour this batter into a bowl with a cup or so of flour spread on bottom and up th' sides. Then mix together a teaspoon baking powder, three-fourths teaspoon salt, an' a fourth teaspoon baking soda with another half-cup flour. Sprinkle this mix over th' batter and stir in easy. Knead flour in from sides an' bottom of th' bowl to make dough. Pinch off biskits or roll them out on a floured board an' cut with a cutter. Crowd 'em close together in a greased nine-inch pan. Let 'em raise half an hour an' bake in a medium-hot oven 'til golden brown.

Cooking with Wine

The use of wine in cooking can change dull meals into gourmet dishes. There is nothing that equals wine to add an exotic touch to a marinade, piquancy to a stew, or new zest to an unexciting sauce.

Wine can be used generously because the alcoholic content evaporates in cooking. The full flavor will remain if the wine is not heated above simmering. Wine is an excellent tenderizer, and can make less expensive cuts of beef tender and economical when used in a marinade. Avoid using metal utensils for marinating because they will react with the acid in the wine.

If you serve wine with the same meal in which wine has been used in cooking, be certain the wines are compatible. Don't serve a sweet red wine if you put dry vermouth in the stew.

Although red wine is traditionally served with beef, veal tends to be overpowered by its rich and hearty flavor. Try a more delicate, dry white wine with veal in deference to its tender age.

WINE CHART

Soup	Beef and vegetable	1 tablespoon per cup	Sherry or Burgundy
Sauces	Cream sauce	1 tablespoon per cup	Sherry or Sauterne
	Cheese sauce	1 tablespoon per cup	Sherry or Sauterne
	Brown sauce	1 tablespoon per cup	Sherry or Burgundy
	Tomato sauce	1 tablespoon per cup	Sherry or Burgundy
Beef	Pot roast	¼ cup per pound	Burgundy
	Pot roast gravy	2 tablespoons per cup	Sherry, Dry Vermouth or Burgundy
	Stew		
	Beef	¼ cup per pound	Burgundy
	Veal	¼ cup per pound	Dry Vermouth
	Liver, braised	¼ cup per pound	Burgundy or Dry Vermouth
	Tongue, boiled	½ cup per pound	Burgundy

Note: *Where Sauterne is suggested, Dry Vermouth, Chablis, Rhine wine or any other dry white wine may be substituted. Claret, or any other dry red wine, may be substituted for Burgundy. Do not use sweet wines in cooking beef.*

Cooking with Cheese

There are thousands of types of cheese, from the blue-veined Roquefort to the sweet, nutlike Emmentaler. Experiment with different cheeses. You will find them delightful companions to beef as in the traditional cheeseburger, as an elegant sauce, or in a peppy side dish.

Do not overcook cheese, as the high protein content will make it tough and stringy. Always add cheese at the last moment possible, and cook over low or medium heat, or several inches from broiler, just until cheese melts.

CHEESE CHART

Family	Cheese	Characteristics
Cheddar	Cheddar	Firm, smooth; mild to sharp flavor
	Colby	Softer than Cheddar; mild flavor
	Longhorn	Firm; mild flavor
	Monterey (Jack)	Semisoft, smooth; mild flavor
Provolone	Provolone	Firm; usually smoked; mild to sharp flavor
	Mozzarella	Semisoft, pliant; mild, delicate flavor
	Scamorze	Semisoft when young, sliceable when aged; salty, sometimes smoked; mild flavor
Swiss	Swiss (Emmentaler)	Firm, smooth, large gas holes; sweet, nutlike flavor
	Gruyère	Firm, tiny gas holes; sweetish, nutlike flavor
Blue	Blue	Semisoft, crumbly; marbled with blue-green mold; piquant, spicy flavor
	Gorgonzola	Semisoft, less moist than blue; marbled with blue-green mold; piquant, spicy flavor
	Roquefort	Semisoft, pasty or crumbly; marbled with blue-green mold; sharp, piquant flavor
	Stilton	Semisoft, crumbly; marbled with blue-green mold; milder than Roquefort
Parmesan	Parmesan	Hard, usually grated; sharp, pungent flavor
	Romano	Hard, aged, usually grated; sharp, piquant flavor
Fresh, Uncured	Cream	Smooth, buttery; mild
	Cottage	Soft, moist, small or large curds; mild
Whey	Sapsago	Hard, greenish; flavored with clover leaves; sweetish flavor
	Ricotta	Soft, moist, and grainy; dry when aged; bland, semi-sweet flavor

Herbs and Spices

A good meal without seasonings is almost impossible. Herbs and spices are "the variety of life," or at least of cooking. The proper use of seasonings can turn eating into a culinary adventure—don't let them stand neglected on the spice rack.

Have the courage to experiment with herbs and spices, but exercise restraint. It is much easier to correct an underseasoned dish than it is to rescue an overseasoned one.

Spices should be kept tightly sealed in a cool place. Fresh grinding, especially of peppercorns, is a vast improvement over preground spices. Fresh herbs are preferable to dried, and should be used in a ratio of 1 tablespoon for every teaspoon of dried herbs.

Unfortunately, domestic paprika, a bland and cowardly substitute for the real thing, is still used by many American cooks. Hungarian paprika is preferable and the difference will be obvious to any cook who uses it.

Here is an herb and spice chart with suggestions for seasonings in beef and veal dishes, variety meats, marinades, and sauces. As a general rule, ¼ teaspoon per pound of meat or pint of liquid is a good starting point. Amounts may be increased as you determine which flavors appeal to you.

Allspice: pot roast, stew, ground beef; mincemeat; marinades; soups
Anise: stew
Basil: stew, meat loaf, meat pies; liver; tomato sauce; soups
Bay leaf: pot roast, sauerbraten, stew, goulash; liver; smoked meats; tomato sauce; marinades
Caraway: sauerbraten; soups
Cardamon: meat loaf
Cayenne: stew; barbecue sauce, Italian sauces
Celery seed: roasts, stew, meat loaf; sauces
Chervil: veal
Chili powder: beef dishes; chili
Cinnamon: stew; ground beef, boiled beef; corned beef
Clove: stew; tongue; smoked meats; soups
Coriander: stew, ground beef; frankfurters; chili, curried dishes
Cumin: stew, meat loaf; kidneys; chili
Curry powder: curry sauce
Dill: ground beef, boiled beef; corned beef; sauces
Fennel: stew, meat loaf; spaghetti sauce
Garlic: most meat dishes; sauces; marinades
Ginger: pot roast, ground beef; Chinese dishes; curried dishes; soups
Green onion: alternative to onion
Horseradish: roast beef, boiled beef; tongue; sauces
Juniper berry: veal
Leeks: brisket; tongue
Mace: meat loaf; veal chops
Marjoram: pot roast, stew, ground beef; liver; veal; chili; gravy, sauces
Mint: Greek dishes
Mustard, dry: Chinese dishes; kidneys; sauces; marinades
Nutmeg: ground beef; veal
Onion: most beef and veal dishes; sauces; marinades
Oregano: meat loaf; veal; kidney stew; Italian dishes; Mexican dishes; chili; barbecue sauce, tomato sauce; soups
Paprika: goulash; veal; gravy; garnishes
Parsley: all beef dishes; garnish
Pickling spice: boiled tongue; corned beef; marinades
Rosemary: stew, meat loaf, broiled meat; veal; kidneys; marinades
Saffron: veal; rice
Sage: roasts, stew; veal
Savory: ground beef; veal; gravy, barbecue sauce, tomato sauce
Sesame: meat balls
Shallots: use as onion, more subtle flavor
Tarragon: roast beef, steak; sweetbreads; sauces
Thyme: meat loaf, boiled beef; veal; veal kidneys; tomato sauce

Note: When a beef dish calls for a bouquet garni, tie parsley, thyme, and bay leaf in a piece of cheesecloth. Add to liquid during cooking and remove before making gravy or serving. Several sweet herbs may be added, such as basil, celery, marjoram, oregano, rosemary, sage, or savory.

BASIC BEEF STOCK 2 QUARTS

4 pounds shank soup bones
2 pounds marrowbone, cut in
    3-inch pieces
1 calf's foot or veal knuckle
3 leeks
1 onion, studded with 3 whole cloves
2 cloves garlic

1 stalk celery with leaves
1 carrot
1 teaspoon thyme
1 bay leaf
12 peppercorns
4 sprigs of parsley
Salt to taste

Place 4 quarts cold water in an 8-quart pot. Add all ingredients except salt. Bring to a boil. Remove scum as it accumulates on surface. Allow stock to boil about 20 minutes. Lower heat, cover, and simmer 2 hours. Skim off any additional scum, add salt, and . simmer 1½ hours longer. Cool. Place in refrigerator until cold enough to skim off fat. Strain and store in freezer for future use.
If storing in refrigerator, leave fat on top of stock during storage. Skim before using. It will keep about 4 days. Reboil for longer refrigerator storage.
NOTE: *To make Brown Stock, brown bones in oven before adding to pot. Since the best stock flavor is obtained if all ingredients are the same temperature when cooking begins, be certain to cool browned bones before adding them to stock pot.*

SAUCE BEARNAISE 1½ CUPS

¼ cup dry white wine
¼ cup wine vinegar
1 tablespoon minced shallots or
    green onions

½ tablespoon tarragon
¼ teaspoon salt
⅛ teaspoon pepper

Combine all ingredients in a small saucepan and bring to a boil. Reduce to moderate heat and simmer until liquid is reduced by half. Cool, strain, and set aside. Complete sauce by either of the following methods.

BLENDER METHOD

3 egg yolks

8 tablespoons butter, melted

Place egg yolks in blender jar. Add cooled vinegar mixture, cover, and blend at high speed 2 minutes. Remove center portion of blender cover and very slowly pour in hot foaming butter while maintaining high speed on blender. Adjust seasoning and serve immediately or set blender jar in tepid water until ready to use.

SAUCEPAN METHOD

3 egg yolks
2 tablespoons cold butter

⅔ cup melted butter

Beat egg yolks until thick in heavy saucepan over very low heat or in double boiler over hot water. Add cooled vinegar mixture and blend. Beat in cold butter, one tablespoon at a time, until blended. Pour in hot foaming butter very slowly, beating constantly. Adjust seasoning and serve immediately or keep warm over tepid water.
Serve as fondue sauce, with steak, or over large beef patties for an elegant ground beef dish.
NOTE: *Maximum amount of butter safely used in making any sauce in the Hollandaise family is three ounces (or 6 tablespoons) per egg yolk. When sauce is made in a blender, amount of butter used must be reduced to a maximum of 1½ ounces (or 3 tablespoons) per egg yolk.*

BORDELAISE SAUCE 2 CUPS

¼ cup beef marrow, diced °
2 tablespoons minced shallots
1 tablespoon butter or margarine
¾ cup dry red wine
1 teaspoon salt

⅛ teaspoon freshly ground pepper
1½ cups brown gravy
2 teaspoons lemon juice
2 teaspoons minced parsley

Gently simmer beef marrow in water a few minutes. Drain and set aside. In a large skillet, sauté shallots in butter until soft but not browned. Add wine, salt, and pepper. Simmer until reduced by half. Add brown gravy. Stir and simmer 5 minutes longer. Add beef marrow, lemon juice, and parsley, and heat thoroughly.
Serve hot over steaks or beef patties.

° To prepare beef marrow: Have beef marrow bones sliced by butcher. Wrap in foil and bake 30 minutes. Scrape out marrow in one piece. This can be done ahead of time and kept in refrigerator until ready to use.

SPAGHETTI SAUCE 8 TO 10 SERVINGS

1 pound lean ground beef
6 slices bacon
4 medium onions, chopped
2 stalks celery, chopped
2 green bell peppers, chopped
4 cloves garlic, crushed
1 can (8 ounces) sliced mushrooms

2 cans (20 ounces each) stewed tomatoes
4 cans (6 ounces each) tomato paste
2 cans (8 ounces each) tomato sauce
2 teaspoons sugar
2 teaspoons basil
Salt and pepper to taste

Sauté meat until brown. Drain off fat and set aside. Fry bacon until crisp. Drain and crumble. Sauté onion, celery, peppers, garlic, and mushrooms in bacon fat until soft but not browned. Drain. Combine all ingredients in large saucepan and simmer about 1 hour.
NOTE: This sauce can be poured over hot spaghetti or mixed with cooked spaghetti, turned into a 2-quart casserole, topped with grated Parmesan Cheese, and baked 30 minutes in a 350° oven.

MUSHROOM GRAVY 1 CUP

2 tablespoons minced onion
5 tablespoons butter or margarine,
     divided
6 tablespoons dry red wine
2 tablespoons dry sherry
½ cup tomato purée
Small piece bay leaf

Salt and pepper to taste
1 tablespoon flour
1 cup Basic Beef Stock (see page 202)
     or canned beef broth
Dash of thyme
Browning sauce (optional)
½ pound mushrooms, sliced

Sauté onion in 1 tablespoon butter in saucepan until soft but not browned. Add wines, tomato puree, bay leaf, salt, and pepper. Bring mixture to a boil and cook until reduced to ⅓ cup. Melt 1 tablespoon butter and blend in flour. Add beef stock and cook, stirring, 3 to 5 minutes. Lower heat and simmer 10 minutes, stirring occasionally. Stir in wine mixture and cook until reduced to ⅔ cup. Remove from heat and stir in 2 tablespoons butter and thyme. Add browning sauce for color, if desired. Sauté mushrooms in 1 tablespoon butter. Strain sauce and add mushrooms.
Serve over ground sirloin steak, London broil, or brochettes.

BARBECUE SAUCE 1⅓ CUPS

3 tablespoons catsup
3 tablespoons vinegar
3 tablespoons butter or margarine
3 tablespoons Worcestershire sauce
3 tablespoons lemon juice
5 teaspoons prepared mustard

5 teaspoons salt
5 teaspoons paprika
1 teaspoon cayenne
2½ teaspoons chili powder
3 tablespoons dark brown sugar
7 drops liquid smoke

Mix ingredients with 6 tablespoons of water and simmer about 20 minutes.

Skim fat off a sauce or soup by putting it in the refrigerator. Fat will rise to the top and harden, making it easy to remove.

TENDERIZER MARINADE 1½ CUPS

¾ cup salad oil
6 tablespoons soy sauce
2 tablespoons Worcestershire sauce
1 tablespoon dry mustard
1 teaspoon salt

½ teaspoon pepper
¼ cup wine vinegar
1 teaspoon dried parsley flakes
⅓ cup lemon juice
1 clove garlic, crushed (optional)

Combine all ingredients in glass jar. Marinade may be made ahead of time and stored, covered, in the refrigerator. It may be saved and used again.

Save leftover marinades for sauces, bastes, gravies, and soups. Whoever guesses where that mysterious delicious flavor comes from gets a prize!

SHERRY BASTE FOR BARBECUING 1½ CUPS

⅔ cup dry sherry
⅔ cup soy sauce
¼ cup dark brown sugar, packed

1 clove garlic, mashed
2 tablespoons grated onion

Combine all ingredients in glass jar. Shake to blend. Let stand several hours to mellow flavors. Use as a barbecue marinade and to baste.

PICKLED PAPAYA 6 TO 8(8-OUNCE) JARS

2 cups vinegar or sweet pickle juice
4 cups sugar
½ teaspoon salt
1 hot red chili, chopped fine

1 tablespoon finely chopped ginger root
6 to 8 firm green papayas (with some yellow streaks), peeled and sliced

Simmer vinegar, sugar, salt, and spices together until sugar is dissolved. Add papaya slices, bring to a boil. Simmer several hours until thickened. Put into sterilized jars and cover.

204 NOTE: *Do not double this recipe. It will not cook down properly.*

YORKSHIRE PUDDING 6 TO 8 SERVINGS

2 eggs, beaten
1 cup milk
1 cup sifted flour

1 teaspoon salt
Pinch of white pepper
2 tablespoons roast drippings

Combine eggs and milk in a bowl. Sift together flour, salt, and pepper and add to liquid gradually. Beat with a rotary beater until smooth. Batter will keep several hours in refrigerator. As an alternative, place all ingredients in container of blender, cover, and process approximately 20 seconds, or until batter is completely smooth. Ideally, Yorkshire Pudding should be baked in an oven hotter than the roast beef it usually accompanies. Therefore, if a second oven is available, preheat it to 400°. If Yorkshire Pudding is to be baked in the same oven in which roast is cooking, remove meat when almost done and allow to stand while Yorkshire Pudding bakes. Reset oven to 400°. Cover bottom of an 8-inch pie plate with drippings. Place plate in hot oven until drippings bubble. Remove from oven and pour batter into hot drippings. Return to oven and bake 30 minutes, or until golden brown. Leave space above pie plate for pudding to rise. **Do NOT OPEN OVEN DURING BAKING!** Serve immediately, or pudding will collapse.
If desired, batter may be poured into an 8-inch square pan or into 8 muffin cups. Cut baking time to 20 minutes for muffin cups.
NOTE: *The real secret to superb Yorkshire Pudding is to have very hot drippings into which the batter is poured.*

 Did the Yorkshire pudding fall flat on its face? Either you didn't beat it long enough, the drippings in the pan in which the pudding baked were not hot enough, or the family didn't come to the table THE MINUTE you called. Try again!!

FARINA WITH CHEESE 4 SERVINGS

2 cups milk
½ cup Farina
1 teaspoon salt
2 teaspoons sugar

1 cup grated Cheddar cheese, divided
3 tablespoons butter or margarine,
   divided
2 eggs, beaten

Preheat oven to 350°. Scald milk in top of double boiler. Stir in Farina, add salt and sugar. Steam, covered, 20 minutes. Remove from heat, stir in ¾ cup cheese, 2 tablespoons butter, and eggs. Turn into 8- x 8-inch pan. Dot with remaining cheese and remaining butter. Bake 25 minutes.

 When making up a large batch of stock (and it's not easy to make a small batch), you will probably want to store most of it in the freezer. Measure one or two cups into each of several plastic bags, seal securely, and label; indicating contents, volume, and date frozen. Then when you need some stock for a recipe you don't have to chip at a 10-gallon container with an ice pick.

CORN TORTILLAS 16 6-INCH TORTILLAS

4 cups dehydrated masa flour
(corn tortilla flour)

Mix flour with 2⅔ cups warm water until dough holds together well. Form into 2-inch balls (¼ cup each). Shape into a flat, round 6-inch cake by patting between hands, rolling with a rolling pin between two damp cloths, or using a tortilla press. Bake on ungreased medium-hot griddle or heavy skillet about 2 minutes on one side, turn and cook 1 minute or until lightly browned. Use two spatulas or a pancake turner to press tortillas flat for even browning.

FLOUR TORTILLAS 20 8-INCH TORTILLAS

4 cups flour	*6 tablespoons shortening*
2 teaspoons salt	*1 teaspoon baking powder (optional)*

Using your hands, mix dry ingredients, add shortening, and work into flour. Add 1 cup lukewarm water and form into soft ball. Use more water if needed to clear bowl of flour. Knead dough until smooth, 3 to 5 minutes, on lightly floured board. Pinch off egg-size pieces. Let stand 15 to 20 minutes, then roll into *very* thin round discs on lightly floured waxed paper. Cook on ungreased hot griddle or skillet (water drops should bounce) about 2 minutes on one side, turn and cook 1 minute or until lightly browned. Use two spatulas or a pancake turner to press tortillas flat for even browning.

TO STORE: Wrap well and refrigerate or freeze for future use.
TO REHEAT: Place on medium-hot griddle about 30 seconds, turning once. If tortillas are dry, wet your hand and rub surface of tortilla lightly before heating. Wrap in cloth and keep warm until ready to use.

Hot green or red chilies are available fresh, frozen, dried, or canned. To prepare for cooking, wash fresh chilies, place in 400° oven until skin pops, remove from oven, cover with damp cloth to steam, peel, remove seeds and devein. Wash dried chilies, remove seeds, devein, soak 1 hour in hot water, and purée. Rinse canned chilies, remove seeds and devein if necessary.

SOUR CREAM TACOS 6 TO 7 SERVINGS

12 to 15 Corn Tortillas (see page 206)	*1 small onion, chopped*
Cooking oil ½ inch deep in small pan	*1 clove garlic, minced*
1 pound Monterey Jack cheese,	*1 can (16 ounces) stewed tomatoes*
* cut in strips*	*1 teaspoon salt*
2 cans (7 ounces each) green chilies,	*1 teaspoon oregano*
* seeded and cut in strips*	*2 cups dairy sour cream*
2 tablespoons cooking oil	

Dip tortillas, one at a time, in heated oil until softened. Drain. Place cheese and chili strips in center of tortilla and roll. Arrange 1 layer deep in baking dish. Preheat oven to 350° Heat 2 tablespoons cooking oil in medium skillet. Add onion and garlic. Sauté until onion is soft but not browned. Add tomatoes, salt, and oregano. Simmer uncovered about 20 minutes. Stir in sour cream. Pour over filled tortillas (tacos). Cover and bake 30 minutes.

RANCH STYLE BEANS 15 SERVINGS

2 pounds pinto or pink beans
2 onions, chopped or thinly sliced
2 cloves garlic, finely diced
½ teaspoon pepper
½ teaspoon cumin

1 can (4 ounces) diced green chilies
1 can (16 ounces) tomatoes
1 can (7 ounces) taco sauce or chili salsa
1 tablespoon salt
1½ teaspoons chili powder (optional)

Wash beans. Soak in 3 quarts cold water overnight or bring to a boil in a large kettle, turn off heat, cover, and let stand 1 to 2 hours. Add enough water if necessary to cover beans by about 2 inches. Boil gently 1 hour. Add remaining ingredients except salt and chili powder. Continue cooking 1 to 1½ hours, or until beans are tender. Add salt and chili powder.

Catsup won't pour? Maybe it's just as well. Catsup poured on a carefully seasoned casserole—or worse, on steak—offends a good cook's sense of creativity. However, if you need it for a sauce or marinade, put a straw down to the bottom of the bottle and blow—gently, unless you want a catsup eyewash.

MEXICAN BEANS 6 TO 8 SERVINGS

1 pound pinto or pink beans
2 medium onions, diced
½ cup hot bacon drippings, butter,
    or margarine

Salt to taste

Wash beans. Soak in 1½ quarts cold water overnight or put beans in a large kettle and cover with 5 cups water, bring to a boil, cover, remove from heat, and let stand 1 to 2 hours. Return to heat and simmer slowly until beans are very tender, about 3 hours. Sauté onion in drippings until soft but not browned. Mash beans with potato masher and add onions, drippings, and salt. Mix well. Continue cooking, stirring frequently, until beans are thickened and drippings absorbed.

Onions will keep their shape during cooking if you prick them around the top with a fork before parboiling.

BEEF NUT BREAD 1 LOAF

½ pound lean ground beef
2 cups flour
½ cup sugar
3 teaspoons baking powder
1 teaspoon baking soda
½ teaspoon salt

½ cup chopped walnuts
1 egg
1 cup buttermilk
3 tablespoons butter or margarine,
    melted
1 teaspoon vanilla

Preheat oven to 350°. Sift dry ingredients into large mixing bowl. Stir in walnuts. Mix raw beef, egg, buttermilk, butter, and vanilla. Add to dry ingredients and mix until all flour is moistened. (Sweet milk can be used, omitting the baking soda.) Pour into greased 5- x 9- x 2½-inch loaf pan. Bake 40 to 50 minutes, or until brown and crusty. Serve hot.

BEEF BREAD 2 LARGE OR 4 SMALL LOAVES

1 cup coarsely ground cooked roast
    beef, or ½ pound cooked ground
    beef
⅓ cup plus 1 teaspoon sugar, divided
1 cup seedless raisins
2 packages dry yeast
1½ cups potato water
3 tablespoons shortening, melted

1 tablespoon molasses
1 cup All Bran
2 cups graham flour
4 cups white flour (approximately),
    divided
1 tablespoon salt
½ cup chopped walnuts

Mix together 1 cup water, ⅓ cup sugar, beef, and raisins, and bring to a boil. Cool. Soak yeast and 1 teaspoon sugar in ½ cup warm water. Add potato water, shortening, molasses, All Bran, graham flour, and 2 cups of white flour. Mix, cover with clean cloth, place in warm, draft-free place and let rise 10 minutes. Add salt, nuts, and enough additional white flour to make a moderately stiff dough. Knead well. Cover, and allow to rise 10 minutes and knead again slightly. Cover and let rise to double in bulk, punch down. Cover, and let rise 20 minutes more. Divide and shape into 2 large or 4 small loaves. Place in well greased, lightly floured loaf pans.° Cover and allow to rise 1 to 1½ hours. Preheat oven to 350°. Bake large loaves 45 minutes. Smaller loaves should take about 30 minutes.

° For large loaves use 2 loaf pans, 9 x 5 x 3 inches; for small loaves, use 4 loaf pans, 4½ x 2½ x 2½ inches.

Oops! Halfway through a bread recipe you find an empty baking powder can sitting apologetically on the shelf. To the rescue: for each cup of flour mix 2 teaspoons cream of tartar, 1 teaspoon baking soda, and ½ teaspoon salt. Use immediately.

MEXICAN CORN BREAD 6 TO 8 SERVINGS

1 cup cornmeal
1 can (17 ounces) cream-style corn
    or whole-kernel corn, drained
¾ cup milk
½ teaspoon baking soda

⅓ cup butter or margarine, melted
1 teaspoon salt
2 eggs, slightly beaten
2 cups grated sharp Cheddar cheese
1 can (4 ounces) diced green chilies

Preheat oven to 400°. Combine all ingredients in a large bowl and mix well. Pour batter into a greased 9- x 9-inch baking dish. Bake 30 minutes.

EASY MINCEMEAT TWO 9-INCH PIES

1 pound lean ground beef
4 cups peeled chopped apples
2 cups dark brown sugar, firmly packed
1 cup seedless raisins
1 cup vinegar

1½ teaspoons salt
1 tablespoon cinnamon
1 tablespoon allspice
1 tablespoon cloves

Combine all ingredients in large pan and mix well. Add 1 cup water and boil slowly 2½ to 3 hours. Fill pie shells or store covered in refrigerator.

Eggs or sour cream should never be added quickly to a hot sauce. Instead, add a little hot sauce to the beaten eggs or sour cream and mix thoroughly. Then slowly pour the mixture back into the rest of the hot sauce.

BEEF MINCEMEAT 7 TO 8 QUARTS

2-pound round rump roast, boneless
1 pound beef suet
5 pounds tart apples, peeled and cored
2 pounds seedless raisins
2 pounds currants
2¼ cups finely diced, mixed citron,
    candied orange and lemon peel or
    fruit cake mix
3 pounds dark brown sugar, firmly
    packed

2 tablespoons cinnamon
2 tablespoons mace
1 tablespoon nutmeg
1 tablespoon cloves
1 tablespoon salt
1 quart apple cider
1 quart grape juice
1 cup brandy

Put meat in large kettle and add water to cover. Simmer until meat is tender, about 1½ hours. Remove from pan and cool. Grind or finely chop with suet and apples. Add remainder of ingredients, except brandy, bring to a boil, and cook 15 minutes, stirring frequently. Add brandy. Put in sterile jars and seal.

BAKED SUET PUDDING 6 SERVINGS

¾ cup finely diced beef suet
4 to 5 slices stale bread
1 cup sugar
1 teaspoon cinnamon
½ teaspoon nutmeg
½ teaspoon cloves
½ teaspoon allspice

½ teaspoon salt
2 eggs, well beaten
1 cup seedless raisins
1 cup chopped walnuts
1 cup cooked apples (optional)
½ cup light cream or condensed milk

Preheat oven to 350°. Put bread in a large bowl and pour 1 cup hot water over it. Add all other ingredients and mix well. Pour into greased 7- x 11-inch baking dish and bake until firm, about 45 minutes.
Serve with hard sauce seasoned with Cognac.

CARROT PUDDING 4 TO 6 SERVINGS

1 cup finely chopped beef suet
1 cup grated carrots
1 cup grated potatoes
1 cup dark brown sugar, firmly packed
1 egg, beaten
1 cup flour
1 teaspoon baking powder

½ teaspoon baking soda
½ teaspoon salt
½ teaspoon cinnamon
½ teaspoon cloves
1 cup raisins
1 cup currants
½ cup chopped walnuts (optional)

Combine suet, carrots, potatoes, sugar, and egg in large bowl. Sift dry ingredients and add. Add fruits and nuts. Mix thoroughly. Pour into greased 2-quart mold, cover with tight lid or foil. Place on rack in large kettle, add boiling water halfway up mold, cover, and steam 3 hours. Or, use pressure cooker following manufacturer's directions. Serve with brandy, rum, or hard sauce.

OLDE ENGLISH CHRISTMAS PUDDING
4 PUDDINGS (1 POUND COFFEE CAN SIZE EACH)

1 pound beef suet, finely chopped
1 teaspoon salt
½ teaspoon nutmeg
½ teaspoon cinnamon
½ teaspoon cloves
2 cups flour
6 cups currants
2 pounds seedless raisins
1 pound white raisins

1 pound mixed candied fruit and peel,
 finely chopped
1 cup chopped almonds, blanched
3½ cups dry bread crumbs
2¼ cups sugar
8 to 10 eggs, beaten
Milk as needed (about 2 cups)
1 jigger brandy or 1 tablespoon vinegar

Add spices to flour, set aside. In a large dishpan, mix all remaining ingredients except eggs, milk, and brandy. Use hands to separate fruits. Mix together eggs, milk, and brandy. Add to fruit mixture. Add flour to fruit mixture, adding more milk if it seems too dry. Use hands to mix thoroughly. Grease molds or four 1-pound coffee cans. Line with waxed paper. Grease paper. Fill with mixture to 1 inch from top. Cover with waxed paper and lid. Place on rack in large kettle, add hot water halfway up mold, cover, and steam 3 hours, or use pressure cooker following manufacturer's directions. Remove lid and top paper. Place in preheated 300° oven 30 minutes to dry out. Cool, cover, and store in cool place, or freeze. Should age 3 to 4 weeks before eating. To reheat, steam as before at least 1 hour, 2 hours if frozen.

Serve with hard sauce or favorite pudding sauce.

MINCEMEAT PUMPKIN PIE ONE 9-INCH PIE

1½ cups mincemeat
Pastry for one 9-inch pie
1 cup mashed, cooked pumpkin
½ cup sugar
½ teaspoon cinnamon

¼ teaspoon nutmeg
2 eggs
¼ teaspoon salt
½ cup milk

Preheat oven to 425°. Fill pastry-lined 9-inch pie pan with mincemeat. Combine remaining ingredients, using a rotary beater. Pour over mincemeat. Bake 35 to 40 minutes. Serve either slightly warm, or cool.

BEEFLET CONFECTIONS APPROXIMATELY 48

1 cup cooked ground beef
1 cup chopped apple
½ cup seedless raisins
½ cup dark brown sugar, firmly packed
¼ cup fruit jelly
1 tablespoon brandy
¼ teaspoon salt
¼ teaspoon cinnamon

⅛ teaspoon cloves
⅛ teaspoon nutmeg
⅛ teaspoon mace
1 envelope unflavored gelatin, softened
   in ¼ cup cold water
½ cup coarsely chopped nut meats
Confectioners sugar

Combine beef, apple, raisins, sugar, jelly, brandy, salt, and spices. Cook over low heat 10 to 15 minutes, or until apple is soft. Stir softened gelatin into hot mixture until thoroughly dissolved. Add nuts. Spread in small pan (approximately 8 x 4 inches). Chill. When firm, cut into 1-inch cubes. Roll in confectioners sugar. Store in refrigerator.

BEEF BROWNIES APPROXIMATELY 18

½ cup finely ground cooked beef
3 eggs
1 cup sugar
½ teaspoon salt
1 teaspoon vanilla
½ cup butter or margarine

2 squares unsweetened chocolate
¾ cup flour
½ teaspoon baking powder
½ cup chopped nut meats
Confectioners sugar

Beat eggs, sugar, salt, and vanilla together until fluffy. Melt butter and chocolate. Cool and add to egg-sugar mixture. Add ground beef and mix well. Preheat oven to 350°. Sift flour and baking powder together and stir into beef mixture. Add nut meats. Spread in an 8- x 8-inch pan lined with wax paper. Bake 35 minutes. Cool. Sprinkle with confectioners sugar, cut into squares, and remove from pan.

VARIATION: Substitute ¾ cup mincemeat for ground beef.

MINCEMEAT MARVEL COOKIES APPROXIMATELY 36

1 cup mincemeat
⅓ cup butter or margarine, melted
1 teaspoon rum or rum extract

3 cups fine vanilla-wafer crumbs
Confectioners sugar

Mix all ingredients well. Shape teaspoonfuls into small balls and refrigerate several hours or overnight. Before serving, roll each ball in confectioners sugar. Will keep best if stored in refrigerator.

MINCEMEAT DROP COOKIES APPROXIMATELY 90

1 cup mincemeat
2 cups dark brown sugar, firmly packed
1 cup shortening
2 eggs, slightly beaten
½ cup sour milk or buttermilk

½ teaspoon salt
1 teaspoon baking soda
1 teaspoon baking powder
3 cups sifted flour

Preheat oven to 350°. Cream sugar and shortening. Add eggs, mincemeat, and sour milk. Sift remaining dry ingredients together and add to mincemeat mixture. Drop by teaspoonfuls onto greased baking sheet. Bake until browned, 10 to 12 minutes.
May be frosted with confectioners sugar mixed with orange juice.

Index

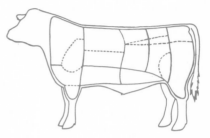

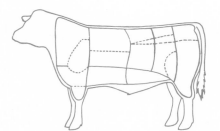